WOMEN IN THE COVENANT OF GRACE

Talks Selected from the
1993 Women's Conference
Sponsored by
Brigham Young University
and the Relief Society

Edited by
Dawn Hall Anderson and
Susette Fletcher Green

Deseret Book Company
Salt Lake City, Utah

Other volumes in the Women's Conference Series:

Women and Christ (1993)
Women Steadfast in Christ (1992)
Women and the Power Within (1991)
Women of Wisdom and Knowledge (1990)
As Women of Faith (1989)
A Heritage of Faith (1988)
Woman to Woman (1986)

Library of Congress Cataloging-in-Publication Data

Women in the covenant of grace : talks selected from the 1993 Women's Conference / edited by Dawn Hall Anderson and Susette Fletcher Green.
    p.   cm.
    Includes bibliographical references and index.
    ISBN 0–87579–829–2
    1. Women, Mormon—Congresses. 2. Grace (Theology)—Congresses.
I. Anderson, Dawn Hall. II. Green, Susette Fletcher. III. BYU Women's Conference (1993)
BX8641.W658   1994
234'.1'082—dc20   93–42368
                                      CIP

Printed in the United States of America

10 9 8 7 6 5 4 3 2 1

Contents

ON THE ERRAND OF ANGELS

CHILDREN'S VOICES:
WHO IS LISTENING?

GRACE AND THE RISK OF AGENCY

Preface

This book is the eighth in the series from the annual Women's Conference, sponsored by Brigham Young University and the Relief Society of The Church of Jesus Christ of Latter-day Saints. Selections in this volume were presented at the 1993 conference.

We are deeply grateful to Carol Lee Hawkins, chair of the conference, and her committee of BYU faculty and Relief Society representatives, who spent many hours planning and coordinating the conference presentations.

We thank Dawnmarie S. Lunnen, of the Women's Research Institute at BYU, who helped prepare this volume for publication. She transcribed hours of audiotape, coordinated transcripts, manuscripts, and page proofs between the authors and the editors, helped track down citations, and provided all the computer skills. We appreciate her personal interest in this project and her perceptive suggestions.

We are also grateful to Suzanne Brady of Deseret Book for her endurance, advice, and superb editorial assistance in turning the manuscript into a book.

Above all, we thank the authors for the time and energy they have devoted to preparing their conference presentations for publication in this volume. We are grateful for their honesty, intelligence, and willingness to share their lives with our readers.

"From Grace to Grace"

ELAINE L. JACK

Each year I look forward to the Women's Conference, anticipating seeing your faces, feeling your spirits, sensing your intensity of testimony and your commitment to Christ. What a blessing such conferences are for us, to share a time together—and in the company of angels.

The 1993 conference theme, "From Grace to Grace," refers to the Lord's grace, that all-encompassing love that knows no bounds. As the conference progressed, I gained a greater understanding of the grace of God in my life. To me, grace is much more than a word. It is an eternal principle with major force in our lives today. In her keynote address, "In the Covenant of Grace," Carol Madsen made grace very real when she said, "We all yearn to feel the touch of grace in our lives, moments that capture the soul and hold it, a willing hostage, away from the assaults and demands of the unjust world in which we live."

By prayerful study, we can appreciate more fully our "Covenant of Grace." We are a covenant-making people. A covenant is a mutual agreement or promise between two people. Our covenants hold great significance because we make them with the Lord. Each week as we take the sacrament, we covenant always to remember him. We covenant at baptism to take his name upon us, we covenant to pay our tithes, and we covenant in our temple ordinances.

The Savior has told us, "As I have loved you . . . love one another." (John 13:34.) During his earthly ministry he showed us how to apply "grace for grace." (Helaman 12:24.) To the woman at the well he offered kindness and concern. So can we. To Peter, Christ reached his hand over the waters, to lift his faltering disciple. To those who jeered at him, scourged him, and hung him on the cross, he said simply, "Father,

Elaine L. Jack grew up in Cardston, Alberta, Canada. She and her husband, Joseph E. Jack, are the parents of four sons and have twelve grandchildren. Sister Jack serves as general president of the Relief Society of The Church of Jesus Christ of Latter-day Saints.

forgive them; for they know not what they do." (Luke 23:34.) To the Nephites, he blessed their little children one by one and prayed unto the Father for them. These are our models of grace.

We are Latter-day Saint women not because of what we do but because we know who we are—daughters of God. We value such definition. While some choose to march or shout or trample others to find their place, we are secure. We are women of covenant. Our attention to "grace for grace" is not a strident shout for a rank in the world, a scramble for recognition or acclaim. It is a quiet reassurance speaking softly to our souls that peace and love, hope and gentility, reverence and joy bring about change and good works. Indeed, we stand before the world today to rejoice in the grace of God, the greatest power on earth. Our goodness reaches out to all around us. It changes lives and touches hearts, heals souls and lights the path for others to follow.

In the jumble of priorities in this world, I want you to know where I stand. I have always found direction in a poem of Relief Society General President Louise Y. Robison, which reads,

> God, give me sympathy and sense
> And help me keep my courage high.
> God, give me calm and confidence
> And please—a twinkle in my eye. [1]

Today we see all around us the adversary at work—and succeeding. He has twisted truths to his purposes, and throngs have followed. But there are amid the masses those who stand out, who witness by their lives the covenants they have made to the Lord. Sisters, we're in a different position than women of the world. We have made covenants with the Lord.

These covenants include our willingness to "lay aside the things of this world, and seek for the things of a better." (D&C 25:10.) I am dedicated to that charge. The merging of sacred and secular in every field and in every endeavor is a major contribution of our people in this challenging era. From gatherings such as the BYU-Relief Society Women's Conference, we can take into the world an understanding of eternal principles applied to earthly needs and measures.

I want you to know that I embrace the blessings that come from working with those who hold the Lord's priesthood in these last days. We must stand united as a people for the Lord to call us one. This is a church of eight and a half million people, a force for good yoked by priesthood power to accomplish the Lord's will. It was in response to the Lord that the sisters of the Relief Society put in place 151 years ago the call to action, "Charity Never Faileth." Today righteous women are making a difference in their homes, wards, governments, businesses, and neighborhoods. Often we feel the Savior's love in the touch of a friend, a note from a neighbor, a dandelion bouquet picked by a small child, a smile and a wave from across the street, or, while reading the scriptures, a silent but clearly enunciated answer to a pressing problem.

His cause is our only cause in these latter days. His work is not cluttered by other agendas. We are on the path of eternal life, and we must not be deterred.

I know that the Lord is with us, that his grace abounds in our lives. I have felt his love and support, his purpose, his consistency, his mercy, and his peace. I think of instances when the Lord has reached into my life. He didn't right the wrongs or fix things, but I have learned that his grace transcends circumstances that are mortal and reminds us of the joy of salvation and the sustaining power of righteousness. He has told us, "Be faithful and diligent in keeping the commandments of God, and I will encircle thee in the arms of my love." (D&C 6:20.) His grace is sufficient for us all. We have no need for more.

As we learn together of our Savior's love and the gift of grace in our lives, let us value that promise in Moroni 9:26, "May the grace of God the Father, whose throne is high in the heavens, and our Lord Jesus Christ, who sitteth on the right hand of his power . . . be, and abide with you forever." Forever, my sisters, is the Lord's "grace for grace" to his people.

NOTE

1. Jill Mulvay Derr, Janath Russell Cannon, and Maureen Ursenbach Beecher, *Women of Covenant: The Story of Relief Society* (Salt Lake City: Deseret Book Co., 1992), p. 249.

In the Covenant of Grace

CAROL CORNWALL MADSEN

An old Hebrew legend relates a conversation that Moses had with the Lord. In the story, Moses asked God to grant him three wishes, one of which was to explain by what law He governed the world. Why, Moses wondered, did He allow the just to suffer and the unjust to enjoy happiness or, at other times, permit both to be happy or both to suffer? In answer, God showed Moses His great treasure troves and explained the destination of each, including the various rewards for the good and the just—those people, He said, who give alms to the poor and care for widows and orphans. "But for whom is this treasure?" Moses asked when they came upon one of immense size, and God answered: "Out of the treasures that I have shown thee I give rewards to those who have deserved them by their deeds; but out of this treasure do I give to those who are not deserving, for I am gracious to those also who may lay no claim to My graciousness, and I am bountiful to those also who are not deserving of My bounty." Then he said to Moses, "Thou canst not grasp all the principles which I apply to the government of the world, but some of them I shall impart to thee. When I see human beings who have no claim to expectations from Me . . . but who pray to Me and implore Me, then do I grant their prayers and give them what they require for subsistence."[1]

Moses expected an answer expressed in terms of logic and law, but the Lord answered him with spiritual truths that defied logic and transcended law. "I will meet the demands of justice and reward the good for their deeds," the Lord was saying to Moses, "but I will also serve the claims of mercy. My love extends to all, deserving of it or not." We

Carol Cornwall Madsen is an associate professor of history and research historian with the Joseph Fielding Smith Institute for Church History at Brigham Young University. She and her husband, Gordon A. Madsen, are the parents of six children. She serves in her ward Relief Society.

can recognize the truth of this legend as we begin to understand the place of grace in our lives.

We have probably at times asked the same questions Moses asked. Like him, we tend to be justice oriented, programmed to expect rewards for good behavior and punishment for bad. But the equation begins to break down, and with it our sense of certitude, when our good efforts seem to go unrewarded and the undeserving seem to prosper. Only when we recognize that we ourselves are often undeserving of God's goodness do we begin to see the blessing it is that life is not wholly governed by our concept of justice, that there is, thankfully, a superior law by which God governs his world.

Paul explained to the Romans the transcendent power of this higher principle. "As by the offence of one judgment came upon all men to condemnation; even so by the righteousness of one the free gift came upon all. . . . For as by one man's disobedience many were made sinners, so by the obedience of one shall many be made righteous. . . .Where sin abounded," Paul concluded, "grace did much more abound." (Romans 5:18–20.) Christ's sacrifice, he explained, allows grace to rule our destiny.

I believe we can learn something about this free gift from the parable of the prodigal son. (See Luke 15:11–32.) Our attention and empathy frequently focus on the faithful older brother, who stayed at his father's side, tending his own inheritance but receiving no celebration and feeling that his erring brother was unjustly rewarded. Perhaps we even tend to identify with him as we seek to live good lives ourselves. But who of us can claim to be the older son? Who of us has not left the Father's presence to tarry awhile in a sin-filled world, succumbing to our own weaknesses but yearning to return one day to our Father's house, even as a servant? The operative power in this story is grace, not justice. The parable is a reminder to us of the limitless reach of God's grace, and God's grace is our hope.

We are rightly taught that most blessings are earned, but as a result we sometimes come to see them as our "right." Such a concept, Lowell Bennion has cautioned, blurs our "vision of God's grace," so freely given.[2] We learn in Ephesians 2:8–9 that "by grace are [we] saved through faith," but "not of [our]selves: it is the gift of God: not of works, lest any man should boast." "What we do by our own effort," Brother Bennion has suggested, "is to prepare ourselves to receive the gifts of Deity. . . . Grace," he says, "precedes, accompanies, and completes individual effort and merit."[3] Our faith is manifest in our works, in both our acceptance of the saving ordinances of the gospel and our Christian service. Our efforts show our willingness to follow God's plan for our salvation and to heed his word to "be not weary in well-doing." (D&C 64:33.) They are expressions of gratitude for his blessings, for that unmerited gift of life itself, which he has so graciously given us. They are opportunities to return good for good.

Remember the story of Jean Valjean, the major character in Victor Hugo's *Les Miserables,* the novel that has become such a moving musical production in recent years? At the beginning of the story, Jean Valjean has been released from prison after serving nineteen years for stealing a loaf of bread. As a former prisoner, he is unable to find a place to stay but is finally given refuge in the home of the bishop of Digne, who kindly offers him food and rest. During the night, however, Jean in desperation steals the bishop's silverware and flees. He is immediately captured and returned to the good bishop. Without any censure, the bishop not only gives Jean what he has stolen but also adds his silver candlesticks to the gift, asking only that he use the silver as a means of living an honest life. After nineteen years of undeserved punishment, Jean is given a new life through undeserved mercy. He commits his life thereafter to proving worthy of that merciful act. Grace begets grace.

There is a beautiful symmetry in the doctrines of grace and works. Balancing the Lord's counsel to be engaged in good works are comparable scriptural reminders that "it is by grace that we are saved, after all we can do." (2 Nephi 25:23.) The two are complementary. God's grace unlocks the door to salvation, and our faith and works lead us through it and take us closer to him. Both grace and works are freewill offerings—doing for others what they cannot do for themselves: God for us through his grace, and we for others through our works.

Sometimes, in our zeal to do well, we upset the symmetry. We tend to magnify works and forget grace. By defining well-doing as something beyond our daily commitments to family, work, and Church, as many of us do, we diminish the meaning and value of our good works on behalf of those nearest to us, our first responsibilities. In a recent reading of Proverbs 31, which describes the virtuous woman, I found that out of sixteen verses that enumerate her qualities, fifteen praised her good works in behalf of her husband, her children, her servants, and the household for which she was responsible. (Proverbs 31:10–31.)

Whether our primary duties are in or out of the home, or whatever the makeup of our families or households, each of them makes its own claims on us, often leaving us little time and energy for additional well-doing. But life continually changes, and opportunities to serve beyond the needs of our immediate circle really do knock more than once. Were we to look in on our lady of Proverbs some years later, with her children grown and her household cares lessened, perhaps the ratio would be reversed and most of the verses would praise her good works beyond her household.

What I am suggesting, sisters, is that we remember that in our cycle of life there is a season for everything, and whatever we do that produces good, at home or abroad, can be counted as good works and well-doing. Even Eliza R. Snow, who continually urged the sisters to attend to their "social duties," also cautioned them to "let [their] first business be to perform [their] duties at home." "But," she promised, "inasmuch as you are wise stewards, . . . you will find that your capacity will increase, and you will be astonished at what you accomplish."[4]

I would hope that when our need to be engaged in well-doing outpaces our physical capacity, the feelings of guilt that often beset us at those times would surrender to feelings of peace and gratitude for the place of grace in our lives. How often has God told us, My grace is sufficient for you? (See Ether 12:27.) Do we ever really ponder what that means? I think he wants us to give grace its due in our lives, to yield ourselves to that unearned blessing more often so that it might lighten our spiritual load and diminish our sense of inadequacy. I think it means to depend more than we do on the enabling power of God's grace to accept and meet our daily commitments, to realize, in short, as the popular hymn tells us, "Grace shall be as your day."[5]

I also think that the Lord would have us remove the emotional and spiritual impediments we create for ourselves that hedge up our souls and deprive us of his Spirit. Perhaps you recall the dream of Martha Cragun Cox that was included in a Relief Society lesson some years ago. Martha was a plural wife and a schoolteacher in St. George in the 1880s, forced to support her children herself because of the federal prosecution of polygamists during that period. In her dream, Martha was bowed down by a heavy chain about her neck from which hung bundles containing the sorrows, disappointments, and resentments that she had allowed to grow and weigh so heavily upon her. Martha was told to place the heavy chain on a rod above the fireplace; then she removed the bundles and examined them one by one. She began to see how embittered she had become and how her resentments had grown far out of proportion to the wrongs she had sustained. She began to realize that the federal marshals, whom she had so bitterly resented, had not done nearly as much harm as they had the power to do; that the mail delivery service that had been imposed on her family to provide, though hard on her young sons, brought them needed income; that those who owed her money were just as poor as she was; and that the 10 percent of her students' tuition kept by the attorney who collected it for her was a small price to pay for relieving her of that burden.

One by one, as she examined them, the bundles began to disappear until she came to the last one, which held her unrelieved sorrow at the loss of her infant. The bundle reminded her of how she often spread out the little baby clothes "on [her] bed on lonely stormy nights when there was no one there to see or hear [her] weep over them." But that bundle also disappeared as she took it from the chain. At last she felt free. When she awoke, she resolved to be truly free. "I made it a rule [from that day on]," she wrote, "to sing a song to the little children on my lap. To the little Indian boy who shared a scolding with [my son] Edward one night and went supperless to his camp, I gave a handsome new shirt to make amends. One day," she noted, "when an Indian woman came to my door with an almost naked child held under her fur robe, I got out the box [of baby clothes] and a feeling of shame came upon me as I gave the little flannel dress and other things to put upon the child, a shame for the tears I had shed over it. I told her to tell the others who had babes to come and get the rest of the things— all but the little shoes—I felt I must keep them. But when I saw the blue feet and legs of one of the little babes I said, 'That bundle must come, all of it, from my chain.'"[6]

When Martha no longer demanded justice from life, she reached a pivotal point in her spiritual understanding. Often forgiving is as difficult as repenting, but Martha experienced a spiritual rebirth when she let go of her catalogue of injustices and allowed herself to forgive. She had made room in her soul for grace when she exchanged bitterness and resentment for kindness and understanding. Through her change of heart, she experienced the transforming power of grace. As she extended it to others, she invited it into her own life. As the Lord said, "You shall receive grace *for* grace." (D&C 93:20; emphasis added.)

May I mention an experience of my own. Some years ago, a series of unfortunate circumstances came my way. I could have coped with any one of them by itself, but collectively they overwhelmed me. I had known discouragement and despondency before and thought that time would be the healing power once again, but as days turned into weeks and weeks into months and more without a change, I knew I had begun to slip into a depression I could not wholly manage. My mind could not let go of the "what ifs" and "if onlys," and the regrets immobilized me. Though my mind told me I had to adjust to what I could not change, I nonetheless felt undeserving of these misfortunes and entitled to some resolution, some compensation, and certainly, at the very least, some comfort or peace of mind. But my demands brought no relief, and I became bitter and resentful.

Through it all I mechanically met the requirements of each day, thinking I could hide my growing sense of helplessness behind a veneer of everyday busyness. But one day my astute daughter asked, "Mother, how long do you intend to go on this way?" I was stunned. My secret, I discovered, was not as secret as I had so foolishly assumed. But more than that, her piercing question let me see, through her eyes, what I had become. I had been broken in mind and spirit by circumstances I could not control, but I had responded with self-pity and, worse, self-righteousness. I was yet to learn that in the Savior's lexicon, self-pity is not the same as a broken heart nor is a bruised ego the same as a contrite spirit. Her question began a long, hard journey in which I learned much about the Savior's patience, love, and efforts to keep us close to him.

Like Martha, I had let bitterness and pride create a barrier between me and the Lord. There was no way that his Spirit could break through that barricade and bring the comfort and strength I so longed for. Only with my daughter's question did I really begin to understand myself, my dependence on God, and especially on his mercy—his forgiveness of my pride and self-righteousness and his willingness to help me find the way back. Each step became an act of faith, of reliance on his guidance and help. I made no more demands, no defiant indictments of the Spirit, no self-righteous outbursts. I had, in a miraculous way for me, experienced a change of heart and, like Martha, felt the transforming power of God's grace. I came to know that in the end, whatever our store of good works and pile of accomplishments, or whatever our weaknesses, mistakes, and unfulfilled intentions, God looks on the heart and knows us by what he sees there.[7]

When we feel inadequate to meet the challenges life throws our way, we ought to consider this passage from Ether: "I give unto [you] weakness that [you] may be humble; and my grace is sufficient for all [who] humble themselves before me . . . and have faith in me." (Ether 12:27.) God knows we are weak. He gave us our weaknesses. And he knows that most of us will demonstrate our weaknesses many times over before we leave this life. This is the risk of agency. But as he so wisely knew, it is through our weakness that we discover humility, and it is through humility that we find God.

We are probably never more humble than when we reach the point of acknowledging our weaknesses in that process we call repentance. Repentance means swallowing our pride, acknowledging our failures, admitting our mistakes, and recognizing our dependence on the Lord. This is not a very easy task, especially at a time when society extols independence, self-reliance, and individual rights. True humility, the scriptures tell us, is a broken heart and a contrite spirit, the elements of repentance, and repentance opens our hearts to receive God's grace. The power of God's grace, in turn, enables us to overcome our weaknesses. Christ's atonement broke the tyranny of justice and opened the way for God's mercy to claim "all those who have a broken heart and a contrite spirit; and unto none else can the ends of the law be answered." (2 Nephi 2:7.)

Let me tell you about the transforming power of humility and grace in the life of Waltrout Jeromin of Hamburg, Germany. A child of the war displaced from her home and left without material resources, and worse, without faith, she eventually married, only to lose her husband several years later in an accident. Her sons helped her as they grew older, but life was never easy for the Jeromins. One day Waltrout reached a point where she saw no solution, felt no hope. For the first time in her life, she turned to prayer. In one of those missionary miracles, two elders just happened to be on her street that day. Within the hour of her prayer, they rang her doorbell. When she looked out the window of her apartment, she saw two young men, their figures clearly visible in a glow that set them apart from the gathering darkness of the evening, even though the porch light was not on. When the missionaries told her they had come to bring a message of hope and peace, Sister Jeromin brought them into her small apartment and with unabating tears listened as they taught her of God's love for her and the atoning sacrifice of his Son. As the missionaries later explained, "We were not sure she heard anything we said; she just cried through the whole lesson. But she accepted the gospel right from the beginning, and her life changed completely."[8] A broken heart, a contrite spirit, and a life touched by grace.

We are living in a time of dramatic social change, much of it directly related to women. It has raised unanswered questions and unresolved issues for many of us, leaving us at times angry, confused, frustrated, and even discouraged. Each of us, I believe, must seek our own answers to the troubling questions and find our own peace. Mine came as my son and daughter went into the mission field. As I saw through them the gospel's power to transform lives, like Sister Jeromin's, I began to rediscover the central place of the gospel in my life. I began to reassess my hierarchy of spiritual needs and to let go of those issues that seemed to me to be secondary to that basic truth. I felt a few of the bundles begin to slip off my chain.

We may not fully understand the theology of the Atonement nor completely comprehend the depth of God's love and mercy for us in giving us the free gift of life by the sacrifice of his Son. But I think we all yearn to feel the touch of grace in our lives, moments that capture the soul and hold it, a willing hostage, away from the assaults and demands of the unjust world in which we live.

My missionary daughter discovered that the moments may be fleeting and unexpected but powerfully moving and life changing. New to the town of Newport, Wales, she and her companion were asked to accompany the elders in their district to visit a man named Brian. Brian was sixty-five years old, a former army surgeon who had served in the Persian Gulf War. He told the missionaries that his only child, a daughter, had been brutally raped and murdered by a man the family knew. A few weeks later, he had been diagnosed with acute leukemia. His wife, unable to cope with such overwhelming tragedies, took her own life. In the year since then, Brian had given up their home, distributed his belongings among relatives, and moved into a housing development for the poor. He spent most of his time in the hospital undergoing painful treatments for his disease. In the evenings he read the Bible, often taking it with him as he walked along the road, standing under a streetlight to read, mainly to help keep his mind from the constant pain. That was where he met the missionaries.

"So much happened that day in his room," my daughter Marianne wrote, "but basically he just opened his heart up to us. He was finally able to be honest with someone about his pain because the Spirit so strongly touched him. He said that he felt as though we had brought Jesus into the room with us. He is such a humble man, and I just cried as he told us about his life. He has such a strong belief in God and Jesus, and he is so forgiving. He is praying for an opportunity before he dies to see the man who murdered his daughter and to be able to forgive him face to face. As we sat there listening to him, he said to us, 'You are truly disciples of Christ, and I know you are an answer to my prayers. Each night I pray to God to ease my pain, and today you have done that. My body still aches, but my heart has been lifted, and my burdens are gone.'" My daughter concluded, "I saw the Spirit change a suffering man's life . . . for a few hours he had peace, and I was able to be a part of that." Brian had eased his emotional pain through his tremendous act of forgiving, and God had lifted his spirit through the power of His grace.

I believe that our need to feel those moments of grace is like Susan Greene's, who, after a long, hard winter in Cache Valley in 1874, wrote: "I begin to feel almost impatient for the snow and frost to quit the earth, and let the sun warm and prepare it for the labors of the husbandman and the reception of seeds and plants. You know I must have my little flower-garden if there is the least chance for such a thing, wherever I am."⁹

Moments of spiritual connection are like Susan's garden. They comfort, inspire, and refresh the spirit, and we must have them wherever we are. They are the power that lifts us from the bench to bear testimony, the feeling of wholeness that follows honest prayer, the sudden illumination when we recognize spiritual truth in words we hear or read, and they are the healing of our souls when we can truly forgive those who have wronged us. But, like the garden, they are not always self-generating, and they have need of constant nurturing. We can be catalysts for such moments in each other's lives if we follow the counsel of Peter to the Ephesians: "As every [one] hath received the gift," he said, "even so minister the same one to another, as good stewards of the manifold grace of God." (1 Peter 4:10.)

If I have learned anything from my study of our Latter-day Saint foremothers, it is that they were good stewards of that gift. They exhibited through the most ordinary acts of their daily lives an abiding consciousness of the blessings of the gospel. It was their defense against adversity and their impetus to serve. Such simple things as a Sunday sermon, a neighbor's testimony, a friend's visit, a gathering of sisters, their diaries attest, were moments of reaffirmation of God's goodness in bringing the gospel to them. As good stewards, they ministered to one another in a myriad of ways because they needed each other, drawing together in a community of faith, love, and support. As Emmeline Wells said of the women with whom she had worshipped and worked throughout her long life, "I loved [them] as much as if bound by kindred ties, closer, perhaps, because our faith and works were so much in tune with our everyday life."[10] Their problems are our problems. They worried about their children, struggled as single parents or working mothers, battled crises of faith, and often felt lonely and overwhelmed with work and responsibility. But they were linked together as sisters in the gospel, willing to share one another's burdens as well as joys in whatever way their circumstances permitted.

I think of the women who donated their Sunday egg money to send their sister saints to medical schools, or to pay the publishing costs of a friend's book of poetry, or to send their beloved leader, Eliza R. Snow, as their proxy on a pilgrimage to the Holy Land.

I think of those women who ministered to one another through their Church callings. One of the most memorable times in Mary Ellen Kimball's life was the day she received the temple ordinances from her sister-wife Vilate in the Nauvoo Temple. "I was overwhelmed by love and admiration for her," Mary Ellen wrote. "I knew her to be a Saint. No one could fill that position so well without the Spirit of our Saviour to assist them to do it."[11] The Logan Temple was the setting for another spiritual exchange. On Mary Ann Maughan's birthday in 1894, seventy of the Logan Temple and Relief Society sisters commemorated the day with her by acting as proxies for her kindred dead.[12] What an act of love that was, not only for Mary Ann but for the seventy deceased women who were given a gift of eternal value that day.

I think of Elizabeth Ann Whitney, who opened her home to Emma and Joseph Smith, total strangers to her, when they arrived in Kirtland, Ohio, in the harsh winter of 1831, a home that would become the setting of some of Joseph Smith's most significant revelations. It was the beginning of a relationship of loyalty and love between Emma and Elizabeth Ann. And I think of Sarah Cleveland, whose home in Quincy, Illinois, provided a place of rest and refuge for Emma, a stranger to Sarah, when she fled Missouri with her young children, leaving her husband behind in Liberty Jail. Is it any wonder that Emma Smith chose these good women to be her counselors in the Nauvoo Relief Society, the organization devoted to compassion and caring?

Ministering one to another as good stewards, even in such modest ways, became a binding act for both giver and receiver. Martha Needham was only one of many who relished these intimate and spiritual experiences with the women she served and declared that she "wanted to spend the rest of her life in doing good to others and blessing and confirming them."[13]

These were not extraordinary women, and their lives, like ours, unfolded against all the exigencies of daily living. But their faith in the reality of eternal life and their understanding of God's mercy as the operative power in this life gave transcendent meaning to each day's experience. Indeed, like the Savior, in whom their lives were centered, they lived from grace to grace, growing in knowledge and faith through their daily struggles and depending on the enabling power of grace to meet the challenges that always lay before them. Each said in her own way, "I have done the best I can and leave the rest to the Lord."

The words of Zina Young, taken from her testimony at a women's meeting in Salt Lake City in 1874, are for me the consummate metaphor for Peter's admonition. "It is a blessing to meet together," she said to the sisters assembled. "The Spirit of God is here, and when we speak to one another, it is like oil going from vessel to vessel."[14] All of the comforting, healing, and empowering qualities of consecrated oil are invoked in that image of woman ministering to woman.

Now, let me return to the Hebrew legend. In his dialogue with the Lord, Moses had hoped to penetrate God's inscrutable ways. The Lord's answer, however, was just as inscrutable to Moses. But the answer revealed the nature of God, and if Moses was listening with spiritual ears, he heard a clear and indisputable message in the *unspoken* words of God's answer. The Lord said to Moses in words he could hear: "I am gracious to the deserving and also to those who make no claim to my graciousness. I extend my love, my forgiveness, and my compassion to all, and give them what they need for their sustenance." His unspoken words were "Now go, and do thou likewise." (See Luke 10:37.) That is the covenant of grace.

NOTES

1. Louis Ginzberg, *The Legends of the Jews,* trans. Paul Radin, 6 vols. (Philadelphia: The Jewish Publication Society of America, 1987), 3: 134–36.

2. Lowell L. Bennion, "For by Grace Are Ye Saved," *Dialogue: A Journal of Mormon Thought* 1 (Winter 1966): 102.

3. Ibid., pp. 102, 101.

4. Eliza R. Snow, "An Address," *Woman's Exponent* 2 (15 September 1873): 68.

5. "Come, Come, Ye Saints," *Hymns of The Church of Jesus Christ of Latter-day Saints* (Salt Lake City: The Church of Jesus Christ of Latter-day Saints, 1985), no. 30.

6. Martha Cragun Cox, "My Dream of a Chain," Journal, typescript, LDS Church Archives, Salt Lake City, Utah.

7. As 1 Samuel 16:7 says: "Man looketh on the outward appearance, but the Lord looketh on the heart."

8. My son, Grant, shared this account with me from his missionary experiences.

9. "Letter to the *Woman's Exponent,*" *Woman's Exponent* 2 (1 April 1874): 166.

10. *Relief Society Magazine* 3 (February 1916): 68.

11. Mary Ellen Able Kimball, Autobiography, holograph, LDS Church Archives.

12. "Journal of Mary Ann Weston Maughan," in Kate B. Carter, comp., *Our Pioneer Heritage,* 20 vols. (Salt Lake City: Daughters of Utah Pioneers, 1959), 2:413.

13. Cache Valley Relief Society Minutes, Book B, 1881–1914, 5 Mar. 1910, p. 438, LDS Church Archives.

14. Minutes of the Senior and Junior Co-operative Retrenchment Society, 3 Oct. 1874, LDS Church Archives.

"Eve Heard All These Things and Was Glad": Grace and Learning by Experience

BRUCE C. HAFEN
MARIE K. HAFEN

Bruce: We testify that because of the Atonement of Jesus Christ, we may learn from our experience without being condemned by our experience.

Soon after Adam and Eve found themselves in the lone and dreary world, the Lord told them, "As thou hast fallen thou mayest be redeemed." (Moses 5:9.) He urged them to accept the Atonement by repenting and calling upon God in the name of the Son forevermore. He promised not only to forgive their transgression in Eden but also to cause the sorrow and the bitterness of both Eden and mortality to become the source of great meaning and joy. When Adam realized that his experience with sin and suffering could enlighten and exalt him rather than condemn him, he exclaimed: "Blessed be the name of God, for *because of my transgression* my eyes are opened, and in this life I shall have joy, and again in the flesh I shall see God." (Moses 5:10; emphasis added.)

Eve had the same astonishing insight: if only they accepted the gospel, their sad experience would not destroy them—it would actually sanctify them! "Eve, his wife, heard all these things and was glad, saying: Were it not for our transgression we never should have had seed, and never should have known good and evil, and the joy of our redemption, and the eternal life which God giveth unto all the obedient." (Moses 5:11.)

This insight is a central message of the temple endowment, taught to us through the story of Adam and Eve. A friend once said to me, "If

Bruce C. Hafen and Marie K. Hafen are the parents of seven children. Sister Hafen has served as a member of the general board of the Young Women organization of The Church of Jesus Christ of Latter-day Saints. She holds a master's degree in English from Brigham Young University and has taught courses part-time at Ricks and at BYU in composition and Shakespeare. Brother Hafen, formerly president of Ricks College and dean of the BYU law school, is the university provost and a professor of law at BYU.

the temple is our holiest place of worship and learning, shouldn't it teach the Atonement, our most sacred and central doctrine? And to do that, shouldn't the endowment focus on the life of Christ rather than on the lives of Adam and Eve?"

The temple endowment does teach the Atonement, but it focuses on Adam and Eve to teach the story of receiving the Atonement. The Savior's life is the story of giving the Atonement. We who must receive the Atonement can identify with the Adam and Eve story so fully as to say, "That is the story of my life." When we see how much their story is our story, perhaps we too will exclaim, as Eve might have, Blessed be the name of God! Because Christ came, mortality is not my enemy. It is precisely because of my mortality that in this life I shall find joy, understanding, and even the presence of God! That is because the Atonement is not a doctrine of simply erasing black marks; the Atonement is fundamentally a doctrine of human development.

A woman who was preparing a lesson on the Atonement told me that she had always believed Christ's atonement plays no role in our lives until we stand before the judgment bar of God. She said our lives and sins would then be weighed in the balance and measured against the degree of our repentance. If we have repented, she thought, the Atonement would remove the stain of our sins and we could be exalted. If that is how it works, she wondered, what can the Atonement possibly have to do with our daily mortality? I believe that the Atonement blesses us not only on Judgment Day but also in the here and now of daily life. It is not a mere abstraction for some other place and time.

Moreover, because of the Atonement's developmental purpose, it also sanctifies all of our distress, not just the distress caused by our sins. One woman told me that as a child she had been the victim of extensive sexual abuse. Years later, as she tried to cope with the wrenching psychic and spiritual trauma caused by this experience, she prayed and searched the scriptures to find healing and relief. She knew that the Atonement is the source of God's most potent healing power, but she thought the Atonement compensated only for our sins. In the dark time of her childhood, she was not a sinner but had been sinned against. How could she repent when she was the victim? Yet her pain and her sense of shame felt much like the "exquisite pain" that Alma says is suffered by those who commit serious sin. That pain somehow made her feel like a transgressor. She also felt, as did the sinful Alma, shut out by feelings of estrangement from the presence of God. She yearned, as did Alma, for the healing and forgiving balm of Christ's love. Could she find what Alma found in our Lord's atonement? Could the Atonement heal her from being hurt by the sins of another person? She longed for understanding.

There are endless variations on this theme. I know parents who ache from losing children, both physically and spiritually, and they wonder, Did they fail their children, or did their children fail them? And I know a good and spiritual man who lost his business and his self-respect through misjudgments that were caused by a serious emotional disorder, not by his conscious choices. Yet, even when it is unclear just what they are accountable for, good people among us take upon themselves admirable responsibility for whatever happens to them. Much of that is as it should be. But not all of it, for we suffer not only from acting but from being acted upon. The bumptious bumper sticker version of this problem might be, "Utah—guilt without sin."

We hear today that those who are hurting can be helped by therapy. And often they are—there is, in fact, a healer's art at work in much professional treatment. Some people, however, assume that religion is of little help in solving serious personal problems; to them religion is just so many clichés and abstractions, so much history, so much irrelevance. In that view of religion, the Atonement is a sterile set of philosophical abstractions that deal only with sin and apply only after death.

But Jesus is the Great Healer, and his atonement is the heart of our theology. No therapist can match that healing power. When is the power of the Master Healer accessible to us? Should we be surprised to discover that the Atonement, the core doctrine of the gospel, applies to the core problems of our mortal lives—all of them?

The story of Adam and Eve teaches us that the Atonement is for all of life, each day of our lives. The Savior's gracious power not only heals and comforts but is also a source of personal growth and development, leading to an understanding of life and a fullness of joy. The Atonement is thus developmental and practical, not static and abstract.

According to Lehi, "If Adam had not transgressed he would not have fallen, but he would have remained in the garden of Eden." He and Eve "would have had no children; wherefore they would have remained in a state of innocence, having no joy, for they knew no misery; doing no good, for they knew no sin." (2 Nephi 2:22–23.) This passage seems to say what many parents have long suspected—if they had no children, they would have no misery. Yet without children and without misery, they would also have no joy. But, taught Lehi, the Fall—with its misery, its sorrow, and even its sin—was not a mistake or an accident. The Fall was consciously designed, misery and all, to bring us joy and freedom: "Adam fell that men might be; and men are, that they might have joy. And the Messiah cometh in the fulness of time . . . that they . . . become free forever, knowing good from evil; to act for themselves." (2 Nephi 2:25–26.)

The Lord taught Adam this same understanding of life. He said Adam's children would experience the bitterness of mortality, but "they taste the bitter, that they may know to prize the good." (Moses 6:55.) Indeed, "If they never should have bitter they *could not* know the sweet." (D&C 29:39; emphasis added.) And the role of the Atonement in that process is to compensate for—to heal us from—the effects of the bitter, after we do all we can do by ourselves: "It is by grace that we are saved, after all we can do." (2 Nephi 25:23.)

Thus does the grace of Christ, unlocked by his atoning sacrifice, heal us from the wounds of our sins and all our other infirmities. As we repent of our conscious sins, accept the gospel, and do all else we can do, we enter into a holy relationship with our Savior based on the two-way covenants made possible by his atonement. Through our covenant relationship with him, celebrated each week by the sacrament, he heals us in at least four distinct ways. First, he satisfies the eternal law of justice, relieving us of the burden of paying for our sins, so long as we repent of them. Second, his influence interacts with our righteous yearnings and our repentance to change our hearts until we desire goodness continually. Third, he bridges any chasm that separates and estranges us from God. Many things can create this sense of alienation—unintentional mistakes or undeserved discouragement and confusion, as well as sin. Regardless of whether his sheep run away or lose their way or are stolen away, the Good Shepherd will search for them when they are lost, pick them up, and carry them home, making them "at one" with him and his Father. That is the work of the great "at-one-ment." And, fourth, once we have done all we can do to make restitution, the Savior will help to compensate for the harm we may have done or the harms done to us, repairing and restoring our spiritual and psychic losses, whether caused by sin or other factors.

Among these four sources of healing, only the first two deal exclusively with the effects of conscious sin. We may become alienated from God or we may injure other people, not only through sinful acts but also by careless mistakes or by the consequences of unavoidable adversity. From the cumulative effect of these causes, we experience the bitter, which can teach us to know the sweet and prize the good. The grace of Jesus Christ makes that sweetness both possible and lasting by purging, healing, and cleansing us from the stains of all mortal bitterness, so long as we in good faith do "all we can do." (2 Nephi 25:23.) His grace lets us learn from our experience without being condemned by that experience. Thus does the Atonement enable our growth and our understanding. No wonder "Eve . . . heard all these things and was glad." (Moses 5:11.)

Beyond these ways of healing, the Lord's grace also adds a fifth, more affirmative dimension: he endows and blesses us with hope, charity, understanding, and joy as we move beyond forgiveness and healing toward the eternal life of possessing a divine nature. At that crowning stage, not only will we desire the good or even do good but we will, as the Lord said to Adam, "prize the good"—savor it, enjoy it, comprehend it. A developmental perspective helps us see that, desirable as it is for us to avoid evil or repent from it, it is not the same as doing—let alone prizing—the good.

A father once scolded his son a few days before Christmas because the little boy was terrorizing the house and creating a constant mess. The father said, "If you aren't good, Santa won't bring you anything." Soon the father wondered where his boy had gone—things were too quiet. He found him lying very still on his bed, looking stonily at the ceiling. "What are you doing?" the father asked. "I'm being good," said the boy. He was avoiding evil by avoiding movement. That is not what it means to prize the good. We seek more than neutrality, more than avoidance. We seek to be good, as the character of God himself is good in its very nature. And that state of being is, like charity, ultimately a gift of Christ's atonement, bestowed upon the humble followers of Christ after they learn from experience all they can discover alone about prizing the good.

Marie: So does the Atonement work in our lives as an event or as a process? If it is an event, life is a simple test that we either pass or fail. We compile a certain number of black marks and white marks. At life's end, we add up the marks, compute our repentance points, and check the score. Above some fixed level, the Atonement applies, our sins are paid for, and we go back to square one. From that perspective, repentance is essentially another white mark—something we do to *earn* forgiveness. But something is missing. For one thing, if the Atonement simply returns Adam and Eve to Eden, theirs is a story with no plot, no character development. Nothing really happens to them, because the Atonement erases what happens to them. There is nothing in this perspective about what it means to have learned to recognize evil and to prize the good.

Moreover, this view sees our repentance as mechanically earning enough grace to offset our black marks. If that is how we think the Atonement works, we are unlikely ever to feel the full freedom and meaning of forgiveness. As long as we believe that we earn forgiveness, we will still feel guilty, because we will sense intuitively that we do not have the power to make ourselves completely whole. The Lord's forgiveness is ultimately an act of grace. It comes as his gift, not as something we have a right to, even though we must repent as a condition of receiving it.

Consider the Atonement as a process in our lives rather than as an event. The process of atonement applies not just once but, potentially, each day of our lives. From this perspective, Adam and Eve did not simply return to Eden; rather, they moved onward from Eden through the telestial world. And because they accepted the gospel and then learned to cast Satan's influence from their lives, they kept moving with the blessings of the priesthood into the terrestrial world and finally to the celestial presence of God. In that arduous journey, our first parents learned from their own experience to distinguish good from evil. By the sorrow and sweat of earthly life, they learned the taste and, ultimately, the very meaning of the sweet and the good. They did not arrive at that understanding merely by partaking of the forbidden fruit. Their first taste of the tree of knowledge was but the beginning of a lifelong quest for meaning—not an event, but an extended process marked by having children, discovering misery, sin, goodness, joy, and the very meaning of eternal life.

When, after all that, Adam and Eve returned to the Lord's presence, we could describe their homecoming in the lines of T. S. Eliot:

> We shall not cease from exploration
> And the end of all our exploring
> Will be to arrive where we started
> And know the place for the first time.[1]

To illustrate, consider Eve's experience. Eve must have carried within her the aspiration of each living thing to become like its parent. As God's literal spirit daughter, Eve probably desired to become like him. Perhaps the serpent in the garden played to that natural desire when he told Eve that if she would eat of the tree of knowledge, she would "be as gods, knowing good and evil." (Moses 4:11.) The Lord had forbidden them to partake of this fruit. But, Elder John A. Widtsoe taught, that commandment was primarily a "warning," simply disclosing to Adam and Eve that the choice to seek knowledge would bring death and great sorrow.[2] But they freely made the brave choice, perhaps sensing that that was the pathway not just to knowledge but to eternal life—which is to become like God.

The last line in the song "I Am a Child of God" originally read, "Teach me all that I must *know* to live with him someday." It was later changed to "Teach me all that I must *do.* . . ."[3] Perhaps it might read, "Teach me all that I must *be* to live with him someday." Satan cunningly misled Eve when he said she would become as the Gods by simply knowing good and evil. Partaking of the tree of knowledge destroyed her innocence, but that was only the beginning of her quest to be as the Gods. She and Adam had to leave the security of the Garden and face the full fury of mortality. They needed to repent and obey God rather than wandering in Satan's misery-bound search for knowledge without obedience. Through the interaction of their obedience and God's mercy, they could then actually become like him, moving beyond just knowing "about" the good toward literally "being" good.

The interaction between our effort and God's grace is represented by the covenants of the Atonement, described in the sacrament prayer. Our part of that covenant is not that we may never make a mistake; it is, rather, that we are willing to take upon ourselves his name, willing to always remember him, and willing to keep his commandments. That willingness shows where our hearts really are. On that condition, he will always be with us to heal, to compensate, to strengthen us by the gifts of his Spirit—for those gifts are "given for the benefit of those who love me and keep all my commandments, *and [those] that seeketh so to do.*" (D&C 46:9; emphasis added.) The Lord offers the gifts of the Spirit not only to those who do but also to those who, "willing" but struggling, seek to do God's will.

What must it have been like for Eve, the first woman, whose willingness to live a good life was constantly tested and battered by the growing pains of mortality? She had no precedent, no one who had already been through her experience. She couldn't call her mother on the phone and ask, "Mom, what did you do when your kids argued?" She and Adam had only each other—and the Spirit of the Lord. How they grew in that total interdependency! Early in their time together, Adam was defensive about his choice to eat the forbidden fruit. Under the Lord's firm questioning, he said, "*The woman* thou gavest me, and commandest that she should remain with me, she gave me of the fruit and I did eat." (Moses 4:18; emphasis added.) But after their shared experience brought them, together, into the depths of humility and the heights of marital commitment, we read, "And Adam *and his wife* mourned before the Lord, because of Cain and his brethren." (Moses 5:27; emphasis added.) Their love grew. They learned *together* the tastes of bitter and sweet and the joy of their redemption.

Arta Romney Ballif once wrote a poem in which she imagined Eve's experience as a mother and a wife—her questions, her cries for understanding, her quest to know God.[4] Sister Ballif, who died earlier this year, was a sister to Marion G. Romney, the wife of Ariel Ballif, and the mother of Jae Ballif of the BYU faculty. Jae read this poem at his mother's funeral. Note the symbols—the fruit of both the garden and the body, the storm, the repetition of *multiply* and *sorrow*. Consider how the Atonement could help Eve with the anguish she describes here:

Lamentation

And God said, *"BE FRUITFUL, AND MULTIPLY—"*
Multiply, multiply — echoes multiply

God said, *"I WILL GREATLY MULTIPLY THY SORROW—"*
Thy sorrow, sorrow, sorrow—

I have gotten a man from the Lord
I have traded the fruit of the garden for fruit of my body
For a laughing bundle of humanity.

And now another one who looks like Adam
We shall call this one "Abel."
It is a lovely name, "Abel."

Cain, Abel, the world is yours.
God set the sun in the heavens to light your days
To warm the flocks, to kernel the grain
He illuminated your nights with stars

He made the trees and the fruit thereof yielding seed
He made every living thing, the wheat, the sheep, the cattle
For your enjoyment
And, behold, it is very good.

. . .

Adam? Adam
Where art thou?
Where are the boys?
The sky darkens with clouds.
Adam, is that you?
Where is Abel?
He is long caring for his flocks.
The sky is black and the rain hammers.
Are the ewes lambing
In this storm?

Why your troubled face, Adam?
Are you ill?
Why so pale, so agitated?
The wind will pass
The lambs will birth
With Abel's help.

Dead?
What is dead?

Merciful God!

Hurry, bring warm water
I'll bathe his wounds
Bring clean clothes
Bring herbs.
I'll heal him.

I am trying to understand.
You said, "Abel is dead."
But I am skilled with herbs
Remember when he was seven
The fever? Remember how—

Herbs will not heal?
Dead?

And Cain? Where is Cain?
Listen to that thunder.

Cain cursed?
What has happened to him?
God said, *"A fugitive and a vagabond?"*

But God can't do that.
They are my sons, too.
I gave them birth
In the valley of pain.

Adam, try to understand
In the valley of pain
I bore them
      fugitive?
      vagabond?

This is his home
This the soil he loved
Where he toiled for golden wheat
For tasseled corn.

To the hill country?
There are rocks in the hill country
Cain can't work in the hill country
The nights are cold
Cold and lonely, and the wind gales.

Quick, we must find him
A basket of bread and his coat.
I worry, thinking of him wandering
With no place to lay his head.
Cain cursed?
A wanderer, a roamer?
Who will bake his bread and mend his coat?

Abel, my son dead?
And Cain, my son, a fugitive?
Two sons
Adam, we had two sons
Both — Oh, Adam—
    multiply
    sorrow

Dear God, Why?
Tell me again about the fruit
Why?
Please, tell me again
Why?

This poem movingly depicts Eve's anguish, yet it does not tell us why she and Adam lost their sons. They may not have known why. They must have wondered if those losses were their own fault. Had they failed as parents? The poem imagines that in her very uncertainty, Eve felt estranged from God, cut off, not at all "at one" with him. And it is fair to assume that Adam's and Eve's questions and fears in losing Abel and Cain were multiplied on other dark days throughout their lives. Like Eve, sometimes we don't know—perhaps cannot know—how fully we are at fault for the bitterness we taste. When we taste the bitter, we, like Eve, can only keep trying, and wondering, and asking for understanding, perhaps in Joseph Smith's words: "O God, where art thou? And where is the pavilion that covereth thy hiding place?" (D&C 121:1.) Does the Atonement speak to such questions? I testify that it does.

Carlfred Broderick, a former stake president and well-known psychotherapist, relates the following incident. He was invited to participate in a Young Women program in his stake. The program theme was based on the *Wizard of Oz* story, hoping to teach young people that if they will follow the yellow brick road of the commandments, they will find their way safely to Oz. As the program ended, a leader asked President Broderick to say a few words. He told them that even if they keep the commandments, life will not always be a yellow brick road. He said he had just come from two wrenching hours of counseling with two faithful, devoted women in their stake. Despite their faithfulness, they found life crumbling around them. So he taught the young women and their parents what he had tried to teach the two women:

the gospel of Jesus Christ was not given us to prevent our pain. The gospel was given us to heal our pain.

That is the promise of the scriptures: the Atonement not only can heal us but it can sanctify our trying experiences to our growth. Alma summarized the breadth and depth of this awesome healing power: "And he shall go forth, suffering pains and afflictions and temptations of every kind; and this that the word might be fulfilled which saith he will take upon him the pains and the sicknesses of his people. And he will take upon him death [and the] infirmities [of his people], that his bowels may be filled with mercy, according to the flesh, that he may know according to the flesh how to succor his people according to their infirmities." (Alma 7:11–12.) Note the words *pain, sicknesses, infirmities,* and then *mercy* and *succor.*

I know a deeply religious woman who could not pray for months after losing her seventeen-year-old son in a motorcycle accident. She said to her husband, "What can I say to the Lord?" She was asking the questions Eve asked. But her faithfulness was stronger than her anguish, until she, like Eve before her, found that the healing balm of the Atonement began to soothe and heal her wounded heart.

This healing, strengthening power is not a vague abstraction of distant hope. This power flows from the fully developed theology of the Atonement. Our most fundamental doctrine truly does speak to our most fundamental problems. Listen to the Lord's words from Isaiah, noting that his promises flow from his atonement: "O Israel, fear not: for I have redeemed thee, I have called thee by thy name; thou art mine. When thou passest through the waters, I will be with thee; and through the rivers, they shall not overflow thee: when thou walkest through the fire, thou shalt not be burned; neither shall the flame kindle upon thee." (Isaiah 43:1–2.)

The Lord can and will sanctify our experience for our growth and development. Remember the fourth and fifth verses of our hymn "How Firm a Foundation":

> When through the deep waters I call thee to go,
> The rivers of sorrow shall not thee o'erflow,
> For I will be with thee, thy troubles to bless,
> And sanctify to thee thy deepest distress.

When through fiery trials thy pathway shall lie,
My grace, all sufficient, shall be thy supply.
The flame shall not hurt thee. I only design
Thy dross to consume and thy gold to refine.[5]

As this song from the first LDS hymnbook, published in 1835, suggests, the doctrines of the Restoration are full of Atonement theology. But often we don't see the breadth and strength of our own theology. The doctrine is not just that adversity can help us learn and grow; rather, it is that Christ, because of what flows from the redemption, gives us the power to make weak things strong, to sift beauty from the ashes of our fires.

When it is our turn to ask Eve's questions, let us "always remember him," for he will never forget us. His sacrifice for us binds his heart to ours. His words from 1 Nephi 21:14–16 etch an indelible impression: "But, behold, Zion hath said: The Lord hath forsaken me, and my Lord hath forgotten me—but he will show that he hath not. For can a woman forget her sucking child, that she should not have compassion on the son of her womb? Yea, they may forget, yet will I not forget thee, O house of Israel. Behold, I have graven thee upon the palms of my hands; thy walls [symbols of our barriers and needs] are continually before me." Note the symbolism of the palms of his hands. The heart of his doctrine and the heart of his love find their source in his having bought us with his blood.

Not long ago, after two frustrating years of infertility, our son and his wife were excitedly expecting their first baby. Then they were devastated to learn that their unborn baby had a serious congenital heart defect. When he was born, their little Devin weighed more than eight pounds, and he had a headful of silky, dark hair. He was, however, quite literally, born with a broken heart. I watched through the window of the ICU unit as the doctors hooked up the wires and tubes that became Devin's lifeline. I watched while his mother held him and his father and others placed their big, adult hands on his tiny newborn head to give him a name and a blessing.

Our Devin struggled mightily for three weeks, but when his struggle ended, we gathered under a large and lonely tree in the Lehi city cemetery. Family and friends and a few flowers surrounded his little coffin. The wind "galed" as my daughters played on their violins "I am a child of God" and "Teach me all that I must do"—and I thought, "All that I must be." We watched then and thereafter as Devin's parents followed in the footsteps of Adam and Eve. We watched as their unanswerable anguish turned gradually into a mellow bonding with their child beyond the veil. Now, even with the questions that remain, they know and feel and understand in ways that are otherwise undiscoverable. Their lives bear witness that the Savior takes upon him our infirmities and that without those infirmities, we, like Eve, "never should have known good and evil, and the joy of our redemption, and the eternal life which God giveth unto all the obedient." (Moses 5:11.)

Bruce: Eve's experience as a mother opens our understanding of the Atonement's developmental nature. She found that the Lord heals our separation to make us "at one" with him, not by returning us magically to Eden but by leading us through a process of learning and growing day by day toward spiritual maturity. The Lord also draws on our understanding of a woman's perspective when he teaches us that he feels toward us the way a mother feels for her child: "For can a woman forget her sucking child, that she should not have compassion on the son of her womb?" Just as a mother could never forget her child, he said, "Yet will I not forget thee." And just as a mother's body may be permanently marked with the signs of pregnancy and childbirth, he said, "I have graven thee upon the palms of my hands." (1 Nephi 21:15–16.) For both a mother and the Savior, those marks memorialize a wrenching sacrifice, the sacrifice of begetting life—for her, physical birth; for him, spiritual rebirth.

How does such a mother view her child's mistakes? Certainly not as the child does. I think of a frustrated little girl, crying and miserable because she always makes mistakes, loses her shoes, and leaves messes around the house. But her mother does not view her mistakes as hopeless disasters. She views them as growing pains. Her mother holds her, dries her tears, and tells her not to be discouraged. She will learn. She will grow. Everything will be all right. With mother's encouragement, she picks up all she can from the debris of her travail. And when she is exhausted, her mother picks up after her. Mother picks up what her daughter can't reach, what she can't find, what she can't see. Cleaning up everything can be so hard when you're little.

The Lord views our mistakes—our messes around the house—as a mother would. What seem to us like overwhelming failures are small growing pains to him. He will hold us. He will comfort us. And then, if we do our best, he will pick up after us.

A little girl I know was once so tired that she just lay down and fell asleep on the edge of a dangerously busy road. Prompted by inspiration, her mother saw her there, picked her up, and carried her to safety. I thought of her when hearing another woman describe her worry about Lehi's dream and the iron rod leading to the tree of life. She said, "My problem is not that I might leave the iron rod and wander off into the mists of darkness. My problem is that sometimes I just get so tired that I sit down in the middle of the path, unable to go on, though still clinging with my hand to the iron rod." She might have sung, "Sometimes I feel like a motherless child, a long way from home." But the Lord, like a mother, will pick up a tired child and take her by the hand toward home.

So we grow and learn, and he leads us along, saying, "Behold, ye are little children and ye cannot bear all things now; ye must grow in grace and in the knowledge of the truth. [But] fear not, little children, for you are mine. . . . And none of them that my Father hath given me shall be lost." (D&C 50:40–42.) That is how Eve and Adam gained a full knowledge of good and evil. And that is how they found the joy of their redemption—not just in one grand gesture that balanced the scales at the end of their lives, but gradually: they grew in grace and in their knowledge of the truth. This understanding of life's developmental nature tells us that even in looking for the meaning of Christ's atonement in our lives, we should focus on ordinary, accumulated experience more than on such bottom-line judgments as whether we are saints or sinners or whether society thinks of us as visible or invisible people.

The Russian author Leo Tolstoy teaches this difference between small-scale development and heroic moments on a grand stage. The real heroes of his novels are not the generals, the great aristocrats, or the dramatic figures. Rather, the characters he admires are the ordinary people who "lead undramatic lives, [but lives that] are rightly lived moment to moment and which unfold only as a background to" the stories of the visible heroes.[6] In this vision of life's meaning, writes Tolstoy scholar Gary Morson, one of the best examples of the moral and spiritual life is "the moment-to-moment conscientiousness of a good mother."[7] A good mother—like other good people—is always working, reaching, responding to others' needs. Of course she will make mistakes, many of them. She can't always be right in her judgments, can't always anticipate other people's responses. But over time, her "moment-to-moment conscientiousness" moves her along, through growing pains, through sunshine and shade, tears and troubles, until she, with the constant help of the Lord, becomes a moral virtuoso. We develop moral virtuosity the way we develop musical virtuosity—by daily, demanding practice.

Would such a mother then be aware of her goodness? Probably not. One of Tolstoy's stories, "Father Sergius," tells of "a proud man" who "trains himself to attain sainthood by grand gestures and noticeable acts of self-sacrifice." But "his quest fails, because no matter what he does to humble his pride, he is still proud of his very humility. When he at last meets a true saint, he discovers that she is unaware of her exceptionality. She is a mother who supports her daughter and the daughter's [very ill] husband," and she "reproaches herself for not going to church. She lives a life of daily kindnesses that are entirely undramatic, undiscerned, and inimitable."[8] That reminds me of what I overheard Elder Neal A. Maxwell once say of President Spencer W. Kimball: "Part of what makes him so special is that he has no idea of how special he really is."

Tolstoy believed that women often seem to understand better than men do that the moral, spiritual life is most fully lived at the prosaic level of daily toil. He believed that the typical abstract interests of men— politics, sports, the military, and philosophizing—are really quite unimportant compared to "moment-to-moment conscientiousness." I know a few men who feel such a need to worry about the "big things"—like who will win the Super Bowl, the election, and the latest far-off civil war—that they happily leave to their wives the "little things," like seeing that the children are fed, educated, and exalted. In distinguishing between the abstract world of "the great" and the everyday world of "the prosaic," Tolstoy believed that the exquisite quality of the prosaic life well lived is best described in "women's language." For him, "almost everything important" and especially "anything that has positive moral value" occurs most naturally within the world of marriage, family, and daily labor that some people commonly regard as the realm of women.[9] That is the realm of greatest moral value, not only for women but also for men. The Lord himself said that it is the realm of "my work and my glory—to bring to pass the immortality and eternal life" of his children. (Moses 1:39.)

If the Atonement is concerned with the process of our spiritual and moral development, where is its meaning most likely to be found?

Is it in long discussions of philosophical implications? Is it to be found in knowing every detail of the Savior's last hours? As valuable as such knowledge may be, the true knowledge and personal meaning of Christ's atoning sacrifice are to be found in the resolution of some person's secret sorrow, as in the story of Adam and Eve.

Consider this symbolic example. The first mortal to see the resurrected Jesus was Mary. Why had Mary and the other women gone to the tomb so early that hushed Easter morning? Did they go in search of grand theological fulfillment? No. They went to care for the body and change the linen. Some would call that "woman's work." And Mary found him there, in the midst of her workaday tasks of compassionate drudgery. We too will most likely find him there—not in abstract experience detached from mortal cares, not solely at the end of life before the grand judgment bar, but here, now, in the tears and needs of obscure and lonely sorrow.

I thank King Benjamin for clarifying this thought in our theology of the Atonement. In his final address, Benjamin spoke of God's goodness and his atonement and then he described the conditions on which we find salvation: "Repent of your sins and forsake them, and humble yourselves before God; and ask in sincerity of heart that he would forgive you; and . . . if ye have . . . tasted of his love, and have received a remission of your sins, which causeth such exceedingly great joy in your souls, . . . ye should . . . always retain in remembrance, the greatness of God, . . . and his goodness and long-suffering towards you, . . . and humble yourselves . . . , calling on the name of the Lord daily." (Mosiah 4:10–11.) Benjamin then taught that the daily cultivation of the attitude of a meek and lowly heart after our baptism is "for the sake of retaining a remission of your sins from day to day, that ye may walk guiltless before God." (Mosiah 4:26.) And "if ye do this ye shall always rejoice, and be filled with the love of God, and always retain a remission of your sins; and ye shall grow in the knowledge of . . . that which is just and true." (Mosiah 4:12.) This passage describes, in its highest sense, the moment-to-moment conscientiousness of a good mother— or father, or any child of God.

The atonement of Jesus Christ allows us to learn from our experience without being condemned by that experience. When we repent and come unto him daily in lowliness of heart, he will take upon himself all our infirmities. He himself, like a conscientious mother, will pick up after us and even at times pick us up from our collapses of fatigue along the path of the iron rod. As we move through each growth stage of life, we will experience the bitter, so that we may know to savor the sweet and prize the good. The conversion of bitter to sweet is like a catalytic process of energy creation. It leaves behind some toxically bitter wastes. After we clean up as much of that waste as we can, the Lord himself absorbs the residue, for he alone drank the bitter cup. He continually nourishes and heals us from all our losses and all our pain, whether caused by our acts or by our being acted upon. Each member of the Church is his spirit child, and he will not forget the child of his compassion, for he has graven us upon the palms of his hands. May we, like Eve, hear all these things and be glad.

NOTES

1. T. S. Eliot, "Little Gidding," *The Complete Poems and Plays, 1909–1950* (New York: Harcourt, Brace & World, 1952), p. 145.

2. John A. Widtsoe, *Gospel Interpretations: Aids to Faith in a Modern Day* (Salt Lake City: Bookcraft, 1947), p. 77.

3. *Hymns of The Church of Jesus Christ of Latter-day Saints* (Salt Lake City: The Church of Jesus Christ of Latter-day Saints, 1985), no. 301; Virginia B. Cannon, *Our Children's Songs: Teaching the Gospel with the Children's Songbook* (Salt Lake City: Deseret Book Co., 1992), pp. 82–83.

4. Arta Romney Ballif, *Lamentation and Other Poems* (Arta Romney Ballif, 1989), pp. 3–7. Used by permission.

5. *Hymns*, no. 85.

6. Gary Saul Morson, "Prosaics," *The American Scholar* (Autumn 1988): 522.

7. Ibid., p. 523.

8. Ibid., p. 522.

9. Ibid., p. 524.

Healing What Really Hurts: He Will Ease Our Burdens

STEVEN C. WALKER

ARDITH W. WALKER

Steve: When I taught a course entitled "The Problem of Pain," our then-eight-year-old daughter Rebecca, seeing that title, said, "I know what the problem of pain is: it hurts."

Ardith: The other problem is that there's so much of it. As the poet W. B. Yeats put it, "The world's more full of weeping than [we] can understand."[1] When you're human, hurting comes with the territory.

Steve: One trick to handling pain is to realize that it's not necessarily your fault. Men tend to be good at knowing that; women often aren't.

Ardith: Sometimes the hurting is our own stupid fault, and we have to stop what's causing the hurting.

Steve: But mostly it isn't our fault, and we just have to get over the hurting. Attitudes don't cause cancer. Our children's failings don't mean we've failed them. Just because loved ones no longer love us does not necessarily mean we are unlovable. One profound moral of the book of Job is that a lot of our hurting is just not our fault.

Ardith: And even when it is, it's possible to get over the hurting. I like the way Helen Keller, who knew something of suffering, said it: "Although the world is full of suffering, it is also full of the overcoming of it."[2]

Steve: So how do we manage that overcoming? Where, in the practical pains of our everyday lives, do we find comfort?

Ardith: We'd like to share some of our homemade remedies for

Steven C. Walker and Ardith W. Walker are the parents of three children. Sister Walker teaches first grade and serves as the Spiritual Living teacher in her ward Relief Society. Brother Walker is a professor of English at Brigham Young University and teaches the Gospel Doctrine course in Sunday School.

hurting—some simple, field-tested ways of applying a little first-aid for the soul.

EXPECT IT

Steve: Maybe the simplest help for dealing with hurting is to expect it.

Ardith: We don't want to put a damper on any fun you may be having, but if you're not hurting right now, you soon may be. No one is immune, so brace yourself for it.

Steve: The worst football injuries come not so much from the biggest collisions but from the unexpected hits, from getting blindsided.

Ardith: A botanist once said that by late summer you cannot find a single leaf that isn't somehow damaged—wind torn, insect bitten, sun rotted, bird scarred.

Steve: An entomologist friend of mine who studies grasshoppers claims the same is true of them—most of those tough little insects by August are missing limbs, all of them damaged somehow by life.

Ardith: Some of us may have more damage than others.

Steve: But none of us escapes unscarred.

Ardith: So expect it. I try to soak in the good times for energy to weather the hard times that will come. And then during the bad times, we have to realize things will get better.

Steve: Or maybe worse. The hurting comes, no matter how good we are. Remember when we were good, back when we first moved to Provo after graduate school, just getting our feet on the ground?

Ardith: I had saved two hundred dollars in my own little savings account toward a piano. Our bishop gave one last plea in sacrament meeting for money for the new chapel. I decided to invest one hundred dollars of that piano money with the Lord and gave it to the bishop, feeling I'd be rewarded.

Steve: During the next ten days the drapes we couldn't afford to get cleaned in the first place came back in shreds from sun rot.

Ardith: I lost a contact lens.

Steve: Our tithing check to the Boston Ward bounced, and the left rear tire on the car got a nail in it—twice. Can you remember what you said?

Ardith: "I guess the Lord wanted the whole two hundred dollars."

ENDURE IT

Steve: A second way to deal with hurting is to endure it, not give in to it but be heroic in the face of it.

Ardith: C. S. Lewis thinks "the form of every virtue at the testing point" is courage.[3] There's real power in just plain refusing to give in to the pain.

Steve: During my mission I met Sister Bean of Hartford, Connecticut. Bent double by rheumatoid arthritis, her hands so misshapen she could not feed herself, she simply kept on smiling. She was, I think, the most cheerful person I have ever known.

Ardith: Viktor Frankl, a Jew imprisoned in a concentration camp during World War II, lived on watery soup and dry bread and never knew when it would be his turn to go to the gas chambers.

Steve: Frankl was not only physically but emotionally abused; his captors sought to dehumanize him. They shaved all the hair from him, even his eyebrows.

Ardith: He refused to submit in spirit: "It becomes clear," he said, "that the sort of person the prisoner became was the result of an inner decision, and not the result of camp influences alone. . . . Any man can, even under such circumstances, decide what shall become of him—mentally and spiritually. He may retain his human dignity even in a concentration camp. . . . It is this spiritual freedom—which cannot be taken away—that makes life meaningful."[4]

Steve: "If thou art called to pass through tribulation; if thou art in perils . . . if thou shouldst be cast into the pit, or into the hands of murderers, and the sentence of death passed upon thee; . . . if the very jaws of hell shall gape open the mouth wide after thee, know thou, my son, that all these things shall give thee experience, and shall be for thy good. The Son of Man hath descended below them all. Art thou greater than he?" (D&C 122:5–8.)

Ardith: As nineteenth-century clergyman Phillips Brooks said, "O, do not pray for easy lives. Pray to be stronger [people]! Do not ask for tasks equal to your powers. Pray for powers equal to your tasks!"[5]

Steve: If it's brave we decide to be, we don't have to be brave forever—just for the next little while.

Ardith: "Courage," claims a Russian proverb, "is hanging on one minute longer."

LAUGH WITH IT

Steve: If you're not too hot on endurance and courage, a defter way to handle pain is to dodge it.

Ardith: Some pains that won't yield to the most courageous head-on facings can be distracted.

Steve: And the surest surefire way we've found of distracting ourselves from our sufferings—better than pruning roses or reading a Gerard Manley Hopkins poem, better even than smashing overheads in tennis—the best way to distract ourselves from suffering is to laugh.

Ardith: Our son Scott was almost twenty when he finally decided to go on a mission. We were ecstatic but kept our fingers crossed that he wouldn't change his mind.

Steve: The day he entered the Missionary Training Center, Scott was so depressed and ornery that we were sure he was about to change his mind.

Ardith: Everyone was supportive and kind at the MTC, but that didn't help. In the orientation meeting, Scott put his elbows on his knees and his face in his hands and reeked negativity.

Steve: In the middle of all that pain, Scott's and ours, and all that potential for worse pain, Ed Pinegar came out and spoke.

Ardith: Ed, who is shiny bald, asked a new missionary to stand up and said, "When I came here I looked just like this elder. Then they gave me a missionary haircut."

Steve: Eight jokes later, Scott laughed, leaned back in his chair, put his foot on his knee, and relaxed. The laughter took him out of his anguish into acceptance, moved him from a position of enduring pain to one of being willing to listen.

Ardith: We had my father, ill with Parkinson's disease and suffering from senility, in our home for eighteen months before he died.

Steve: The older I get, the more I think old folks' sufferings may be the saddest of sufferings.

Ardith: Daddy had been a lively church and civic leader in his day, and to see him senile was extremely difficult. We shed many tears over his condition and could have spent every day crying.

Steve: The only way we were able to keep Reed in our home was to laugh with him—and sometimes at him.

Ardith: He would forget our names and rarely called me Ardith. One day as he spoke to me he said, "Well, Mildred, Phyllis, Gwen, I mean Ar—Ar—Arthritis."

Steve: You must have been something of a pain for Reed. Another time, when we were cutting his toenails, Reed said, "Now don't be putting those toenails in the soup. Last time you did that it didn't help the soup any."

Ardith: But our favorite was one of the sermons he gave to the philodendron plant.

Steve: Reed stood before the plant and in his fullest preacher's voice said: "My dear brothers and sisters, there is only one thing you have to do to gain eternal life."

Ardith: I was at the kitchen sink, and I stood perfectly still, thinking that perhaps out of his confusion had come some profound spiritual insight. Daddy went on to say to a breathless audience of me and the philodendron:

Steve: "And that one thing, my dear brothers and sisters, is to keep all of God's commandments."

Ardith: According to *Prevention* magazine, "Laughter serves as a blocking agent. Like a bulletproof vest, it may help protect you against the ravages of . . . disease." In fact, one study reported that "finding something funny results in a significant increase in antibodies . . .

Steve: " . . . Pleasant moods . . . are associated with changes in levels of stress hormones. . . . Laughter was as effective as biofeedback in reducing stress." And laughing "requires no special training."[6]

Ardith: Humor is tragedy plus time.

Steve: The sooner we can get to the humor, the less time in the tragedy.

GROW FROM IT

Ardith: If you can't anticipate the suffering, can't endure it, can't distract it—

Steve: or even if you can—

Ardith: one of the best things to do with pain is to grow from it.

Steve: Life has a way of trading us wisdom for pain. The Norse god Odin worried about the frost giants waiting to devour his people. Desperate for a better defense against giants, he journeyed clear to the witch at the end of the world for wisdom. The wise old witch promised to trade the needed wisdom for his eye. So Odin handed over his left eye, and the witch said:

Ardith: "The wisdom you need against giants is: Keep both eyes open always."

Steve: Sometimes we can trade pain for wisdom. But the learning is not automatic. Experience may be not the best teacher for some of us but the worst.

Ardith: Anne Morrow Lindbergh looked back on the sorrows of her life and decided: "I do not believe that sheer suffering teaches. If suffering alone taught, then all the world would be wise, since everyone suffers. To suffering must be added mourning, understanding, patience, love, openness and the willingness to remain vulnerable."[7]

Steve: What if what we thought was the worst part of life—the struggling and the hurting—were to turn out to be the best part?

Ardith: What if the best things God created were deliberately designed for struggle?

Steve: What if he invented relationships not so much for compatibility and companionship and contentment as for confrontation?

Ardith: What if God designed families not for security and nurturance but for what happens most regularly in families: struggling to get along?

Steve: In families we are tutored by daily irritations, struggle, and heartaches in "mourning, understanding, patience, love, openness and the willingness to remain vulnerable."

SHARE IT

Steve: Sometimes you can ease the pain by getting something out of it.

Ardith: Sometimes you can distract it.

Steve: Sometimes you can be heroic.

Ardith: Sometimes you can avoid it.

Steve: Sometimes you can reduce the anguish by anticipating it.

Ardith: Sometimes—quite a lot of the time, when you're really hurting—none of those works.

Steve: The best way we've found?

Ardith: Share your hurts. Share your pain with someone.

Steve: I used to think the human body could not hurt more than it could stand, that when things got really painful there was an automatic shutoff system, so you just passed out.

Ardith: It was a terrible disappointment to Steve to discover that there's no such protection, that it's entirely possible to hurt more than you can endure.

Steve: With knee problems that had already given me considerably more pain than I wanted, I was dismayed to find myself in a doctor's office facing the prospect of dye being injected into the bone with a needle that looked as big as my finger. As I looked away from that needle, my eye caught a nurse standing in the doorway. She leaned her head on her hand in anguish for me. Somehow her hurting for me made it possible for me to bear the pain. Somehow she took some of my pain.

Ardith: I think we can do that for each other.

Steve: I think we can literally bear each others' burdens.

Ardith: Our daughter Emily—the youngest, sweet seventeen—was raped last summer.

Steve: She was jogging on the road above our house.

Ardith: A man wearing a stocking over his head handcuffed her hands behind her back and dragged her into the oak brush.

Steve: I guess I thought I knew what rape was about, realized it was a crime of violence, but I wasn't prepared for the bruises on her face and back and arms.

Ardith: I wasn't prepared either for the aftermath, the five-hour police debriefing and medical check, the "morning after" pill, the checking for AIDS.

Steve: I've had some trouble dealing with my feelings toward the rapist. I'm not used to feeling hatred, and I keep choking it down instead of working through it—however you do that. And it won't stay choked. I keep dreaming variations of a single dream: I get to the oak brush in time to stop the rape, but then I do very bad things to the rapist, hurtful things. The dream I like best is the one where I blast him with my father's twelve-gauge shotgun in the knees at close range. We were in California when Emily was attacked, and I keep imagining ways I could have stopped it had I been here. I keep thinking I shouldn't have moved to Edgemont and shouldn't have had any children in the first place and shouldn't have encouraged Emily to get out into God's good world.

Ardith: For a while every man in the world looked like a potential rapist. I couldn't look at a little girl because I kept thinking she might grow up to be raped—and a fifth of women in this country will be; many who read this have been.[8]

Steve: In that dark time, my soul clouded with hate, haunted by an unremitting murderousness that took great pleasure in the fact that in the good old days of William the Conqueror, rape was punished by castration and blinding—don't even let them look—the thing that saved me was recognizing there are still good people in the world.

Ardith: And people have helped, have been heartwarmingly supportive. It's not natural for me to share my problems. My first instinct was that our family should go out of town the Sunday after the rape to avoid people asking or wondering or looking. But Emily wanted people in the ward to know about the rape in hopes of deterring future attacks. So she and I talked with the Young Women in our ward that next Sunday morning and then with the Relief Society . . .

Steve: . . . and I with my Gospel Doctrine class. It was like a burden lifted—it was a burden lifted. Those good people in our ward took some of the anguish off our shoulders and helped carry it. The tears that day on the faces of Anna Tueller and Carol Lee Hawkins made my own tears less bitter.

Ardith: Emily's entire class, one by one, hugged her, and so many flowers were sent that our living room smelled like love.

Steve: Mal Oveson, a feisty eighty-seven-year-old in our ward, encapsulated for me how amazingly people manage to help even when there's no way in the world to help: she walked down the hall at church with Emily and said (as I also so often so frustratingly feel), "I just don't know what to do." Then she took off her gold bracelet, inscribed "I love you," and slipped it into Emily's hand.

Ardith: You can't get much of that sort of direct emotional support without having your faith in humanity healed.

Steve: I'm a whole lot less bitter than I was—less angry at me, and at God, and even at rapists. I am determined to be henceforth more actively loving, to do some real things for others, to do unto as I have been so lovingly done by.

Ardith: So when you're hurting, particularly when you're hurting beyond what you can handle, share. Sometimes just thinking about a friend can help, as Shakespeare reminds us.

Steve:

> When in disgrace with fortune and men's eyes
> I all alone beweep my outcast state,
> And trouble deaf heaven with my bootless cries,
> And look upon myself, and curse my fate,
> Wishing me like to one more strong in hope,
> Featured like him, like him with friends possessed,

Desiring this man's art and that man's scope,
With what I most enjoy contented least;
Yet in these thoughts myself almost despising
Haply I think on thee, and then my state,
Like to the lark at break of day arising
From sullen earth, sings hymns at heaven's gate:
For thy sweet love remembered such wealth brings
That then I scorn to change my state with kings.
(Sonnet 29)

Ardith: Sharing helps. Not being used to sharing my problems, I was overwhelmed with how much sharing helps. If I hadn't shared my anguish about Emily's rape, I wouldn't have made it through.

SHARE IT WITH THE LORD

Steve: There's only one surefire, never-fails, always-comes-through way to ease our backaches and heartaches and soul aches—

Ardith: And that is by sharing our pain with the Lord.

Steve: Even a spouse can't always help. One of the most painful episodes in our marriage was the infertility drama. We were married six years before Scott was finally born.

Ardith: I handled it pretty well during the first two years of marriage, but during the third year I became a basket case.

Steve: Ardith was desperate to have a baby; I spent a lot of time reading in Genesis about how Rachel seized Jacob by his robe collar and shouted, "Give me children, or else I die." (Genesis 30:1.)

Ardith: I was constantly reading the symptoms of being pregnant. I spent hours looking in the mirror to see if the whites of my eyes were somewhat gray because that was one of the signs.

Steve: Ardith would get her hopes up and then cry for two days, and then get her hopes up again. Then cry again.

Ardith: One summer night as Steve said our prayer, he told God (as usual) that we would like to have a baby, "if it be thy will." When he finished praying, I got mad and told him not to say "if it be thy will" anymore because it just undid all the good of my prayers. I wanted to have a baby now, not wait around for God's will. A few days later I came upon Proverbs 3:5: "Trust in the Lord with all thine heart; and lean not unto thine own understanding." A peace came over me. Something in me changed. I lost that desperate, frustrated feeling. It was still three more years before we had Scott, but those three years were filled with peace.

Steve: And quiet. "For I am persuaded, that neither death, nor life, nor angels, nor principalities, nor powers, nor things present, nor things to come, nor height, nor depth, nor any other creature"—

Ardith: no matter how bad—

Steve: "shall be able to separate us from the love of God, which is in Christ Jesus our Lord." (Romans 8:38–39.)

Ardith: "Come unto me, all ye that labour and are heavy laden, and I will give you rest.

Steve: "Take my yoke upon you, and learn of me; for I am meek and lowly in heart: and ye shall find rest unto your souls." (Matthew 11:28–29.)

Ardith: "Fear not, little children, for you are mine." (D&C 50:41.)

Steve: "Be of good cheer, and do not fear." (D&C 68:6.)

Ardith: "In the world ye shall have tribulation: but be of good cheer; I have overcome the world." (John 16:33.) I like the way Anne Frank put it: "I can feel the sufferings of millions and yet, if I look up to the heavens, I think that . . . this cruelty too will end, and that peace and tranquillity will return again."⁹

Steve: I like the way a fifteenth-century English lyric puts it:

> Ther bloweth a cold wynd to-day, to-day,
> The wynd bloweth cold to-day;
> Crist suffred his passioun for [our] salvacioun
> To kepe the colde wynd awey."¹⁰

Ardith: I like the way the Lord—

Steve: He with whom we best share our suffering and our sorrow—

Ardith: I like the way the Lord put it: "Many are the afflictions of the righteous: but the Lord delivereth [you] out of them all." (Psalm 34:19.) "I will turn their mourning into joy, and will comfort them, and make them rejoice from their sorrow." (Jeremiah 31:13.)

Steve: "They that wait upon the Lord shall renew their strength; they shall mount up with wings as eagles; they shall run, and not be weary; and they shall walk, and not faint." (Isaiah 40:31.)

Ardith: "Yea, though I walk through the valley of the shadow of death, I will fear no evil: for thou art with me; thy rod and thy staff they comfort me." (Psalm 23:4.)

Steve: "Peace I leave with you, my peace I give unto you: not as the world giveth, give I unto you.

Ardith: "Let not your heart be troubled, neither let it be afraid." (John 14:27.)

Steve: "I am come that they might have life, and that they might have it more abundantly." (John 10:10.)

Ardith: There's a lot of hurt in life, but the more life, the better.

Steve: Maybe even the more hurt the better, provided we can share our suffering with each other and with the Lord.

Ardith: God's peace, the peace that passeth understanding, is as likely to come to us in our hurts as in our happiness.

Steve: Likelier.

Ardith: Maybe that's the process.

Steve: Maybe that's the plan.

NOTES

1. W. B. Yeats, "The Stolen Child," in *Poems Lyrical and Narrative: Being the First Volume of the Collected Works in Verse and Prose of William Butler Yeats,* 4th ed. (New York: Oxford University Press, 1992), p. 113.

2. Helen Keller, quoted in *I Am with You Always,* ed. Douglas Bloch (New York: Bantam Books, 1992), p. 122.

3. C. S. Lewis, quoted in *The Unquiet Grave: A Word Cycle by Palinurus,* rev. ed. (New York: Persea Books, 1981), p. 99.

4. Viktor E. Frankl, *Man's Search for Meaning* (New York: Simon and Schuster, 1963), pp. 105–6.

5. Phillips Brooks, "Going Up to Jerusalem," in *Twenty Sermons* (New York: E. P. Dutton, 1980), p. 330.

6. "Comic Relief," *Prevention,* Mar. 1988, p. 40; Blair Justice, "Think Yourself Healthy," *Prevention,* June 1988, p. 108.

7. Anne Morrow Lindbergh, quoted in *Great Quotes and Illustrations,* comp. George Sweeting (Waco: Word Books, 1985), p. 243.

8. Our source for this figure is duplicated materials given by the rape crisis center to our daughter after her rape. One in five is perhaps conservative. Many studies claim one in three American women will be raped or sexually abused during their lifetimes.

9. Anne Frank, *Anne Frank: The Diary of a Young Girl,* trans. B. M. Mooyaart-Doubleday (Garden City, New York: Doubleday & Co., 1952), p. 278.

10. Robert D. Stevick, ed., *One Hundred Middle English Lyrics* (Indianapolis: Bobbs-Merrill, 1964), p. 162.

The Way Back

NEIDY MESSER

August, hiking the Tetons, I'm breathless
in an hour and light-headed from altitude.
On an open rise of grass and amber clumps
of fiddler's necks, I lie down, still
dizzy, everything swirling blue
and green. Even after I close my eyes
the colors shimmer to the wind's unhurried
rhythm, a wind that seems, up here,
like the cool breath of this mountain—
so quiet, only the sound
in trees, a low, sweet hum, as if
the wind were a bow playing in the forest,
adagio, andante. How easy
to forget, lying here, the traffic
of another life. How easy to lose myself,
to be lost, wander hopefully, aimlessly
under the spell of wind and tangled
cover of trees to a stream,
follow its eventual spill
into the wide valley
I have just come from
and find there the shining, silver car
and know where to go, what to do.

Neidy Messer lives in Boise, Idaho, with her husband, Bill Messer, and their two sons. She teaches English at Boise State College and was the Idaho Writer-in-Residence, 1990–91. A book of her poems, In Far Corners, *has been published, and she is working on another volume. Sister Messer serves in her ward Relief Society.*

Perspectives on Divorce

Divorce is a unique personal experience, so it is with some risk that we share our individual perspectives. We hope our thoughts will help some of you.

PEACE AFTER DIVORCE
Elaine Shaw Sorensen

I have put aside traditional self-help lessons on how to live happily ever after divorce. I, like all of you, divorced or not, do not live happily ever after, but I have begun to find peace.

My problems in dealing with divorce include an aversion to the word itself. I have been divorced almost eight years and still find great difficulty in saying the word *divorce*. Instead, I usually say, "I am alone," or avoid comment. This is the first time that I have publicly and directly addressed the issue of my divorce. The word is still difficult for me to face.

My divorce languished legally for nearly two years before a two-day trial. Just as I hoped it was over, the decision was appealed to the Utah State Court of Appeals and then on to the Utah State Supreme Court. The entire litigation process lasted almost eight years. It was heard by two domestic commissioners and nine judges, two of whom were women. I have often wondered what might have happened if four or five judges had been women, or even if the proportion of men to women had been reversed, and nine women had heard our case. I have wondered if a larger perspective from women might have changed the focus from property to personal welfare, from hearings to healing. As the years passed, similarity between the legal "facts" and

Elaine Shaw Sorensen is the mother of four children and serves as the associate dean of the College of Nursing at Brigham Young University. Sister Sorensen filled a mission in Colombia and is the education counselor in her stake Relief Society.

"arguments" and our lived reality diminished, numbing my perception of the outcome. The final settlement seemed fair enough. It is hard to remember who "won."

When the divorce began, I was vulnerable and exhausted, almost extinguished, as I was forced to face the end of the most significant part of my life. Seeking employment, I went back to a nursing friend for whom I had previously worked. She had been good to me, and she knew a little about my situation. She had experienced her own divorce two years earlier. This time my interview with her was more serious than before. I wasn't looking for a part-time job to help pay for summer vacation. I now needed a career.

I was wounded, weepy, and philosophical—consumed by fears and burdens in trying to hold my children together emotionally and spiritually and simply trying to survive. Uncharacteristically aloof to my tears, my friend said something like, "Elaine, what you need is money." I was shocked. Her statement seemed irrelevant and brutal. At that point, money meant little to me in comparison to my overwhelming emotional and spiritual hurts.

She continued, "I can see you are not getting the message." She then drew a dollar sign on a sticky note and pasted it to my chest. I left her, thinking that for the first time since I had known her she really did not understand. I soon revised my opinion, however, as I discovered the harsh reality of supporting a family on significantly decreased resources while also facing the major costs of divorce recovery: legal fees, school tuition, a car, selling a house and buying a house, child care, and a hundred other things.

Another surprising shock of divorce was the adversarial nature of the legal system itself. I am a nurse, so the sensitive care of sick or hurting people had been my professional obligation. I had anticipated that the judicial system would treat me and my family with similar careful concern. I was wrong. I was stunned to find the process to be absolutely—and requisitely—adversarial. My hopes of achieving any semblance of conciliation, resolution, or equanimity were out of step with the legal process. Being thrown into a costly public arena left me reeling with the sudden need for another difficult adjustment for survival. The requirement of the system for me to prepare and represent myself as an adversary against husband and father, rather than as advocate for the relief and healing of my family, impeded my early hopes for peace.

There are a few other things that those of us who are divorced wish were more widely understood. First, divorce is neither the beginning nor the end. It is only one chapter in the story. Divorce usually follows some very long, painful passages within a marriage, of which others are often unaware. Divorce often follows a long, draining history of hurt or betrayal. The divorcing person then must enter a threatening, new, life-changing scene at a time when he or she is already depleted, vulnerable, and suffering. The people who knocked at my door with offerings of help at the time I faced divorce came very late in the trauma chapter of my life story. I am grateful to such friends, but I wish that *I* had reached out to *them* earlier.

Second, healing and peace after divorce take time. Divorce is the loss of a dream, survival from trauma. Much time must pass before emotional, spiritual, physical, and social healing is possible. Be patient with us who divorce.

On the other hand, time alone will not heal. It is what you do with that time. For a divorcing person, most of that healing is done alone, but another part is done at the side of good friends. You need friends who will listen, people whose simple presence nurtures. Some friends do not need to do or say anything—they nourish by simply being there. Two friends walked with me for an hour every morning during the first year of separation. My memory is that I talked for the entire hour. We walked, I talked, and my friends listened. That was one of the greatest gifts of my life.

Finding peace after divorce requires life changes and some new areas of family focus. I was amazed at the resilience of my children and at their hunger for our recovery as a family. We started new, healing traditions. We had regular sleepovers in my bedroom, with one of us in the bed and the rest on the floor, rotating on different nights. Once forbidden territory became a campground for renewal. We now have regular prayer and family home evening. Such activities say, "We're still together and we are okay. We can grow through this together."

In divorce you need to face the reality of the situation, without denial, without trying to change or hold back the truth. I don't think children need to know everything about the process of divorce, but what they are told always needs to be true. Their questions need to be answered.

Understanding and using resources appropriately can be critical, especially in divorce. The confidence and support of a bishop or stake president are important for spiritual counsel, of a lawyer for legal counsel, of a therapist for emotional help, of an accountant for financial guidance, of friends and family for love. But it is equally important not to confuse the roles of such valuable relationships. The bishop is not the accountant; the lawyer is not the therapist. Under emotional stress, a divorcing person will often mistakenly want all needs met by each resource.

Don't be surprised when other realities continue alongside divorce. Children still get chicken pox, the car breaks down, the family reunion is still scheduled. Sometimes divorce seems an unfair complication to such events. The world should stop during a divorce. Nothing that taxes mind or spirit should be allowed to occur in a life coping with divorce. But life continues, with floods and snowstorms, with flat tires on the way to work, and with the school carnival needing cookies. Your divorce does not cause such events, make them worse or better, include or excuse you. Such things just happen.

Forgiveness is always an issue on both sides of marriage and divorce. But not distinguishing between what is and what is not forgiveness prevents healing. Tolerance of abuse is not forgiveness. If you need distance for safety, then get it. Excusing and rationalizing are not forgiveness. Sometimes the hardest thing you do is face up to the reality of assault and then forgive. Only then will forgiveness be a freeing release rather than unrealistic hope for change. We need to honor the truth of our own experiences and feelings, whether they be fear, betrayal, or relief.

Peace and healing require continued efforts toward growth. Occasionally, the divorced person confronts bias or disappointment from those who do not understand. Fortunately, I have found amazing acceptance from the people in my life. I probably get most hurt by distant media reports of the characteristics of our deteriorating society, listing increases in crime, in immorality, and in single-parent families. To be listed parallel with all of the ills of the world is difficult. I take it personally when I find myself among the top problems in America.

I am also bothered by conversations about women who work or women who do not work, though my situation is accepted as exceptional and therefore "justified." I don't like to feel I am living a life that needs to be explained, excused, or justified. For one thing, if I am in an exceptional situation, I feel pressure to perform exceptionally. In other words, my children must behave better than my neighbors' children who live with two parents, my house has to be cleaner, my yard must look tidier. At work, I have to be smarter, quicker, and more productive. When there are only twenty-four hours in my day, it becomes a trap to think that because I feel different, I must always perform beyond the norm. I must try not to do that to myself—and we ought to not do that to each other.

When I told my family I was writing about peace after divorce, they laughed and said, "Tell them there isn't any!" I'm not telling you that. There is peace. Peace after divorce comes in the process of living. It happens after learning hard lessons. It occurs over time alongside family, friends, and professionals who care. It happens privately but also with many others who share the experience and understand. Peace emerges from pain and accompanies healing. It comes from confronting and accepting truth, from being willing to live and love and forgive and move forward. *Divorce* is still hard to say, but it has not closed the gate on my own path to life, love, and peace.

WHEN A MARRIAGE IS NOT CELESTIAL
Nedra Hardy

I don't recall meeting another divorced person, inside or outside of the Church, who professes to believe in divorce. Neither do I believe in divorce, but I am divorced.

I marched in the parade of starry-eyed brides at the Salt Lake Temple thirty-one years ago next month. I embarked on my eternal marriage with all my idealism in place. Divorce was an unknown. No one in my family had ever been divorced. I did know some people who had been divorced, but the possibility of divorce for me then was as remote as a man going to the moon.

My lofty ideals took a beating from the beginning, but I knew that adjustments were part of every marriage. Readjusting to rolling the toilet paper the other way was easy; financial matters were a little more difficult. My husband spent what money we had and more; my approach was to try to balance the checkbook and establish a budget. We were never to have a financial meeting of the minds. After my husband graduated from law school and I was a full-time mother, I withdrew from

Nedra Hardy is the mother of nine children and is employed as the administrative assistant in the Center for Engineering Tribology at Northwestern University. Sister Hardy serves as secretary in the Primary of the Wilmette Illinois Stake.

all financial matters to preserve our family and my sanity, tried to spend conservatively, and trusted that obligations would be handled judiciously.

As the years went by, my husband's alcoholism became the challenge to overcome. I was not equipped to handle that. For one thing, as active Latter-day Saints we didn't believe in using alcohol. For many years I lived alone with my efforts to adjust. To whom could I turn for help in dealing with the respected Sunday School teacher, high councilor, and pro bono legal counsel to everyone, who had become an alcoholic? He threatened me to keep me from talking to anyone. Even his own children thought he just worked all night quite frequently. On those nights I spent a great deal of time praying for some solution.

Finally my stake president, suspecting problems with his high councilor and tennis partner, confronted me with his suspicions and stepped in to help me over the hurdles. He was on call at all hours of the day and night but freely admitted that he had no idea how to effect the changes we needed. We were dealing with the agency of another person. The possibility of divorce crept in.

After years of living with the alcoholism, I also discovered that my husband had been living a double life. A fellow Church member who was an FBI agent had uncovered hidden files and records revealing that my husband had kept and secreted a very large settlement check relating to the death of this member's son. The devoted husband, father, and Church leader never missed his Sunday meetings. During the rest of the week, however, he lived in a world of diverted settlement checks, unpaid business and personal taxes, and a life filled with drinking, womanizing, and who knows what else.

My husband was indicted for mail fraud involving the theft of his clients' funds, but plea bargaining saved him from serving time in prison. As a part of this bargain, we were to sell our home to partially repay the victims of theft. During this time I spent many wakeful nights visualizing my children all dropping out of school and our living on the streets. Meanwhile, a small house in our community was put on the market "by owner." The house was too small for the six of our nine children who were still living at home, and there was no way I could possibly finance a house, but I went to look at it. During the next six weeks, I gradually fit together pieces of an impossible puzzle, working completely independently from my husband. With some financial backing from my mother, I negotiated a contract with the owner of the house, and we had a roof over our heads—nothing short of a miracle.

The judge allowed my husband to remain with his family to care for them. His purpose, however, was not so much to care for his family as to put us back into place as blindfolded puppets to reestablish his front of respectability. We were all expected to stand beside him in devotion without questioning him or admitting to the existence of the elements of his life outside the confines of our home. He threatened, ridiculed, and belittled us, and he demanded our love and devotion. Those of us who want things to be peaceful and stand ready to absorb guilt are easily controlled by these methods.

Now was my day of decision. I had counted on the jail sentence to give me space to reassess and determine direction. With no separation, divorce seemed to be the only salvation for me and my nine children. Can the forsaking of an eternal commitment save a family? I could not exist in this life of duplicity. He promised to change and reassured me that we would regain our financial position within a few years. I panicked. Was reform possible? Or would he sweep everything under the carpet to go on as we had been? I prayed—on my knees and on my feet, while I walked, while I worked.

I had taken a secretarial job at Northwestern University at its campus on the shores of Lake Michigan. I used my lunch hours to walk along the lake and contemplate. What would a broken family do to my children? What were present circumstances doing to my children? How could I support my children alone and send them to college? The stigma of divorce hung over me. One day as I was walking and sorting and praying, I had the strange feeling of being lifted from the ground and knew at that moment that I had to file for divorce. I also knew that what lay ahead was going to be the most difficult time of my life.

When I informed my husband of my intent, he countered with a plan of his own. He would make the divorce as difficult and as drawn out as possible. (He knew the legal means.) He would file for custody of the children. He would withdraw all financial support immediately as he would need his money for himself, and he would not move from the house I had bought until a judge ordered him to do so.

I filed for divorce and was forced to look to the Church for assistance in supporting my family. I began facing my concerns for my family. I wanted to put all of eternity into order. One of the most difficult things for me to do was to take each day as it came. Whatever could be handled this week I worked with; whatever could wait I put aside. I continually had to remind myself that I couldn't handle everything at once.

My husband held true to his word, introducing me to the world of legal wrangling. One of our first court actions resulted in his being removed from my house; having him under a different roof made all that followed a great deal easier.

Everything I did became the subject of court action: a junior high concert he didn't know about until the day it occurred (parental rights); an overnight retreat when I left my children in the care of my twenty-two-year-old daughter (child neglect). School conferences that he had never before attended became the subject of court sessions. I had to base all of my actions and decisions on whether they were worth going to court for. My first priority was my children; I wanted them separated from this as much as possible, and I would not give up custody.

I was willing to fight for my home, but there were no other material possessions that were worth a fight. At the same time, it was very difficult to sit back and allow myself to be manipulated and taken advantage of. My husband would make unreasonable demands regarding the children. (They were his power over me.) If I did not bend to his will, he would file a motion in court to get a judge to order me to do as he wished. If the demand was not worth a day in court and attorney's fees, I would bend. He constantly forced me to redraw the battle lines. The divorce proceedings were very long and difficult. After the first judge ordered my husband out of the house and ordered his book collection sold to pay attorney's fees, he filed for a change of venue, and we started from the beginning. I received a constant stream of letters from him reprimanding, blaming, instructing, and threatening me.

In a desperate effort to bring everything to an end, one November I agreed to an out-of-court settlement. I would have custody of the children and my home. He would have liberal visitation and vacation privileges with the children and would give no financial support. One element of the agreement was that the children should all spend Thanksgiving with him.

Our Thanksgiving, steeped in tradition, had always begun with playing a morning football game. Being far from any extended family, we had always shared our holidays with several families of close friends, giving us a core group of twenty-one children within the same age range. My children wanted to play football, and the game wouldn't be complete without them. Couldn't they have breakfast with their father, leave to play football for an hour or two, and then go back for the rest of the day? They called to ask his permission. Not only did they not receive his permission, but the next day I received a copy of his motion to the court to quash our entire settlement and custody agreement, which I had "violated" by allowing them to ask.

Our three years of court hearings were filled with continual frustration. When emotions boiled high in the courtroom, my Catholic attorney would often lean to me and suggest something like "Remember, Jesus forgave everyone." I was grateful for his attitude. He did all he could in my interest, and I could trust him to be completely ethical and avoid any underhanded tactics. I had been the subject of too many of those, and I had no desire to reciprocate.

At the end of the trial and the finalization of the divorce, I had custody of my children, my home, and even an order for fifty dollars a month in child support. I had been warned about postdecree motions, so I was not completely surprised by them. Just because my divorce was legally final, my former husband did not stop taking me to court with motions to have me found in contempt for every perceived infringement of his parental privileges. As long as I have children under eighteen, I will inevitably be doing something that will take me back to the courtroom, such as forgetting to inform him at the onset of my daughter's bout with Bell's palsy.

In the beginning, the disintegration of so much of what I had expected of life left me emotionally drained and wondering where and how to begin the readjustment to a new life. Yet help came from unexpected sources, and small pleasures sustained me. When my husband was indicted for his theft, both newspapers and television carried accounts. For two days after the news broke, I did nothing but answer my telephone. Friends from every phase of my life, not knowing what to say, called to let me know they were there. I have never needed friends so much, and their outpouring was voluminous.

These friends have never left me. They've gone to the temple with me, fasted and prayed, and even filled the courtroom. Sometimes they just listened while I ran off at the mouth. My friends have been my constant reminder and the personification of the love of my heavenly parents—parents who will allow us to suffer but will not leave us alone.

My children were an incredible help in getting through the worst of times. We were able to lean on each other. The day after the news stories, my eight-year-old daughter came home from school in tears, wondering if she would ever feel normal again, or if she would always hurt. Her ten-year-old sister compared that pain to the pain they had felt when their grandfather died. "Remember," she said, "the hurt doesn't go away, but it gets better." Even their mundane needs were helpful— the laundry and meals had to go on and required no painful decisions.

I made every effort to keep life on an even keel. Despite our move, we had remained in the same school district, where the children were known for themselves rather than for their father's reputation. When I returned to work outside the home, I had to reorganize my life and discard many activities and obligations. One of the things I made every effort to hold onto for myself was my book club, which gave me a book to read each month and the association of friends at the meeting. It was at the book club where I first really laughed again—a cleansing laugh from my very insides. My sewing machine had always been very therapeutic for me. I got to it as often as I could, even if it was late into the night. It soothed my soul and enhanced our wardrobes.

Today I look back at twenty-four years of marriage, three years and more than fifty court hearings of divorce proceedings, and four years of still more court hearings after my divorce. Although I have three years to go before my youngest child turns eighteen and my husband's legal holds over me have ended, I have not for a moment doubted the prompting I had to file for divorce. It has allowed me to be again the person who had been suppressed in the effort to make a hopeless situation into an eternal marriage.

A marriage is a commitment between two people that is designed to last for eternity. One person cannot carry that commitment to fruition alone. When it is not being upheld by both parties, it ceases to be eternal. It requires dedication on both sides to make it valid. A hopeless marriage need not be forever; an abusive situation need not be tolerated. You can still have worth as a person with an unsuccessful marriage. My marriage ceased being eternal years before we entered the divorce courts.

I have a new life that is both challenging and fulfilling. I feel good about being single. Finances are tight, but aren't everyone's? My relationship with and my love for my children have intensified as we have grown together through our struggle for survival, and we are now able to talk about those parts of our lives that were forbidden subjects for so many years. They all see and correspond with their father regularly.

They like him to be happy, and they refrain from making demands that will bring court sessions for mother and scathing letters to all. I have learned, and they are learning, that letters do not have to be read.

I think that the greatest lesson I have learned is that I can only be responsible for myself. The principle of agency allows us to preserve or destroy ourselves. We cannot ultimately be responsible for anyone else's salvation, nor can we blame or credit anyone else for our own.

TUNA ON BROWN BREAD

Suzanne Little Dastrup

I have been divorced for seventeen years, and I am happy. I would also be happy if I found Prince Charming. But if I don't, I'll still be happy. I didn't understand that fact for a long time. I was divorced after six years of marriage. I had a year of undergraduate work behind me and three young children. Shortly after the divorce, I vividly remember, I was rocking Ben, my youngest, and reading an article in the paper that said children of divorce are destined to be socially and emotionally wounded. I wept in despair. I no longer do that. David is twenty-three, Kim twenty-one, and Ben eighteen: all three are doing well. Statistics are not destiny. There are married people that are unhappy and married people that are happy. The same goes for educated people, for old people, for the handicapped or ill—and for divorced families. Happiness is not guaranteed in any situation or at any age.

My divorce catapulted me into the process that all of us have to go through eventually—the process of discovering that our happiness does not depend on our circumstances or things around us or people we live with; it depends on something internal. We don't know that we've relied on something external for our happiness, until someone or something takes it away. If we're drowning in despair or depression or anger, then our sense of peace has come from some external place. Often our happiness depends on worldly things, on having a successful spouse, successful children, on being liked or admired, or fitting in in some way. When these externals are jerked away one way or anothe—when we lose our health, lose our money, lose our spouse, lose our kids—then we have to find peace internally.

Suzanne Little Dastrup is the mother of three children. She holds a Ph.D. in marriage and family therapy from Brigham Young University and is in practice in Provo, Utah. Sister Dastrup teaches the Family Relations class in her ward Relief Society.

For some of you, that peace may seem so distant that you feel you will never reach it. I too felt that way. I had bitter days; I may again. I'm just not having them now. Having peace within doesn't mean you will never hurt again. It means that you are understanding yourself and liking yourself. We seem to feel this clarity during some stages of life more than others. Without a doubt, however, our personal relationship with the Savior will be an unfailing source of peace.

Divorce is not something you pass through and then it's over. Divorce begins long before the court decree of divorce and lasts a long time after that: it's a process. Just when you think it's past history, a daughter gets married and you're standing in a reception line with your former spouse and his or her new spouse. And you realize that it is still not over.

A very important part of the process is grieving. First you may experience denial: you're going to get back into the relationship, you're going to wait it out, it's going to heal, you'll be back together. You may deny that you're going to be a divorced person. Some people jump quickly into another relationship, thinking, "Well, person A is gone, so I'll just replace person A with person B, and everything will be fine." Research shows that remarriages occurring after at least one year of being divorced or widowed have a much higher success rate than those occurring during the first year. We need time to grieve and rediscover our true selves. That rediscovery requires us to face our aloneness, which is difficult but necessary.

One stage that might follow denial in the process of grieving is anger, including feelings of rage, revenge, bitterness, and hostility. Those feelings may be directed toward the absent spouse, or toward God, parents, church, or the myths of happily-ever-after many of us have been taught. This bitterness may make you hate yourself and even your children. Though this stage is seemingly not very productive, it is normal, as long as you don't get stuck there. Temporary anger serves to finish off any lingering hope about the past relationship.

You may move next to a stage of depression, with feelings of guilt, failure, self-hate, and hopelessness. Usually either anger or depression becomes your most prevalent emotion, depending upon your personality. Depression may actually be anger or other feelings turned inward. If you're better at being expressive, probably you're most inclined to anger. If you're not so good at expressing your feelings, then you could get stuck in the depression stage. Sometimes you bounce back and forth between denial and depression, anger and denial, and anger and depression. As you are swamped first by one feeling and then another, you may feel that your life is forever ruined—but those feelings do end, I promise you. Those feelings are part of a healing process that all people have to go through any time they experience a significant loss or transition in their lives.

After some months of these grieving and healing emotions, a numbness, characterized by low energy, occurs. And after a period of numbness, you reach the acceptance stage, and healing is complete. Often the hardest part about healing, or regaining your equilibrium, is that everybody in the family starts on a different timetable or heals in different ways. For instance, you may be finally past depression and anger and into numbness (or ambivalence), before you've even filed for divorce or separated. Then you file for divorce and have to start back at square one with your children's denial. They're trying to reunite the parents, line you up with their teacher at school, or fix it some other way. Or perhaps they're in the anger stage and you're in the depression stage. Or one of your children will be angry while another is in denial. This emotional smorgasbord makes the first year incredibly complicated.

We used to believe that children of divorce were emotionally, psychologically, and socially damaged. We don't believe that anymore. I am not in any way promoting divorce; however, people do divorce, so it's important to understand that it is neither the actual divorce nor the father's or mother's absence that is devastating for family members. Rather, it is the functioning of the remaining family members that creates either turmoil or success.

Basically we have to watch out for four types of problems in the single-parent home. The first is role or task overload. With one parent gone, the other parent assumes the work of two people. That parent becomes everything from mechanic to breadwinner to cook to homework helper to family home evening preparer to confidant to head dishwasher. That's a whole lot of work! If you are to survive as a single parent, you must learn to lower your expectations about things that aren't so important and not feel depressed and guilty about what you don't get done. You need to pat yourself on the back for what you're completing, concentrating on the most important things. Those important things should include your relationships, especially with your children. Relationships are what we get to take with us. If the living room's cluttered, then it's cluttered. If somebody comes to visit, have them help you clean it up!

One way to avoid role overload is to delegate better. Ask for help. Teach people what you need. I know that is difficult, but think back to the neighborhoods or wards where you lived before you were a single parent. Think about the divorced or single people who lived there. Were you aware of their financial or social needs? Could the widowed mother have used your husband to help build a pinewood derby roadster with her Cub Scout son? Would your best casserole have been appreciated after a long day's work? I had been blind to their needs. I didn't understand the overload until I experienced it. Instead of resenting people for not seeing it, we need to teach them.

Another problem area to be aware of is the destructive effects of lingering anger or emotional poisoning. It's difficult but necessary to let go of bitterness and hostility. I understand that there are reasons to be bitter. But if you hold onto those feelings throughout the next five, ten, or twenty years of parenting, you and your children will pay a terrible price. The atmosphere of the home, throughout most of the child's developmental years, would be one of resentment. Children deserve to feel peace and love rather than resentment and distrust. No excuse for hanging on to bitterness could justify the loss of a Christlike spirit in the home. Prayer, support, or therapy may help you heal.

A third difficulty for most single parents is money. Finances pose a seemingly endless problem, and the stress can seem unbearable. There are no quick solutions for the problems that financial stress creates. I remember coming home from a soccer game shortly after I was divorced and hearing my oldest son object, "Mom! You didn't stop and get a Slurpee!" Well, that was a tradition after a soccer game: we stop and get Slurpees. But I'd had it; I was in acute role overload and financial stress. I remember yelling, "What do you mean? How dare you ask me for a Slurpee! Do you think money grows on trees? Do you think this job of mine is easy?" My six-year-old piped up from the backseat, "Whoa! My mom's flipped out!" It would have been much better (and on other days I did the better thing) to explain, "Look, I know we used to stop for Slurpees, but we can't because we don't have the money. We can go home and try to make one, or we'll make some different kind of treat. We have to start a new tradition now." Sometimes we're in so much pain that it's hard for us to teach our children or to take them into our confidence. Nonetheless, they will feel much more secure if we try to explain.

The fourth problem for single parents is isolation and self-doubt. It's tempting to isolate yourself in this Noah's ark society of ours where everybody's coupled off. You stay home because you don't fit in, or because you can't afford to go somewhere, or because you're exhausted. But isolation breeds depression, self-doubt, and self-criticism. I remember a day, probably five years after I was divorced, walking home from a Church interview—my bishop's annual check-up interview. I could tell that he was watching the clock. "Well, how are you doing, Sister Dastrup? It's so good to see you! I just wanted to check in, see if you're doing okay!" I said, "I guess I'm okay," and he said, "I know the Lord loves you! I feel his Spirit when you're in my office. The Lord is mindful of you!" And I said, "Yeah, yeah, whatever." It had been five years, and I was still single, I was still poor, and I was still in school. I remember walking home from that interview full of despair, feeling that neither my bishop nor the Lord was really mindful of me.

But as I walked home, a memory came back to me of another day, a hot summer day when I was home with the kids. They were outside playing in the sprinkler. When I'm home, I try to do some mommy things—quality versus quantity things. I fixed a good wholesome lunch—tuna fish on whole wheat sandwiches and milk and carrot sticks—and I called the children in. They came slipping and sliding in the back door, saw this great lunch that I had fixed, and all three chorused their appreciation: "Yuck! This is stupid! I hate this! Mom! Everybody gets Wonder Bread, and you've got that brown bread." "I hate tuna fish; milk is dumb. How come we can't have Kool-aid? Jenny's mom just gave her kids Kool-aid and Oreo's, and they're having a picnic." "You're the meanest mom in the whole neighborhood. If you really loved us, you wouldn't make us eat this dumb lunch!"

What are my choices, I thought, trying to maintain my composure. I could smack them all for their ungratefulness and shout, "You'd better appreciate this, because I AM a good mom!" Or, I could send them all to their rooms and eat everybody's lunch myself. Or I could line them all up on the couch and then pull out the encyclopedia, volume "N" for Nutrition. Now remember, they're ages six, five, and two. Should I make them learn about nutrition, so that I could prove to them that I'm a good mom? No, I thought, none of these responses is going to work. Instead, I knelt down to be at eye level with them at the kitchen table and said, "Trust me, guys. I'm giving you this whole wheat bread and milk and carrot sticks, and this tuna fish, because I do love you. You may not get it right now, and you may not trust what I'm saying, but someday you'll understand. I'm giving you this lunch because I love you so very much, and this lunch will make you strong!"

Remember, I was still daydreaming, walking home from the bishop's office, when suddenly it struck me: That's exactly what happens when I kneel to pray. I am asking for Oreos, and the Lord is saying, "Trust me. I'm giving you all this experience because I love you so much!" And I've noticed that he keeps dishing out the tuna fish. Maybe a few side orders of Oreos and Kool-aid, but mostly it's tuna fish on brown bread. I know I have learned more than I ever would have on a diet of cookies and Kool-aid. So at this point in my life I have enough maturity to say, "Okay, I get it! Thank you! I have grown so much! Help me to trust that process here on earth. Teach me to take joy in the growth of each day."

To the Gate

BIANCA PALMIERI LISONBEE

I always thought I'd walk with you to the gate.
Slowly we'd stroll, lingering gently at the place where softly
    it would open and you'd go in.
Perhaps I'd wave, or maybe even catch a glimpse
    of where you went as your image faded on.
Then, I'd go my way. Back to the sameness of my self.
But you went ahead without me. Too soon.
Too quick. No way for me to catch you.
I ran so fast, the gate was locked and you, already gone.
I shake and shake the metal forged latch
But this journeyman knew his trade.
Iron cold crystal shuts me out and my hope begins to fade
    into a vain desire to wait and wait
    and wait.   I can't go back.
I want to stay and keep vigil through the night.
But morning's brightness only shows my blindness in the
    light.
Is there another way for me to see?
A side or back entrance into eternity?
Then I recall the place.
It's high enough I'm told
    that from spired gold one can get a view.
I've been there before and never really saw,
But then I had no need to look for you.

Bianca Palmieri Lisonbee graduated from Brigham Young University in theater arts and worked on the Integrated Arts in the Schools project in Provo. Now a homemaker, she and her husband, David Lisonbee, are the parents of five children. Sister Lisonbee serves as her ward Relief Society president.

This poem is dedicated to her mother, Josephine Palmieri, upon whose death it was written.

Let Your Light So Shine

ALEXANDER B. MORRISON

In the greatest sermon ever spoken, he who is the Light of the world affirmed the responsibility of his followers to show by their actions whose servants they are. "Let your light so shine before men," Jesus proclaimed, "that they may see your good works, and glorify your Father which is in heaven." (Matthew 5:16.) I would like to discuss in pragmatic terms aspects of that supernal task as it applies to the lives of women and children around the world.

One thing seems clear to me: If the status of women and children is to be improved worldwide, as justice and decency demand it must be, women themselves will have to play increasingly significant roles in effecting the necessary changes. In doing so, women will have to stand up and speak out, gently but firmly, against evil and brutality, injustice and oppression. They must be joined by their brothers in a mighty army of righteous men and women united in a common cause. In uniting with their brothers, women must be considered neither inferior nor superior to men but simply their equals. Of course, men and women are different. We must place equal value on their differences and rejoice in them.

We cannot succeed in these efforts unless we keep out of our homes the filth and dross of the world. We will be required to walk in faith and integrity, in love and charity, in courage and hope. Education—both of the intellect and of the heart and spirit—must become our daily joy. There will be neither time nor room for self-pity or despondency.

Alexander B. Morrison, of Edmonton, Alberta, Canada, is a member of the First Quorum of the Seventy of The Church of Jesus Christ of Latter-day Saints. An internationally recognized scientist, he has been particularly interested in public health in Africa and other developing areas. Elder Morrison and his wife, Shirley E. Brooks Morrison, are the parents of eight children.

The natural feelings of sisterhood that bind women together will require constant strengthening and nurturing.

A favorite choice of women's choruses in the Church is the lovely "As Sisters in Zion,"[1] a composition that portrays faithfully the need to "bear . . . one another's burdens, and so fulfil the law of Christ." (Galatians 6:2.) This enduringly appealing work was written by a woman of remarkable faith and accomplishment, Emily Woodmansee. Sister Woodmansee first heard the gospel message in her native England when she was only twelve years old. She was baptized at age sixteen, came to America as a young woman, and in 1856 crossed the plains to Zion under conditions of great adversity as a member of the Willie Handcart Company. She was deserted by her first husband under stark and tragic circumstances and married Joseph Woodmansee in 1864. It was said of this remarkable woman that she possessed a rare combination of talents—"a poetic as well as a practical mind."[2]

The second verse of "As Sisters in Zion" reads:

The errand of angels is given to women;
And this is a gift that, as sisters, we claim:
To do whatsoever is gentle and human,
To cheer and to bless in humanity's name.

These felicitous phrases cogently describe the role and destiny of women. Let us consider in some detail various aspects of "the errand of angels" with which God has entrusted his daughters. In doing so, I shall draw upon examples primarily from Third World nations, where a high proportion of the world's women live.

Women from Third World countries are joining the Church in increasing numbers. If current trends continue, members in the United States, Canada, and Europe will be a minority by the year 2000, representing approximately 40 percent of the total Church membership. The plight of our sisters in Third World nations is of great concern to the leaders of the Church and should be to all members everywhere. We are all part of the family of God, who "hath made of one blood all nations . . . for to dwell on all the face of the earth." (Acts 17:26.)

It has been said that females "are one-half of the world's population, perform two-thirds of the world's work, receive one-tenth of its income and own less than one-hundredth of its property."[3] There can be little doubt that for the vast majority of women, the "errand of angels" is a very difficult task indeed, played out in poverty and adversity, in sorrow and deprivation. The following stories illustrate that point.

"It's 5:00 A.M. and a monsoon rain is falling over the Ershad Nagar slum. Here, at the edge of Dhaka, Bangladesh's capital, more than 50,000 people make their homes in one-room shacks crowded along narrow, garbage-strewn paths.

"Inside a 6-by-8-foot dwelling, a young widow, Ayesha Kharoum, cooks rice and lentils over a clay stove. Water drips from a makeshift roof, woven of thatch and scraps of plastic. A single light bulb [a luxury for the Ershad Nagar slum] casts a dim yellow glow over two children sleeping on a floor mat.

"Outside, the slum's maze of lanes are fast becoming rivers of sewage. Water seeps into Ayesha's home," waking her two children, a girl age ten and a boy age seven. "Ankle deep in the filthy water," she feeds her children their breakfast.

"At 8:00 A.M. Ayesha wades to a neighborhood training center to embroider blouses. With two timeouts for child care, she continues sewing until 11:00 that night. By working 12 to 15 hours a day, seven days a week, Ayesha earns almost $30 a month. It is twice the usual wage for female garment workers, and it enables Ayesha to send her children to school.

"'As a child I dreamed of learning to read and write,' says Ayesha. 'I didn't get this blessing, but I am giving it to my children.'"[4] How impressive is the quiet strength of this good woman who truly lets her light shine! What a tremendous blessing the Relief Society literacy program will prove to be in the lives of so many of our sisters around the world.

In mountainous central Sri Lanka, "women are employed on large tea plantations as pluckers. They work long hours on the steep hillsides, plucking the ripe individual tea leaves from shoulder-high bushes. At the day's end, they carry their harvest to a factory in eighty-pound baskets that have remained strapped to their backs throughout the day."

Their wages for their grueling work? About 4.70 rupees—or 45 cents—per day. One tea plucker, at the end of her day in the fields, was interviewed as she began her second day of work around the home. Thirty-five years old, she was "a thin woman and appeared devoid of energy." She had worked in the fields since she was ten years old. She said she had not seen much improvement in her life. Her entire life had been spent caring for and sustaining her family.

" 'I had nine children, but I lost the ninth just a year ago. The eighth child is three years old. I have five sons and three daughters. I never went to school. I was just twelve when I was married. I had not seen my husband before. My marriage was arranged by my parents. I had my first child at the age of thirteen.

" 'When I was a small child, I was quite all right. . . . But now I find life extremely difficult.' "[5]

Indeed, for many women in the world, life *is* extremely difficult. The old saying that a woman's work is never done is well illustrated by the life of a typical rural African woman. Her days are long, the work unending. She is in the fields before sunrise, and her day does not end until nearly seventeen hours later. After her work in the field is completed, she must gather firewood, pound and grind corn, collect water, cook for the family, and clean the home.

I met such a typical African woman several years ago "in the bush" of northern Côte d'Ivoire. It was early June, and I was in West Africa as part of a World Health Organization team investigating an outbreak of African trypanosomiasis—sleeping sickness. We stopped near a village perched on the banks of the Bandama River. Because it was just at the end of the dry season, the river was shallow and easily forded on foot. We walked down to the river, where the tsetse flies that spread sleeping sickness rested on the riverine foliage. There, crossing the river, coming from the jungle on the far side, was an African woman, up to her knees in the water. She had a baby on her back, another on her hip, two preschool youngsters who paddled alongside, and was heavily pregnant with a fifth child. A chipped enamel basket piled high with bananas was balanced on her head, and in her free hand she carried a rusty machete. She was hot and dusty, her face beaded with sweat. But she smiled and shook my hand before gathering her children to climb the path that wound up the hill to her village—one of the host of unsung heroines amongst my African sisters.

My thoughts turn to another African woman, pounding the hulls from rice on a hot and humid summer's day in West Africa. She, too, was tired and dusty, glistening with perspiration. The muscles in her arms rippled as she rhythmically pounded the raw rice, using a heavy wooden mortar held in both hands and a pestle hewn out of a tree trunk. Around her were the timeless verities of African village life—mud huts with palm-thatched roofs and no windows, children playing in the dirt, the men of the village sitting in the shade, ruminating over the local gossip and the state of the crops.

Many experts agree that women hold the key to ending Africa's hunger. They work more than 63 percent of the small farms and process essentially all the food that small farmers grow. They also carry the water—often over distances of a mile or more—and much of the firewood needed daily. Many rural African women spend up to five or six hours daily carrying water.

Two scenes are forever etched in my memory. One is of two Ethiopian women bent forward grotesquely at the waist, struggling down a village street. Secured by a tumpline around each woman's forehead and balanced on the small of her back was an earthenware water vessel that must have weighed fifty pounds empty. No beasts of burden could have been more heavily laden. The other scene at first glance seemed to be a huge bundle of tree trunks and branches with two dirty brown legs sticking out of the bottom. On closer examination, I found the legs belonged to a frail and apparently aged African woman who was busily performing the never-ending job of collecting and bringing home firewood. African women typically spend at least an hour daily, and often much more, gathering firewood. What a blessing a truly effective and cheap solar cooker would be!

In addition to their domestic responsibilities, women in Africa do up to three-quarters of all agricultural work. They carry out most of the unmechanized parts of farming—harvesting, weeding, processing, and storing crops—as well as essentially all of the domestic work involved with cooking food and caring for children. In Kenya, where 38 percent of the farms are run by women, those women manage to harvest the same amount per hectare (2.47 acres) as men, despite men's greater access to loans, technical advice, fertilizers, hybrid seeds, and pesticides. And when women are given the same level of assistance, they have been found to be more efficient and to produce bigger harvests than men.[6]

Most of the petty traders in Africa are women. They run the roadside markets and gather in the village square to sell foods and other products, much of which they have either grown themselves or harvested from the forest. They are natural entrepreneurs. One such person is Ester Ocloo, a Ghanaian who was the first woman to receive the prestigious Africa Prize for Leadership for the Sustainable End of Hunger. What a shining light she is!

In 1943, Ester borrowed ten shillings from her aunt to buy oranges to make marmalade which she then sold at the market. Her enterprise has since grown to one hundred companies, both large and small. Most of the workers are women from rural areas. Shortly after Ghanaian independence from Britain, she saved enough money to obtain training in England in food processing and preservation. She then taught those skills to others and organized them into food-manufacturing associations. She exemplifies the entrepreneurial skills of African women, from one end of the continent to the other.[7]

Third World women not only work very hard but they also face difficult health and education problems. Women occupy the bottom rung of society in most developing countries. They eat least and last, always serving the men and children first, often having little or nothing left for themselves. In common with impoverished mothers everywhere, they do without for themselves in order to give as much as they can to their children. Consequently, women in developing countries are much more likely to be malnourished than are men. In Southeast Asia and Africa, 65 percent of pregnant women suffer from nutritional anemia, for example. That condition lowers their resistance to infectious diseases, reduces their capacity to work and to learn, and results in a greater risk of death in pregnancy and childbirth. The result is that women in developing countries do not live nearly as long as their sisters in the United States, Canada, or other developed Western countries. In severely impoverished African countries such as Mozambique, Somalia, or Mali, life expectancy of females is only about fifty years, compared to nearly eighty years for women in the United States or Canada. Life expectancy in Ghana is only fifty-seven years and that in Zimbabwe is sixty-two years.[8]

Women in developing countries are routinely denied basic education and the opportunity to learn job skills that could lead to economic self-sufficiency. They long for knowledge that will help them to better look after their families, to grow more food, to prevent illness in their children. As one Sudanese woman explained: "I must learn new skills or I will be left behind and my family will suffer. My children must not remain ignorant like me."[9]

Fewer than one in five women is literate in many parts of Africa. In Mozambique 79 percent are illiterate; in Sierra Leone, 89 percent; in Mali, 76 percent; in Ghana, 49 percent; and in Zimbabwe, 40 percent.[10]

Many fewer girls than boys attend secondary school in most African countries—only 5 percent of the girls in Mozambique attend, for example, and that number drops to 4 percent in Mali.[11] Often, girls' mothers need them at home to care for the younger children while the mothers work in the fields or engage in petty trading.

It is no small thing that Relief Society has championed the cause of literacy for women everywhere.[12] Indeed, I am convinced that teaching women to read and write is part of that "errand of angels" that I mentioned earlier. Substantial evidence indicates that the health and well-being of Third World families is more closely related to the educational status of the mothers than to the economic status of the family. Furthermore, how can a woman learn the gospel if she cannot read the sacred scriptures?

The adversity under which so many women struggle is heightened under conditions that reduce them to the status of refugees. At the end of 1991, according to the U.S. Committee for Refugees, nearly seventeen million uprooted persons needed protection and assistance around the world. That number has increased during 1992, as the horrifying events in the Balkans have continued to shock and sicken people everywhere. Many of these uprooted people are women and children. The United Nations high commissioner for refugees has officially designated women and girls as an especially vulnerable segment of refugee populations. Rape, abduction, torture, forced prostitution, and murder are all common forms of violence against female refugees. Such actions, in addition to being criminal acts, are a deep affront to human dignity and abhorrent in the sight of God.

In all countries, the lives of women are inextricably connected—both by nature and by nurture—with those of their children. In all lands, mothers worry and weep over the health of their little ones. Those sorrows are accentuated, quantitatively, if not qualitatively, in developing countries where so many children suffer untimely illness or death. As would be expected, infant mortality rates are ten to twenty times higher in African countries than in the United States or Canada.

Major causes of death in preschool children in a refugee camp hospital in Ethiopia during the first ten months of 1989 were similar to those found throughout the continent under nonrefugee conditions. Death comes most frequently to African children as "the result of uncontrolled diarrhea stemming from unsafe water, intestinal diseases and parasites, and lack of proper medical care."[13] At least one million African children die each year from diarrhea. Large numbers of children die from such infectious diseases as pneumonia or measles under conditions of poor sanitation, malnutrition, overcrowding, and low vaccination rates. The common infectious diseases of childhood, which almost never kill well-nourished Western children, can and do kill large numbers of malnourished children in the Third World. In 1985 in a refugee camp in eastern Sudan, for example, between one-third and one-half of the children had measurable signs of malnutrition and as many as one in three children suffering from measles died from the disease. Malaria kills an estimated one million African children under the age of twelve each year. The members of society most susceptible to infectious diseases are infants and preschool children, pregnant women, and the elderly, many of whom are already weakened by preexisting nutritional and health problems.[14]

The link between malnutrition and disease amongst Third World children is complex. Malnutrition can increase the risk and severity of diarrhea, and diarrhea in turn lowers the absorption of nutrients from the gastrointestinal tract, increases the loss of nutrients from the body, and reduces food intake. A vicious cycle is set up that often leads to dehydration and death unless it is interrupted by proper medical treatment, such as oral rehydration therapy—administering a simple mixture of sugar, salts, and safe water. This mixture can be given by mouth and is safe and cheap to administer. Sadly, many Third World infants do not receive even this simple, lifesaving treatment.

Mothers play a special role in determining the health of their children. In Bangladesh, if the mother is living, approximately 90 percent of children survive to one year of age. If the mother dies, however, infant survival drops so precipitously and quickly that by four months after birth only 40 percent of such children are still alive. Smaller numbers of children continue to die during the remaining months of the first year of life. Death of the mother doubles the rate of mortality in her sons and more than triples it in her daughters.[15]

It would, of course, be wrong to suppose that only Third World children are in peril or that only Third World mothers weep for their sons and daughters. When we speak of "the errand of angels," we must look to the plight of women and children in this country as well. A chilling series of articles in the 10 August 1992 edition of *Fortune* magazine outlined in grim detail the dangers facing American children. One of the authors, Louis S. Richman, pointed out that "if the well-being of its children is the proper measure of the health of a civilization, the United

States is in grave danger." Mr. Richman noted that "the bipartisan National Commission on Children wrote in 'Beyond Rhetoric,' its 1991 report, that addressing the unmet needs of American youngsters 'is a national imperative as compelling as an armed attack or a natural disaster.'"[16]

The long, lamentable catalogue of perils afflicting the children in this country include the following:

• The infant mortality rate in the United States is higher than that of nineteen other industrialized nations.

• The proportion of nonwhite one-year-olds immunized in the United States against polio, measles, and other preventable diseases lags behind that of fifty-five other nations.

• The parents of nearly 2,750 children separate or divorce each day. More than half of all white children and three-fourths of African American children under eighteen will spend part of their childhood in a single-parent household.

• Every day more than three children die of injuries inflicted by abusive parents.

• There are 1.3 million latchkey children between five and fourteen years of age who come home to an empty house each day.

• A typical fourteen-year-old watches three hours of television daily but does only one hour of homework.

• On average, 2,200 kids drop out of school each school day.

• Every day more than 500 children between the ages of ten and fourteen begin using illegal drugs, and more than 1,000 start drinking alcohol.

• Nearly half of all middle-schoolers abuse drugs or alcohol, engage in unprotected sex, or live in poverty.

• More than 1,400 teenage girls a day, two-thirds of them unmarried, become mothers.

• Among fifteen- to nineteen-year-olds, homicide by firearms is the third leading cause of death for whites and *the* leading cause of death for blacks.

• Some 41 percent of boys and 24 percent of girls are able to get a gun on a whim.[17]

Much of this frightening decline in the well-being of America's children has occurred in the last thirty years. In the three decades since 1960, we have seen a 560 percent increase in violent crime in America, a 419 percent increase in illegitimate births, a quadrupling in divorce rates, a tripling in the proportion of children living with single mothers, a tripling in the teenage suicide rate, and a drop of nearly eighty points in SAT scores, according to the authors of a 1992 report.[18]

To what can we attribute this lamentable turn of events? In a recent perceptive article in the *Wall Street Journal*, William J. Bennett, United States Secretary of Education from 1985 to 1988, hit the nail on the head when he wrote: "Our society now places less value than before on what we owe to others as a matter of moral obligation; less value on sacrifice as a moral good; less value on social conformity and respectability; and less value on correctness and restraint in matters of physical pleasure and sexuality. . . . The social regression of the past 30 years is due in large part to the enfeebled state of our social institutions and their failure to carry out their critical and time-honored tasks."[19]

The social institutions to which Bennett refers include the nation's homes, schools, and communities. Surely, if we value the future, the deplorable results of misplaced personal, family, and societal values cannot be allowed to remain unreversed.

No one would argue with the assertion that there is too much injustice and oppression in the world, too much misery and suffering, too many tears, too little compassion and caring, too little purity of heart. No race, gender, or society is immune to travail and trouble; they are the common burdens of humankind. Yet it is clear that, worldwide, women and children are at a comparative disadvantage. They suffer much more than their share; they receive much less than they deserve. He to whom "all are alike," both male and female, who had a special love for children, who makes no distinction in terms of worthiness between the races, kindreds, tongues, and peoples of humankind, who loves equally his sons and his daughters, must weep at the lack of true humanity manifested by so many.

Let me repeat what I said at the outset: If the status of women and children is to be improved worldwide, as justice and decency demand it must be, women themselves will have to play increasingly significant roles in effecting the necessary changes. In doing so, women will have to stand up and speak out, gently but firmly, against evil and brutality, injustice and oppression. They must be joined by their brothers in a mighty army of righteous men and women united in a common cause.

The work will not be easy nor the way short. There is much to do, much dreaming and planning, service and sacrifice, prayer and labor. Yet the world is full of glorious examples of women who have altered the path of history. One was Florence Nightingale, the founder of the modern nursing profession. Born in 1820 in Florence, Italy, where her well-to-do British parents lived temporarily, she grew to womanhood in England. A child of privilege, she could easily have spent her life in the pursuit of pleasure, as did many of her contemporaries.

But Florence felt deeply that God had a mission for her to accomplish. Against the wishes of her family, she trained in Germany as a practical nurse and became the superintendent of nurses at a London hospital. Nursing at that time had no prestige and did not attract women of good character and breeding. In 1854, when war broke out in the Crimea between Britain and France on the one side and Russia on the other, Florence took a party of nurses to work in the military hospitals for wounded British soldiers.

When she arrived at the hospital in Scutari, Turkey, Florence found appalling conditions of filth, degradation, and gross overcrowding. The walls were thick with dirt; the floors, rotten. Vermin scurried everywhere. There were no basins, no towels or soap, insufficient bedding and bandages, and no hot food. Florence's first requisition was for two hundred scrub brushes.

Blessed with an iron will and unflinching courage, Florence fought the hostility of the medical establishment and the army bureaucracy to obtain supplies needed for proper nursing of desperately wounded soldiers. She reorganized the kitchens and laundries. Prodigious efforts were made to clean the wards and bring to their inhabitants some of the necessities of civilized life. The wounded began to receive nourishing, well-cooked food and the comfort of clean linen. Wounds were dressed regularly, and the men were bathed and given clean clothing.

Florence drove herself hard. She worked eighteen-hour days, making her rounds through the wards late at night, a lamp in her hand, giving comfort and solace to thousands. The soldiers called her the "Lady with the Lamp." They kissed her shadow as it passed and, in an army noted for blasphemy, scrupulously watched their language in her presence. In a few months the mortality rate amongst the wounded fell from more than 50 percent to just over 2 percent.

Florence became a national hero in her native Britain. But she cared little for personal glory, refusing public transport home and every kind of public honor. She was more interested in obtaining improved living conditions for the soldiers. Important and wide-ranging reforms resulted from her efforts.

In 1860 she organized the Nightingale School for Nurses at St. Thomas' Hospital in London, the first of its kind in the world. The justly honored position held by the nursing profession today throughout the world has resulted in no small measure from Florence Nightingale's extraordinary life of unstinting service. I believe she would have agreed with King Benjamin, who knew that "when ye are in the service of your fellow beings ye are only in the service of your God." (Mosiah 2:17.) The lesson of Florence Nightingale's life is clear: one person with vision and indomitable will can accomplish much.[20] Indeed, she can change the world!

The Lord does not expect his daughters all to become clones of Florence Nightingale, leaving family and friends to care for the afflicted of the world. Modern "sisters in Zion," however, have a Christian obligation to do as the Lord instructed the First Presidency: to "succor the weak, lift up the hands which hang down, and strengthen the feeble knees." (D&C 81:5.) This work begins at home and then extends out, as circumstances permit and warrant, to impoverished souls in local communities and elsewhere. The payment of a generous fast offering, as simple and undramatic as that is, remains an effective way to help others.

A First Presidency letter, dated 13 December 1991, also notes, "We receive inquiries from those wanting to make additional contributions to Church humanitarian work that assists people in dire need throughout the world. We feel moved by such compassion and wish to provide an avenue through which this can be done. Therefore, those desiring to assist can write *Humanitarian Service* on the *Other* line of the standard donation slip, enter in the desired amount, and give the slip and their contribution to their bishop or branch president who will immediately forward it to the Church. They may also elect to send such contributions directly to Humanitarian Service at Church headquarters." These funds are earmarked for use in the Church's worldwide humanitarian effort.[21]

Ours is a time when values are inverted, when good is called evil and evil good, when the devil pacifies many and lulls them away into carnal security, whispering that there is no hell. (See 2 Nephi 28:21–22.) In the midst of this darkness, I for one remain optimistic about the future. The reason is simple. The gospel of Christ is again upon the earth in its fulness. God's church has been reestablished, for the last time, never again to be taken from the world. Inspired prophets lead and direct the work, which continues to roll forth to cover the whole earth as the waters cover the mighty deep. My serenity is akin to that of Cyprian, bishop of Carthage, and a Christian martyr of the third century. To his friend Donatus, Cyprian wrote: "This seems a cheerful world, Donatus, when I view it from this fair garden under the shadow of these vines. But if I climbed some great mountain and looked out over the wide lands, you know very well what I would see—brigands on the high roads, pirates on the seas, in the amphitheaters men murdered to please applauding crowds; under all roofs misery and selfishness. It is really a bad world, yet in the midst of it I have found a quiet and holy people. They have discovered a joy which is a thousand times better than any pleasure of this sinful life. They are despised and persecuted, but they care not. . . . These people, Donatus, are the Christians and I am one of them."[22]

With my serenity about the future come deep feelings of gratitude. How grateful I am for the glorious gospel of Christ and for his church— The Church of Jesus Christ of Latter-day Saints—which provide the guidelines and point the way to what must be done to make this world a better place for all of God's children.

I finish where I began, with Christ's admonition to let your light shine forth to the glory of God. May women everywhere rise above the adversity that is too often their lot to the full measure of the divinity within them. May they lift up their lamps and illuminate every corner of our globe. And may their lights coalesce with those of their brethren to form a mighty beacon that will penetrate and sweep away the gross "darkness [which] covereth the earth." (D&C 112:23.)

NOTES

1. Emily Woodmansee, "As Sisters in Zion," *Hymns of The Church of Jesus Christ of Latter-day Saints* (Salt Lake City: The Church of Jesus Christ of Latter-day Saints, 1985), no. 309.

2. Karen Lynn Davidson, *Our Latter-day Hymns: The Stories and the Messages* (Salt Lake City: Deseret Book Co., 1988), p. 462.

3. See *The State of the World's Women, 1985* (New York: United Nations, 1985).

4. Barbara Thompson, "Coming Out of the Shadows: Women in the Third World," *World Vision*, Feb.-Mar. 1993, pp. 3–4.

5. Perdita Huston, *Third World Women Speak Out* (New York: Praeger Publishers, 1979), p. 67.

6. *Women: A World Report* (New York: Oxford University Press, 1985), p. 3.

7. See "Women Hold the Key to End Africa's Hunger," *USA Today*, 27 Sept. 1990, p. A–11.

8. *World Development Report 1993: Investing in Health* (New York: Oxford University Press, 1993), p. 300.

9. Huston, p. 88.

10. *World Development Report 1993*, p. 238.

11. Ibid., p. 294.

12. In 1992 the Relief Society General Presidency initiated a focus on literacy as part of the Relief Society's sesquicentennial celebration. The Gospel Literacy effort is an ongoing plan to help individuals learn to read and write so they can better understand the gospel and participate in all aspects of gospel living. The First Presidency has spoken of the importance of this Gospel Literacy effort: "Now a great new project is to be undertaken. . . . Its consequences will go on and on and be felt in the lives of generations yet to come. It is a program . . . designed to bring light into the lives of those who can neither read nor write." For information on how to implement this program, refer to "Gospel Literacy Guidelines for Priesthood and Relief Society Leaders," distributed December 1992. See also Gordon B. Hinckley, "Ambitious to Do Good," *Ensign*, Mar. 1992, pp. 2–6.

13. *Hunger 1993: Uprooted People* (Washington, D.C.: Bread for the World Institute, 1993), p. 21.

14. Ibid., pp. 17, 21–22.

15. *The Health of Adults in the Developing World*, ed. Richard G. A. Feachem, et al. (New York: Oxford University Press, 1992), pp. 165–66.

16. Louis S. Richman, "Struggling to Save Our Kids," *Fortune*, 10 Aug. 1992, p. 34.

17. Ibid., pp. 35–36.

18. Victor R. Fuchs and Diane M. Reklis, "America's Children: Economic Perspectives and Policy Options," *Science*, 3 Jan. 1992, pp. 41–42.

19. William J. Bennett, "Quantifying America's Decline," *Wall Street Journal*, 15 Mar. 1993, p. A–12.

20. For further information regarding this extraordinary woman, see Lytton Strachey's perceptive essay entitled "Florence Nightingale," in his book *Eminent Victorians* (London: Penguin Books, 1948).

21. As quoted in Presiding Bishopric letter to Regional Representatives and to stake presidents and bishops of BYU stakes and wards, 4 Mar. 1993.

22. As quoted in Marion D. Hanks, *Improvement Era*, June 1969, p. 53.

In a Black Sedan

ELISA PULIDO

In a black sedan, two parents and we
children drove down park-lined avenues,
past Minerva's statue and her streaming fountains,
waving to flower vendors
with long orange yellow pink gladiolas—
leaving asphalt for cobblestone for gravel for dirt
through the mucky streets
of a no-tree bush flower village
whose earthen walls rose three feet
from the car's fenders,
left and right.

In doorless entrances to mud hovels
shawled women, nude children
stood silently watching our passage
until we stopped to wait
for slow-moving tail-swishing cattle
whose taut black and white hides
stretched from bony pelvis
along swayed spine to horned head.
Our windows (quickly rolled) blocked
the onslaught of flies,
odors of dung.

Outside my window I saw a naked boy,
skin the color of Mexican mud,

Elisa Pulido received her bachelor's degree in German from Brigham Young University. She and her husband, Timothy Jay Pulido, are the parents of three children. Sister Pulido served a mission to Switzerland, and she conducts the choir in her Pennsylvania ward.

clinging to the dark skirts
of a small Indian woman
wrapped in a red green magenta striped reboza—
A boy whose black eyes met the magnified blue eyes
of a child in thick glasses
and a pale yellow dress
who stopped in his village
and glided away
in a chrome-trimmed car
when the cows were gone.

Invincible Summer:
Finding Grace Within

MARTHA N. BECK

Have you ever seen someone with a terminal illness, or delinquent children, or a failed marriage, and thought, "There but for the grace of God go I"? That phrase was probably my first encounter with the concept of God's grace. And except for a few hymns that we seldom sing and a few passages of scripture that we rarely read, that is where grace probably enters most frequently into Latter-day Saint thought and language patterns. That sentence—"There but for the grace of God go I"—also sums up much of the common cultural baggage that clouds the concept of grace. Think about the implications of that statement: "There, but for grace, go I." It conveys a powerful message that the primary function of God's grace is to preserve human beings from suffering and misfortune. It suggests that grace is essentially equivalent to luck: God's grace saves us from the miserable fate that we might encounter without its protection.

That is a concept of grace that shapes almost all people's thinking as their faith first develops. Nearly all of us have believed at one time or another that grace is a simple equation: if I obey God's commandments, then God will protect me from misfortune and suffering. That very comforting philosophy gives many individuals a foundation of emotional security on which to build their lives. The problem is that the more one learns and sees, the more God appears to be capricious in the administration of grace.

Let me give you an example. A couple of years ago I heard a story in a church meeting about a woman whose doctors said she was going to have a handicapped child. They urged abortion. The woman held

Martha N. Beck is a researcher and writer living in Provo, Utah, with her husband, John, and their three children. She is completing a Ph.D. in sociology from Harvard University and is a popular speaker on a variety of topics, including gender issues in LDS culture and society.

out faithful, refused the abortion, received priesthood blessings, prayed, fasted, and delivered a perfectly normal, healthy baby. I believe the story, and I know God can intervene in the lives of his children. The problem I had with it, however, was that the same thing had happened to me—almost. I also was told by doctors that I would have a handicapped child and was encouraged to abort that child. I also held out faithful, received priesthood blessings, prayed, fasted, and delivered a beautiful baby, who was and is handicapped exactly as the doctors predicted.

I would bet that dozens of women reading this have similar stories to tell. Women who have waited faithfully for miracles that never happened: ships that never came in, cavalry that never rode over the hill, help that arrived just *after* the nick of time. Women who have then longed to understand the reasons for their losses and found in reply only complexity and confusion. Women who have prayed for a knowledge of God's will and have not seen angels or visions or burning bushes but only their own tears in their own eyes.

The fact is that miraculous redemption from suffering happens a good deal less often than suffering that is not redeemed. If that weren't true, we would have no need to go to doctors, fasten our seat belts, or weep for damaged or lost relationships. But we don't often tell stories over the pulpit about such ordinary things as predictable suffering, because we tell our public stories to inspire each other, to inspire confidence in a God who will keep us from hurting or from making the wrong choices, if we just adhere to his commandments.

Why do we oversimplify like that? Well, part of it is simple psychology: it is very comforting to see the world as straightforward and God's grace as a sure defense against pain. And another important reason is found not so much in psychology as in sociology, the study of social traditions and behaviors. As you probably know, most of the early Mormons came from the lineage of Western European Protestants, among whom the Calvinists provide perhaps the most extreme example of grace defined as an equation. John Calvin and his followers were a religious group who believed that some people were simply chosen, rather arbitrarily, to go to heaven. Others were chosen, equally arbitrarily, to go the other way. Nothing one did could change one's eternal fate. Nevertheless, the Calvinists believed that they could tell who was chosen for heaven because God would grace his favorites with good fortune. By the nineteenth century, Calvinists, as a group, had become almost obsessed with appearing to be favored by fortune, since that determined whether or not they were seen as righteous. If their business did well, if their house was beautifully decorated, if their children were good-looking and well behaved, then everyone in the congregation would know that God approved of them.

Sound familiar? It did to me when I read about the Calvinists. I had seen the same type of reckoning being made by some people in my own hometown. A good many Calvinists were converted to Mormonism in the late nineteenth century and journeyed over the plains, carrying as unintended baggage many of the cultural ideas of Calvinism. They brought the view of grace expressed in the phrase "There but for the grace of God go I": "I am prosperous, healthy, wealthy, and wise, because of God's grace. I have a perfect family with no rebellious teenagers, comfortable finances, a sound marriage, because I am graced by God. And logically, of course, if you do have rebellious teenagers, no income, or a rocky marriage—or no marriage at all—well, God just doesn't like you as much as he likes me." This is a capricious god, the god of Calvinism, who still lingers on to be worshipped in many aspects of our culture. Ironically, that god has nothing to do with the God of Latter-day Saint theology. In fact, he is a cultural and psychological creation in direct opposition to Mormon doctrine.

So what does LDS doctrine have to say about God's grace? What is it, and how can we receive it? I do not claim to be an authority on doctrine, and I speak from my own experience and my own reading of the scriptures. I fumble and fuss over these issues just as you do and probably with less success.

My perspective on grace is straightforward: if it's good, I want it. But to get something, I must first understand what that thing is; and to understand what God's grace is, I must first understand the God who administers it. All of LDS scripture teaches that the God of grace is Jesus Christ. All grace, then, must be seen as a manifestation of the nature and mission of Christ. And what is that nature, that mission? That question returns us to the great story—unique to LDS doctrine—of how Christ became the savior of this world.

According to that doctrine, we all lived with God before we came to earth. The plan of salvation was set up in a great council in heaven in which we all participated. The plan was that we should go to earth and live as mortals for a brief span of time in order to progress toward our divine nature. We all agreed to that much. But there was some disagreement about the details of how such progress should occur. First of all, Lucifer, son of the morning, stepped forward and offered his plan. In Lucifer's version, good and evil would exist on the earth, but Lucifer would ensure that all of us would do good: there would be no choice to do otherwise. Christ sustained the Father's scenario, in which we would be placed on earth in ignorance and allowed to choose whether we would follow good or evil. In brief, Lucifer's plan gets us all safely back home, and Christ's plan, which is not safe at all, virtually assures that many of us will never get back home. And what did we do? We condemned Lucifer's plan and accepted Christ's.

My question is, Why would we do such a thing? Why would we condemn Satan's plan? Why did we reject it, not just as an ineffective or second-rate scheme but as evil itself? I have often heard that the problem with Satan's plan was that he sought glory for himself, whereas Jesus offered his glory to God the Father. That is true, but it wasn't the allocation of credit that we rejected; it was Satan's *entire plan*. We rejected his image of a world where we would have no volition to sin or suffer in favor of a world where sin and suffering are inevitable.

Christ's mission is to put this second plan into operation. And I believe that grace is one of the aspects of his power by which human beings experience his presence and his will. This definition of grace is fundamentally different from the popular, or Calvinist, notions. Although most Judeo-Christian cultures assume that the function of grace is to remove uncertainty and keep us from straying from God, Mormon theology, it seems to me, indicates that the function of grace is to *ensure* uncertainty and to protect at all costs our freedom to stray from God if we so choose.

Now back to my question: Why did we vote for our Father's plan? It virtually guarantees tremendous human suffering, because if people are ignorant and are also free to make choices, some of their choices will inevitably be wrong. When that happens, both they and others will sometimes suffer horrendous consequences. To make a choice in ignorance is a terrifying gamble, yet that is exactly what we opted to do in the premortal existence.

Personally, it's hard for me to believe I voted the way our doctrine says I did, because I hate hard choices. One such choice I could not avoid was whether or not to bring a handicapped child into the world. I remember the frustration I felt when I was being pressured to abort that baby. I thought that I deserved some clear, divine guidance at that

point in my life. I wanted God to give me one clear option and somehow make me certain that there was no other way. Instead, when I
prayed and opened the scriptures, I felt myself being drawn to 2 Nephi
10:23, which reads: "Therefore, cheer up your hearts, and remember
that ye are free to act for yourselves—to choose the way of everlasting death or the way of eternal life."

I was shocked and offended by this directive. Cheer up my heart?
Because of my freedom to make my own decision, without help and
without certainty? That freedom—to choose life or death—felt awful to
me. Why should I have to make the choice? Why should I have to risk
"everlasting death"? *I wanted someone to tell me what was right!*

I think we all feel that way at various times. In the face of really
difficult decisions, it is often easier to turn over to some outside force
one's right to choose rather than take responsibility for frightening consequences. When I was making my decision about my child, I went to
speak to one of my professors at Harvard, a very well-known and influential sociologist and someone I respect very much. I asked her for an
extension on a paper and explained the problems I was having with
my pregnancy. She knew that I was LDS, and she asked me if my
church was pressuring me to refuse an abortion. I told my professor
the truth, which was that the people I knew in the Church had very
explicitly told me that this was my own decision and that they sympa-
thized with my pain but would not pressure me one way or the other.
Thinking I had cast the Church in a flattering, open-minded light, I was
surprised at her response. She said, "Oh, that's awful! They've dumped
all of the responsibility on you." Well, you just can't win for losing with
some people.

Naturally, I had not identified our doctrine of agency in such negative terms, but of course it's true: Agency comes with a sometimes
oppressive load of responsibility. Freedom and responsibility are, in fact,
two sides of the same coin. You cannot have one without the other. As
a sociologist who studies women's history, I have seen that women's
economic and social position has always greatly restricted a woman's
freedom to choose the course of her own life. But restricted freedom
is also a kind of protection. And early in its course, the woman's movement did not recognize that many women do not want to relinquish
that protection. Faced with difficult decisions, many women—and
men—prefer to turn over responsibility to some outside power and
thereby abdicate responsibility for the choice.

According to a story I have been told is true (it may be apocryphal, but I still believe it!), Brigham Young once encountered a woman with that kind of psychology. She went to him in tears. "Brother Brigham, my husband told me to go to hell." And he said, "Well, sister, don't go!"[1] Now the reason that's funny is that the solution to the woman's dilemma was so obvious. She did not need a prophet's okay to disobey her husband and refuse to go to hell—or to defy his authority over her if it took the form of insult. Although her husband might have been, in the hierarchy of LDS authority, responsible for some of her choices, her husband was not responsible for her salvation. Yet Brigham Young's joke has some basis in reality. Some women actually choose, at some level, to accept their husband's authority to direct their lives in all things, even to do wrong.

The results of this kind of abdication of choice, of turning over to other people our freedom to choose, can be far more terrifying than this trivial, humorous example. The history of the world is strewn with the bloody stories of whole groups of people who have turned the governance of their lives over to other people's decisions, whether or not those decisions resonated with the feelings in their hearts. At this point in history, the peoples of the former Soviet Union have taken the opposite track. They are actively engaged in the very process for which we came to this earth. They are willingly suffering the vagaries of a difficult fate to gain the liberty to make their own choices.

Karl Marx, one of the creators of communism, was a sociologist. In Marx's ideal society, property was to be held in common and people were to willingly contribute and cooperate in building a society for the good of all. All people were to be equal, fulfilled, and healthy. All were supposed to contribute to the community, in whatever way best suited their abilities, and take in return what they needed for life. The only problem with that idyllic plan when it was implemented in various nations was that the liberty to make free choices was taken from the people and placed in the hands of the intelligentsia. A trivial distinction, right? Why not let the best and the brightest, the leadership, make choices for the ignorant? It seems logical, but we have all seen how it works out in practice. Many people who have lived under such a system find the coercion of their will so intolerable that they have been willing to die in the struggle for freedom of choice—and please note that their leaders have also been willing to kill to maintain what was supposed to be a benevolent power.

Communism now appears to be failing all over the world for many reasons, but the central reason is its core denial of agency, its siding with Satan's plan to reach a good end by corrupt and coercive means that deny the agency of individual citizens. To ensure control, tyrannical governments remove as many areas of choice from their people as possible.

The same dynamics develop in all social systems invested in controlling the behavior of others, from the Ku Klux Klan to the KGB, from fraternal organizations to dysfunctional families. Patterns of control may exist in any institution, any group or society. Certain rules become very important to the governing parties of such social groups. First of all, blind obedience to authority becomes the highest of virtues, overriding all other virtues. Questioning authority is seen as treasonous and defined as evil. Criticism of the governing elite is strictly forbidden. (Think of the Soviet Union or Hitler's Germany.) In fact, criticism itself comes to receive more severe punishment than any immoral or senseless act that may be criticized. And finally, any information that might undermine the legitimacy of the powerful is strictly withheld from the public, and lies are told to preserve the image of the leadership. All of those elements are strategies to coerce people into surrendering their agency, their freedom to make choices, and to convince them that they should unquestioningly accept the choices made by others. In these systems, voluntarily doing things that go against the individual's deepest feelings is seen as a great virtue—in fact, the greatest virtue, if it is done in obedience to authority.

I have three small children. That means the examples that leap to mind these days are not from Shakespeare or Dante but from Walt Disney. I have already seen *Aladdin* several times. The Disney version of this classic tale portrays a genie who is basically a very good-hearted soul. This genie really wants to be good but is bound by a magical curse to obey the owner of the lamp in which he resides, no matter what that owner asks of him. As long as Aladdin owns the lamp, the genie does the work of good because he obeys a basically good and honest person. But at one point the evil character, villainous Jafar, obtains the lamp. And the genie, though longing to serve Aladdin, must serve evil because his primary directive is blind obedience. He cannot break that directive.

In an authoritarian system, obedience is the supreme virtue. Thus the Nazis at the Nuremberg trials claimed to be innocent of any crime, although they had tortured and killed millions of people. In following orders, they saw themselves as having no right and no capability to choose; to them, their obedience was a virtue no matter what they did because of it. Heinrich Himmler, the leader in the Third Reich who established the concentration camps in which he directed the systematic genocide of Jews, speaking to the SS, said, "Most of you know what it means to see a hundred corpses lying together, five hundred or a thousand. We had the duty to kill this people. By and large, however, we can say that we have performed this most difficult of tasks out of love for our people and we have suffered no harm from it in our inner-self, in our soul, in our character."[2] It was reported that this man sat at his trial and listened unabashed to stories of the most horrendous atrocities committed against innocent people, and yet he blushed furiously when he once forgot to stand up when the judge came in. He was ashamed because he had forgotten to follow the rules of the court, yet not ashamed of the suffering he had inflicted on the people he had murdered.

This mentality seemed so outlandish that for a time psychologists all over the world thought it must be a strange mutation of the German character or society. Americans, in particular, were positive that members of a society based on free thought and individual enterprise could never fall prey to such an abdication of choice. So, shortly after the war, to prove that hypothesis and to study the fearful cultural aberration that had led to the rise of Hitler in Germany, Stanley Milgram, a psychologist, devised an experiment to examine several cultures in order to find out how Germans differed from other cultural types.[3] He arranged for ordinary student volunteers to quiz a stranger, seated opposite them at a table on the other side of a pane of glass. The student, who sat in front of a panel of buttons and a gauge, was given a sheet of questions to ask the person seated opposite. The psychologist remained in the room to give the instructions. If the stranger answered incorrectly, the volunteer was instructed to adjust the gauge and press a button to administer an electric shock. The buttons and gauge were arranged and labeled to show the wattage, which increased from mildly shocking to painful to near-lethal at the highest possible setting.

Even though no electricity was actually transmitted to the stranger on the other side of the glass, this experiment would now be considered highly unethical. It is nevertheless interesting—as so many unethical things can be! The supposed volunteer was, in fact, an actor collaborating with the psychologist. The actor pretended to be in pain while the psychologist encouraged the student volunteer to increase the voltage when the actor persisted in answering questions incorrectly. The psychologist said over and over, "The experiment requires that you go on."

What Milgram expected to find—his working hypothesis—was that almost all people would comply to a certain level, probably the point when the person being shocked expressed mild discomfort, and then object, "I'm not going to do this anymore. I have no obligation to be part of this!" But that is not what happened. Many of the volunteers continued to administer shocks even when the other person appeared to be screaming in pain from near-lethal doses of electricity. The reason seems to have been that the volunteers had abdicated to the psychologist their right to choose. There was no huge financial penalty, no physical force, no threat of punishment. The mere presence of an authority figure to whom they had given responsibility for their actions was enough to get these very normal Americans to torture other human beings. Milgram's terrifying conclusion was that almost all people—some more than others, but virtually all to some degree—are willing to relinquish their right to choose in certain situations. Evidently we are all susceptible to the temptation to follow Satan's plan, to give up our agency.

That is especially true in situations where an imposing authority is giving commands, but it also occurs in situations where no authority figure is present. Another experiment conducted in the 1940s by psychologist Solomon Asch and his collaborators examined the effect of social pressure on behavior.[4] Six people, one the "naive subject" (volunteer) and five collaborators, were asked to perform a very simple task. They were shown a line and asked to identify which of three lines matched it in length. The naive subject was allowed to overhear the responses of the collaborating subjects. The collaborators purposely matched up the wrong lines, just to see what the naive subject would do. (Aren't psychologists sadistic sometimes?) Asch's landmark 1951 paper published a staggering result: most people, when confronted with the decision of a group that opposed their own perceptions, not only would agree with the majority but would actually begin to perceive the wrong line as being the correct one, against the very clear evidence of their own senses. Later, on written questionnaires administered in private, they would continue to answer that the line chosen by their peers was the correct match.

A variation of the experiment involved exchanging the collaborating subjects with true volunteers one by one, so that the starting ratio of five collaborators to one naive subject gradually shifted to all volunteers. By the end of the experiment, no one in the group was a collaborator with the psychologists; yet in many cases all the subjects were still maintaining two very different lines were a perfect match. There was no compulsion at all, no apparent reason for them to falsify their true perceptions. Evidently the power of social shame, embarrassment, desire not to be seen as different, or doubt of our own perceptions in the face of a consensual view of truth different from our own, can sway us to abdicate our right to choose as powerfully as can the presence of an authority figure.

Asch and other social psychologists who verified his work have noted that women are especially vulnerable to this type of pressure. That is so not because women are stupid or have less moral fiber than men but because women typically are socially imbedded beings. We identify ourselves by our relationships and our place in the community. No one knows whether this trait is inborn or socialized, but gender research consistently shows that women are very sensitive to other people's feelings, typically more so than men. Women seem to depend on the social environment to validate their choices. Often we feel we can't make a choice that would put us in opposition to the majority or make us seem odd. We may abandon our own perceptions and feelings because we are afraid to feel, believe, or know something that conflicts with the opinions of others. We may do things we don't want to do and then lie about our feelings of reluctance because we don't want to hurt others' feelings, incur disrespect, or, worst of all, make someone angry.

In my own life I have been dominated by fear of anger or disapproval. I dread conflict, I want to be thought well of, I worry about stepping on people's toes, I even want to impress people. As a result, I've made many choices to please others when my heart told me to do otherwise. I found out how much this trait was affecting me a few years ago after I made a New Year's resolution. I was trying very hard to live the best life I could, but I didn't feel I was doing a particularly good job. So, I decided to go back to basics. My resolution was that I would not lie all year, not once.

At first I was proud of myself because I found out that essentially

I am an honest person. I don't try to shortchange at the grocery store, or shade the truth to manipulate people, or cheat on my taxes. But I found that the more scrupulously honest I became, the more clearly I began to see where I was dishonest. Cultivating an affection for truth highlighted my lies for me, and I found that they were usually in the area of trying to make relationships smooth. I often denied my own genuine feelings and responses when I thought they would offend someone—cause anger, conflict, or stress in a relationship. Far from improving my relationships, however, lying about my feelings harmed them.

I believe that is what Christ means when he says, "Whosoever is angry . . . [is] in danger. . . . Therefore if thou bring thy gift to the altar, and there rememberest that thy brother hath ought against thee . . . first be reconciled to thy brother, and then come and offer thy gift." (Matthew 5:22–24.) I don't think that directive means to pretend you feel no anger. It means to acknowledge it, discuss it with the other person, resolve the causes of it, and move on. Christ deals with his anger by telling us clearly, "I'm angry." The Topical Guide directly references only three instances of God expressing anger, but when I read through the scriptures looking for God's anger, I could find it on almost every page. Perhaps because we believe that anger is antithetical to love we overlook God's expressions of anger when in truth this God who loves us expresses his anger to us very consistently. He says to us, "Please stop that. I get very angry and I will have to withdraw if you continue to do things that disrupt the fabric of our relationship." I found that I often said I didn't feel angry when in fact I did. I came to see that my dishonesty actually increased the anger I carried around with me, and it became a barrier to my having open, honest, healthy relationships. As I became more honest about expressing painful feelings, in the calmest way possible, I found my life changing in frightening but wonderful ways. My inner life became more peaceful. I was thrilled.

As I gained more confidence in my newfound honesty, I one day realized I had to come to terms with a particularly difficult relationship, one in which my choices were motivated mostly by a desire to avoid conflict. I was virtually certain, however, that this person would respond to my real feelings and beliefs with anger—and I am terrified of people being mad at me. I stewed and fussed and tried to put my resolve to be honest out of my mind. I told myself it was a trivial matter, not worth the trouble it would cause, but it wouldn't go away. Finally, I knelt down and pleaded, "Heavenly Father, I'm trying hard to be good here. And I know that to be closer to Thee, I need to make choices that are going to make this other person really angry at me. I don't want to deal with that, Father. Will you take care of this for me? I've worked hard. I don't want the responsibility or the consequences of this choice. Please take the choice away from me." A few times in my life, my prayers have been answered in words, and this was one of them. I heard a clear, calm voice say something that was totally unexpected. The voice said: "I don't just want you to be *with* me; I want you to be *like* me."

It was then that I began to understand the way grace operates. I made the choices that I felt were right, the person I feared did respond with extreme anger, and it did hurt. But I found that growing in my heart was a feeling I had sensed only vaguely before: a sense that my affiliation with Christ was the work of my own agency and that by choosing to follow the truth as I understood it, I had somehow opened my soul to receive comfort and joy that I had never before experienced.

That incident along with many others convinced me that it is by accepting both the freedom and the responsibility to make our own choices that we begin to align ourselves with the power of God—his power and the power he has invested in us as his children. I believe that the full, courageous acceptance of our agency is the step that allows us to take possession of our own hearts and to invite the gifts of grace. Those gifts cannot come to us unless we are consciously and freely electing to follow the truth, because God will never subordinate our recognition of what is right to his own. That is true even though God knows more than we do and knows what is best for us. In our Father's plan, the choices we make may not be as important as our making them freely in accordance with the best estimate of truth that we can achieve at that moment in our lives. I believe, then, that the choice to follow the truth as we see it is the avenue through which we reach toward grace and through which grace is transmitted to us.

The phrase "invincible summer" alludes to the writings of Albert Camus, a French existentialist philosopher. The existentialist thinkers in early twentieth-century Europe struggled to free themselves from the control of false ideologies, false churches, false political parties. In the thick of his own struggle, Camus wrote, "In the depths of winter, I finally learned that within me there lay an invincible summer."[5] Another writer, psychiatrist Viktor Frankl, defined what that invincible summer was for the existentialists: the capacity to choose to hold onto the truth about one's responses, one's beliefs, one's feelings, despite every social and psychological attempt to persuade, seduce, or coerce the mind. Frankl was one of the prisoners of war whom the Nazis so dutifully tortured and violated. In the concentration camps, he grew to believe that there was only one thing that his tormentors could never take from him: his ability to choose to recognize and respond to his own perceptions of truth and goodness. The Nazis, on the other hand, had relinquished their capacity for defining truth to their military and political superiors. Frankl believed that he was therefore essentially free while his captors were in fact prisoners.[6]

Doctrine and Covenants 93:24 states: "Truth is knowledge of things as they are, and as they were, and as they are to come." Do you see the distinction that is being made? Truth is not "things as they are" but "knowledge" of those eternal verities. We have no access to "things as they are" except through the filter of our perceptions, so our knowledge constitutes our truth. In this mortal sphere, everybody's knowledge is different, because everybody's perceptions are different. That is why we are told, "All truth is independent in that sphere in which God has placed it, to act for itself." (D&C 93:30.) To me that passage means that your knowledge of your reality is your own, and your obligation is to act for yourself and not to be acted upon. Indeed, you cannot do otherwise, for the act of surrendering your perceptions is in itself a choice, though not always a conscious one.

I believe that our divinely mandated freedom of choice, or ability to act from our own perceptions, is the universal grace afforded to every individual by Christ's plan of salvation. And because I believe in God, I go a step further than the existentialist philosophers. I believe that accepting responsibility for our own choices and making them in accordance with what we most deeply feel to be true can bring us more than intellectual authenticity. It will bring us joy, progression, happiness, and ultimately salvation. If we adopt that strategy and persist in it, we cannot help but grow in our understanding, so that we correct with later choices the mistakes we made in earlier ones.

My understanding of grace leaves me with more than contemplation: it leads me ineluctably to action. Every morning when I wake up, I am immediately bombarded by a host of choices. So are you. As one who has studied the history of women's roles, I can assure you that never before has any group of people been subjected to a more bewildering variety of choices than are the women of today. Women, urged by both authority and peer pressure toward one choice or another, are often eager to find something or someone to tell them what to do, because that much freedom to choose is a terrifying responsibility.

How do we make those choices? Each of us faces different pressures, different life circumstances, different problems. I have studied LDS women through intensive interviewing for the last seven years or so, and I believe that as a group we are so bombarded by choices that we often search desperately for someone to give us the right answers. I have known many women to seek for the right rule to tell them how to behave. I know women who go to the bishop's office routinely on Sundays to get advice on each new problem that has arisen during the week. I've known women who endlessly wonder and speculate about what will look right to others. Their overriding concern is to determine what will make others think of them as good, loving, righteous people. But everybody's perceptions are different, and you can never, by any act of yours, create anyone's perceptions of you. "Truth is independent . . . to act for itself." It cannot be acted upon.

So I have come to believe that at a time of such tremendously conflicted choices, the surest answers come from the sense of truth, the recognition of joy, that lies in the core of every individual's personality. Camus called it invincible summer. I call it the light of Christ. That touchstone of truth is the purest manifestation of my own identity and of yours. For each of us it is different, responding to the vagaries of our individual personalities and circumstances; and for each of us it is the same, calling us toward joy and wholeness with a cry that is both sweet and frightening. Our ability to perceive the light of Christ is the function of grace, and I believe that if we respond to it in a way that honors it, the other attributes of grace—peace of mind, happiness, health—come to us in ways that are sometimes frankly miraculous.

It is to this light, sisters, that we owe our obedience. And this obedience may take unexpected forms. Christ meekly obeyed when he stood before Pilate and spoke nothing in response to his accusers, when he carried his own cross to Golgotha, when he suffered willingly in Gethsemane. But Christ was meek and obedient not only at the end of his life but throughout his entire ministry. In meek obedience to God, Christ violated some of the most treasured rules of his church and community. In meek obedience to God he took a scourge of cords and drove the money changers from the temple with the strength of his arm and the strength of his anger. In meek obedience to God, he denounced the hypocrisy of the Pharisees. It was for his meek obedience that he was crucified. We cannot be obedient to God without engaging in conflict at some level. We should never be abusive or seek conflict, but conflict will come to us if we obey what is in our hearts rather than just doing what people tell us to do.

Do you seek that light in your heart? Do you honor your ability to know this truth? Do you feel it? Do you taste it? Do you smell it? Do you hear it? I use all forms of sensory perception to describe what it is like, but really it is something we perceive in ways that are spiritual, not physical. The light of Christ is the part of you that knows the truth—the simple truth about what you see, what you know, what you really believe.

Here's a way to know that feeling: ask yourself if you believe the things that I am telling you. Do the things I am saying make sense? Do *all* of them make sense? Of course not. Which of them feel right, feel true? Why do they feel true? I am constantly amazed that when I go to speak somewhere, and I'm introduced by someone of great personal power and institutional authority, and everyone knows that I have three degrees of glory from Harvard University, and I wear my best clothes— and, after all, I *do* have the microphone—people often seem to believe what I say without question! Isn't that bizarre? Of course I'm saying what I believe out of my best thought and experience, but *anything I say might be absolutely wrong*. My experience is not your experience. Does what I say make sense? Does *all* of it make sense? Which parts of it make sense to you? Which parts don't? What resonates with the light of truth in you? What informs that light, what makes it grow? What makes it recoil? Feel those things; respond to them. To do so is the burden of Christ's plan of salvation. That is what we must do to access the gifts of grace. Don't do or believe what others tell you. Listen. Consider. Reason together. Pray. But believe and do only what the best efforts of your heart and mind together tell you makes sense. Listen for Christ's voice, which ultimately is the same as your own deepest voice.

Trust yourself. It is the need to learn to trust yourself that brought you to this life. To have a chance to make your own choices, you came to a place where you are constantly vulnerable to being confused, to feeling lost, to being hurt by the wrongful choices of others. Don't suffer all this for nothing. Don't look for any person or social entity to give you the last word on what you should do. And don't expect God to give you all the answers. He will not coerce you by making your choices for you, when the whole plan of salvation is designed for you to have the opportunity to make them yourself. His grace showers down upon you, leaving you in ignorance, letting you err, allowing you to sin and repent, to be hurt and to heal. And he loves you, loves you measurelessly, through it all.

Even now you may be in the midst of a winter, perhaps an existential winter, a winter of confusion, of bombardment by the demands of peers or authority, a winter of despair. You may perceive no end to the short days, the long nights, or the terrible, discouraging cold. *Know that in you there is an invincible summer.* You can find that summer through accepting the capacity and the responsibility to make choices. For some of those choices, you will be castigated, vilified, and hurt. But that will matter less and less as you draw closer to the truth about yourself, about your own life, which is Christ's truth. Drawing close to that truth invites his presence, and that is a gift that will warm you here until you can live in the summer of his grace forever.

NOTES

1. For other examples of Brigham Young's humorous quips, see Leonard J. Arrington, *Brigham Young: American Moses* (Urbana: University of Illinois Press, 1986), pp. 197–200.

2. Alice Miller, *For Your Own Good,* trans. Hildegarde and Hunter Hannum (New York: Farrar, Straus, and Giroux, 1983), p. 80.

3. Stanley Milgram, *The Individual in a Social World: Essays and Experiments* (Reading, Mass.: Addison-Wesley Publishing Co., 1977), p. 113.

4. Ibid., p. 152.

5. Albert Camus, "Return to Tipasa," in *Lyrical and Critical Essays,* trans. Ellen Conroy Kennedy, ed. Philip Thody (New York: Random House, 1970), p. 169.

6. Viktor Frankl, *Man's Search for Meaning* (New York: Washington Square Press, 1985).

The Gathering of Peace

SUSAN ELIZABETH HOWE

1. STONE

For all the days of the church's life,
the saints had been battered
from home to home, a whole continent
twitching, bucking them on.
"Our temple," they said,
"should be heavy, dense.
To weight us to the land."

They cut and dragged solid granite
from mountains to the east—
four yoke of straining oxen
and four days for every block.
Workers sank foundations
sixteen feet and for decades
shaped and finished pedestals,
buttresses, six great towers. As walls
rose around their covenants,
the saints were welcomed in
to the still, firm silence
at the heart of stone.

Their children, we go up
to temples and back to their source—
granite mountains, eggstone cliffs,

Susan Elizabeth Howe is an assistant professor of English at Brigham Young University. Her poems have been published in Southwest Review, Shenandoah, *and* The New Yorker, *and two of her plays have been produced at BYU. She is the poetry editor of* Dialogue, *and she serves as Spiritual Living teacher in her ward Relief Society.*

great arches of sandstone. Relearning
their devotion, we kneel
on pocks and cracks
as silence pools around us
and grit sticks to our knees. Anchor
and altar, stone gives us space
to pray for the hard cool wisdom
that rises through the bones,
wisdom born
of cataclysm and pressure
and eons of peace.

2. ROSE

The saints left hardwood forests
with their tangled
abundance of roots,
left prairies of deep soil,
to come to a desert
of sand and clay
and a random alkaline crust.
Someone believed this country
would support the rose.
An Englishwoman, perhaps,
tied five or ten or twelve bushes,
their roots wrapped in burlap,
to a prairie schooner's side.
Day after day on her trek
the visionary gardener
hauled buckets to the roses,
soaking the burlap,
moistening the roots.

To survive, the saints
learned to nourish the land
with the mountains' melted snow.
And in a protected corner
this gardener dug a hole,
filled it with clear water

and pieces of raw fish
to feed a rose.

Photos from the moon
show the earth rising,
a blue flower swirling
as it floats up
through the dark, as fragile
as the first rose
on the Mormon desert floor.

3. BREAD

Winter Wheat

October fields
open dark, newly sown,
readied for the weight
of heavy winter snows—
again and yet again,
generation. Melting water
sinks straight down,
bursts waiting kernels
till the whole field is wet
spring grass.

Meal

Children in a field
of heavy wheat bending,
rattling the stalks,
pull up handfuls of the golden
grass. Into their palms they rub
each crest for its small
bright pellets.
Blowing off the chaff,
they bite hard kernels,
chew and chew the mass
into a sticky gum.

But the same kernels harvested,
milled into flour, leavened,

mixed with oil, salt,
rise to become
warm bread, crusty,
that breaks open
to a white, clean heart.
Bread to be savored
bite by bite,
dipped into a stew
of vegetables and lamb,
served at an oak table
in the shine of lamplight.

Communion

In a ward chapel,
or a screened cabin by a lake,
on desert logs pulled into a rough circle,
we saints gather wherever we are.
After prayer
the tokens come on silver
trays. Each of us is served,
serves the next neighbor.
Think of the taste of that crust,
that morsel. Think of wheat
in a fresh field waving
in the rain. Think of your own
hunger. Think of the flesh
torn from the bread,
that we might not destroy
each other. Of Christ come to teach us
how we might have life.

Rummaging in the Attic: Missionary Memos

CLAIRE HAWKINS

Not long ago I returned from a welfare services and proselyting mission in Guatemala. I loved my mission. I have never experienced a period of my life so densely packed with adventure, life, and spirit. I have never felt Christ's presence more immediately or witnessed his guidance more often than I did during those eighteen months. Yet I have spent considerable time lately wondering whether I was an effective missionary.

I was rummaging through some old family files and came across the autobiography of my great-grandmother Maydell Palmer. I vaguely remembered that she had served a mission for the Church in the Northern States Mission at the beginning of the century. I opened the book and found the chapter heading, "My Mission." I believed, as I opened those pages, that her words would capture the essence of being a sister missionary in 1915. Perhaps they would shed some light on my self-doubts. In her account I observed that her love for the Savior seemed infinite. Her life was dedicated to the welfare of humankind, and her whole existence focused upon establishing God's kingdom on this earth; however, she expressed very honestly her frustration over the programs and regulations that restricted her as a sister missionary in 1915.

Let me share with you some relevant passages: "There are three things missionaries must not do. They must not give the gospel to the colored people. And the lady missionaries must not call for repentance when they teach. This is the prerogative of the elders. I was shocked and repelled by such restrictions. My first day of tracting I spoke of the gospel to a kindly looking colored lady who did look a little surprised

Claire Elizabeth Hawkins is a student of anthropology at Brigham Young University. She served a welfare mission in Quetzaltenango, Guatemala, and she has worked with a BYU team in piloting a village literacy program in India.

when she opened her door to see a white woman there who gave her a religious tract to read. My heart ached when I realized the gospel was not for her. I cry out today 'Oh Lord, how long will thou suffer our prejudice to continue?'

"The other restriction was even more distasteful. If the lady missionaries were not to preach the necessity for repentance, why were they called on missions to teach the gospel? Repentance is the second step in that gospel.

"My third hard lesson was that when the elders took the [sister] missionaries on an evening visit they were not to attempt to explain, but just to listen. The elders must do the talking even if the hostess asked that the sisters explain the teaching. It was a difficult lesson to learn. I who had been teaching the gospel to young people for years must now keep still while a new elder with no experience, in poor English, and in ignorance of that principle stumbled through his explanation."

In another passage from her autobiography, my great-grandmother complained about another of her restricted roles: "There was one activity where the lady missionaries were not curtailed and that was to go up into homes where mothers were ill and needed help in the housework or needed a baby sitter to help or to clean her house. Lady missionaries came in very handy on such occasions." She then comments, "I understand that is all changed now as it should have been years ago."

I was comforted to know that my great-grandmother struggled in her mission too. Yet in spite of her struggles, she was able to analyze her experience and discover what it was that caused her discontent. Certainly the principles and ordinances of the gospel of Jesus Christ did not cause her grief. No, that was her utter joy. Rather, what plagued her were the cultural restrictions that limited her role as a representative of the gospel of Jesus Christ: what she, as a woman, could and could not say and do, to whom she could or could not proclaim the gospel and in what way, and the seemingly mandatory maid service reserved to the sisters.

What pained my grandmother in her era is less of an issue now. The gospel can be shared with any man or woman regardless of race or color. We now have many strong black members and missionaries who serve in wards and branches throughout the world. Who can preach the gospel as a missionary today? Any worthy woman or man who is a member of the Church. And I am also pleased to report that sister missionaries these days can talk circles around the elders if they wish.

The policies of Great-Grandma Maydell's mission were established long before she entered the mission field; they were rules that, however unjust, she needed to obey to assure unity and uniformity within the mission. Such unity is called teamwork and is necessary because we live in a community. Our joint effort as part of a community is good. But the collaboration that bonds us to others sometimes also demands that we sacrifice a little individuality—that we compromise. And many times that compromise is very painful. My great-grandma wanted to proselyte. She wanted desperately to preach the gospel to that black woman, to teach *with* the elders, and not to be confined to baby-sitting and housework. Ironically, she felt confined to doing what I longed to do *more* of in my mission: welfare service.

The Church sends welfare missionaries to help local Church leaders assess local needs, and following their suggestions, we begin teaching and learning together. We teach literacy, money management, nutrition, social skills, and hygiene. Best of all, rather than doing the teaching, we teach others to teach. When a woman begins to learn to read, a whole new world opens up to her. She can then read the scriptures and follow the lessons in Relief Society. Her self-esteem skyrockets, and she feels intelligent and useful. As a result of a few reading lessons, a woman can turn into a dynamite mother, Church leader, and contributor to the community. When we teach a mother how to treat her child for diarrhea and how to prevent its recurrence, all of a sudden she no longer has to worry about her child's life from one second to the next. She doesn't have to spend her last centavos on expensive medication and her precious hours in line on the front porch of a doctor's office. Her concerns can turn to others. She can help them as she has helped herself, and the once-desperate little Mormon community can rise together in skill, and knowledge, and unity.

As a welfare missionary sent to a mission that emphasized proselyting, I longed for more assignments to give welfare service. One such opportunity came when my companion and I were asked to assist the wife of an investigator. She had almost died of typhoid fever and whooping cough five months before. When we first met her, she was so emaciated that she could not even sit without her bones digging into the wooden slats of the chair. She was, literally, a walking skeleton. Worst of all, she had lost all hope. With every visit, we watched her move closer to death. It was not just her frail figure that was filled with death; it was her eyes. Little by little, as we helped the family with basic errands and household chores—grocery shopping, picking up the government checks in the city, baby-sitting—we began to teach her the gospel. Her husband was ready for baptism and wanted to be ordained to the Aaronic Priesthood so he could baptize his wife and children. He cared for the four children while we taught her, and eventually we convinced her to go to church.

The meetinghouse, however, was a thirty-minute walk from her home, and she was physically incapable of walking that distance. Each week we scavenged for centavos to pay for a taxi on Sunday to take her and her children to church while her husband biked. We brought pillows, blankets, exercise mats, and anything else soft we could find for her to sit on so that she could withstand the long hours of church. Her deterioration was so great that her husband's care for her wasn't always sufficient. Often, our help was the only break he had from the demands of her sickness. She was still quite discouraged about her health the day of her baptism. But when her husband pulled her up from the waters and the bishopric laid their hands upon her head and said, "Receive the Holy Ghost," she began to live again. She was still the same weak, feverish, thin woman, but her eyes were alive.

Two weeks later, she found the energy to dress her own children and walk to church herself. She now walks to church every week and sits on the hard pews along with the rest of the ward members. Somehow, on the day of her baptism, Heavenly Father allowed her to be born again. And since that day, a divine life force that is not her own carries her body through each week and fills her countenance with light. If we had not helped meet her basic needs first, we would not have been able to teach her. But that was one of the few times I was allowed to serve as a welfare missionary. More and more my calling was diverted from welfare service to strictly proselyting.

Please don't misunderstand me. I am grateful for the opportunity I had to actively preach the gospel—to proselyte. God loves his children. All of them. And he desires that all receive his love and enter into covenant with him. Meeting his children is what makes a mission marvelous. And somehow the Lord works his way into our self-absorbed, young missionary hearts and lets us see and love his Father's children as he does. All in all, that's quite a miracle.

My companions and I had the opportunity to teach many different types of people: soldiers, communist guerrillas, prominent doctors, simple Indian peasants, orphans, prisoners, and prostitutes. We began to love many of them as if they were part of our own family. Some were baptized, and some were not. But those who were baptized and who struggled to honor the sacred covenants they had made began to change miraculously.

I loved to share the discussions, which carefully explain the plan of salvation, the significance of Christ's atonement in our lives, and the reality of eternal families. I loved entering into a one-room home, sitting cross-legged on the bed with four little children on my lap, and telling a humble family in all honesty that they are children of prophets, that their lineage is blessed and they have been preserved for a great and last day, that their ancestors wrote a book of scriptures specifically for them so that they might come to know Christ in his fullness—that he loves them. I loved watching them grow and prepare for the day of their baptism, for the day they would make covenants with God. They became my friends, my family, and I would give my life for them.

Can the knowledge of the gospel and the gift of the Holy Ghost change someone's life? They can and they do. I have seen it happen again and again. The gospel is wonderful. Our Heavenly Father's children are amazing. And it is one of the most marvelous experiences in this life to be a missionary of Jesus Christ and watch these two components meet.

The day of their baptisms we rejoiced together. But that is where a painful paradox began for me and where I first began to question my effectiveness as a missionary, because that same day I cried bitterly and silently inside. Baptism by itself does not bring a soul to Christ. Baptism is only the "gateway." Once we are baptized, the gates are opened. But we often forget that beyond those gates lies a long road we must travel. We all know that the road is hard. The new members are fragile. They feel the Spirit of our Father, realize that they need to change their lives, and with astounding amounts of hope and faith enter into a sacred covenant. It is amazing what people will do, and the degree of sincerity with which they do it, when they are touched by the Spirit. Still, they are fragile.

When they accept the gospel, they also accept the community that accompanies God's latter-day church. In Latin America, religion extends beyond the Sunday church walls. It determines most social activity within the community. Celebrations are based on baptisms, communions, weddings, and saints' days whether the community is Protestant or Catholic. Thus religion determines, for the most part, friends. When a family chooses to be baptized, whether they are aware of it or not, they are severing themselves from their previous ties. They are walking away from their lives in the community. They are utterly alone and need the support of a new community to fill this vast and sudden vacuum in their lives.

Initially the regular missionary visits provide a secure sense of place and community. After baptism, however, the new member is visited less frequently by the missionaries. The missionaries are needed to help other families progress towards baptism. Missionaries visit perhaps once a week to make sure everything is okay. After about two to three months, mission policy in my area dictated that missionary visits should be phased out as the wards and branches integrated these new members through stake missionaries and visiting and home teachers. That is the model.

Reality, unfortunately, proved a little different. I served in four Guatemalan wards during my mission. During that time, only one bishop and one counselor visited either the new or old members in their homes. Visiting and service are the key to keeping the people in the Church: simple human interaction and friendship. But, amazingly enough, very, very few stepped out of their homes and into the doorways of their neighbors. Why? Is it a matter of training leaders and teaching the importance of visiting others? In part, yes. But there is a more fundamental reason why no one visits. People in those countries are living on the edge of existence. At the beginning of a day, a sister member collects water and firewood, cooks beans, takes corn to the mill to be ground to make tortillas, and two hours later cooks breakfast. Then begins the process of making lunch, washing the clothes by hand, and hanging them to dry. If she is a city dweller, much of the process is the same, yet she will also tend the little candy and soap store at the front of her house to supplement her husband's meager wages. Many Guatemalan families work all day long every day of the week to assure food on the table. They do not have the luxury of time in which they can visit one another. They are so crippled by their own economic state that they cannot reach out to others.

New members fall away, and old, inactive members remain inactive. Should we blame the missionaries? Should we blame the members? No. Placing blame is not a solution. Whomever we blame, there is still a problem—we are losing souls. We are losing souls because their basic needs are not being met.

In frustration, as I watched many of my struggling, faithful families fall through the cracks, I wanted to reach out and save them. I wanted to alleviate the burdens of the members by tending their children, washing their clothes, *anything*, so they had time to become the new community for these converts. But my mission assignment had been diverted from primarily welfare to solely proselyting. My revised calling was something I had to accept. As my great-grandmother Maydell had discovered and taught me, we can't restructure the whole mission program worldwide in one afternoon. Policy and program changes evolve over years of feedback, trial and error, earnest prayer, and painful compromises. But sometimes avenues to change individual lives are already there and we miss their significance. The welfare program is tailored to the individual needs of members. This underrated and unappreciated program takes individual members and teaches them spiritual, physical, emotional, and social well-being. It is a program that helps the members help themselves in ways that transform their souls.

Think back to the most meaningful and spiritual moments in your own life. Weren't they somehow tied into human interaction? Maybe someone listened and expressed confidence in you. Maybe someone helped you think through a problem as you bottled peaches together. In my mission, the members who grew to be spiritually and socially strong in the Church were baptized because of similar interactions. We ate the food they ate, husked and dried corn on their patios with them, taught them how to read, and flew kites with their children. We shared their day-to-day trials and joys. Isn't that what the gospel is all about? To make others burdens lighter? My great-grandmother Maydell wanted to be out proselyting, but I wonder if her untallied acts of service didn't bring about more conversions than she knew.

I am a firm believer in the power of service—the converting power, the retaining power of charity. Charity is the pure love of Christ. He is the converting power. He changes lives as we communicate his love through service in his name. Change does not come from big institutions; it comes from the heart. One by one as we can begin to serve others, we will establish Zion across the nations.

Moonlight and Roses

NEIDY MESSER

After school my son washes cars, dazzling new
reds, silver-blue metallics, sticker price
taped to the windows, and each one he wishes
he owned. He comes home at dusk,
driving his dad's dented pickup
hungry, tired, and silent at us
for all we can't give him.

Today he carries a slender, white box,
lifts the lid gently and shows us
a dozen yellow roses, a gift
for his girlfriend. How many washed cars
for each perfect rose? Then I remember
roses some nameless boy gave me
years before my son's first breath, roses
I pressed between pages of a book
and forgot about until now.

On tonight's news, refugees huddle along
hillsides of a far country as soldiers
carry boxes filled with food, milk
for the children. And women, hundreds,
toss their babies into the air, hoping
soldiers will throw them rations.
Tonight some will eat, some
will fill their children's bellies

Neidy Messer lives in Boise, Idaho, with her husband, Bill Messer, and their two sons. She teaches English at Boise State College and was the Idaho Writer-in-Residence, 1990–91. A book of her poems, In Far Corners, has been published, and she is working on another volume. Sister Messer serves in her ward Relief Society.

with dried army dinners, some babies
will fall asleep on the open ground,
dribbled milk on their unwashed faces.

Later, after my son cleans up and rushes out,
the white box under his arm, I picture
refugee women, standing
on tent-cluttered hillsides blushed
by moonlight, their faces tilted upward,
holding roses in their roughened hands
as if something depended on it.

Children's Voices: Who Is Listening?

SHARON P. McCULLY

In Seattle not long ago, I heard the president of the American Bar Association address a gathering of, primarily, juvenile court judges. "An article I read last summer puts the case plainly," he said. " 'If the well-being of its children is the proper measure of the health of a civilization, the United States is in grave danger.' " I thought of my own five-year-old daughter and the questions she asks me regularly. She worries a lot about whether everything is okay—about whether she is safe, or if she should be afraid. He went on, "I wonder, how many adult Americans over the years have said to a concerned child: 'Don't worry; it'll be all right.'

"Well, today, how can we say, 'Don't worry,' when about 415 American children will run away from home during the next *three* hours?

"How can we say, 'It'll be all right,' when 76 American children are abused and neglected *every* hour of *every* day?

"How can we say, 'Don't worry,' when three American children will die in poverty tomorrow morning and *every* morning?

"How can we say, 'It'll be all right,' when 135,000 students in this country go to school every day—carrying guns? And 70 percent of them say they carry guns in order to *protect* themselves!

"How can we say, 'It'll be all right,' when 900 teachers are threatened, and nearly forty are actually assaulted, *every hour* of *every school day?*

"How can we say, 'Don't worry,' when during the course of a typical day, forty children are either killed or injured by gunshot wounds?

"We still might say to a concerned child, 'Don't worry, it'll be all

Sharon P. McCully is a juvenile court judge in Salt Lake City, Utah. She and her husband, Michael D. McCully, have one daughter. Sister McCully is the Laurel adviser in her ward Young Women organization.

right,' but *we* adults had better be worried, because it's *not* going to be all right, unless we work for a safer, healthier, and more productive world for our children."[1]

But these are not *my* children, you may object. They are not my responsibility. I have enough worries of my own. If these are not your children, should you care? Marian Wright Edelman, who heads the Children's Defense Fund, a national organization dedicated to the well-being of children, tells her own children, "Paradoxically, the more I worried about and wanted for you, the more I worried about the children of parents who have so much less. When one of you got a high fever, painful earache, asthma attack, or sports injury, how reassuring it was to pick up the phone and call our pediatrician and take you right in. How enraged I am to think that other parents cannot ease their children's suffering and their own fears because they happen to be born on the wrong side of the tracks, the wrong color, or to lack a job with health insurance or the means to get health care."[2] So many of the problems I see every day in juvenile courts are directly related to economic status, poverty, illness, and still, unfortunately, to race and ethnicity. These are problems tearing at the fiber of so many families. We have to be concerned for their children.

To her sons, who are of mixed African-American and Jewish heritage, Edelman says, "As you have grown toward adulthood, you have become increasingly aware that your educationally and financially privileged lives are not typical of other children in this world, nation, or even our own city. We live in one of the wealthiest neighborhoods of Washington, D.C., while thousands of children ten minutes away are living in a war zone that imprisons them in fear and near-Third World poverty. First World privilege and Third World deprivation and rage are struggling to coexist not only in our nation's capital but all over an America that has the capacity but not the moral commitment or political will to protect all of its young.

"You must walk the streets with other people's children and attend schools with other people's children. You breathe polluted air and eat polluted food like millions of other children and are threatened by pesticides and chemicals and toxic wastes and a depleted ozone layer like everybody's children. Drunken drivers and crack addicts on the streets are a menace to every American child. So are violent television shows and movies and incessant advertising and cultural signals that hawk profligate consumption and excessive violence and tell you slick is real. It is too easy and unrealistic to say these forces can be tuned out just by individual parental vigilance.

"So as a parent I wanted to make sure you had all your physical needs met and a lot of love. But as a parent I could not ignore other people's children or pain that spills over to public space and threatens the safety and quality of life and pocketbook and future of every American."[3]

Even though these may not be your children who are troubled and in trouble every hour of every day, this is your world and your country, your city and your community, your street, your neighborhood, and your ward. These children are your concern.

Let me tell you about the children I saw just this morning. First there was a seventeen-year-old boy who is being held in a detention center in Las Vegas. He will be returned to Utah on my order for shooting a 7-Eleven clerk in the face for eighteen dollars and some odd cents. Should you be concerned? What about the seventeen-year-old girl I signed into detention this morning charged with aggravated robbery, which means she was using a gun or other weapon? She was helping her boyfriend commit a robbery primarily so they wouldn't have to pay for the pizza they had ordered. What about the girl I sent to detention this morning, who at thirteen has lived on the streets for months and needs serious mental health treatment? She first came to our court two years ago for minor shoplifting. She has continued to run away, break the law, and place herself in serious danger on the streets for more than two years now. Or what about the eleven-year-old boy I saw earlier this week who was charged with the rape of a six-year-old girl? What about the ten-, eleven-, and twelve-year-old boys who were recently before me for breaking into, vandalizing, and stealing from more than seventy cars in one neighborhood in one night? What about the boys I had before me last week who did a reverse drive-by shooting? What is a reverse drive-by shooting? Instead of shooting from a moving car, these boys shot at a car that drove by while they were sitting on the lawn in front of their house. Two of these boys had never been to juvenile court before and are now there for attempted criminal homicide.

If these are not your children, should you care about what happens to them? It's relatively easy to care about and even act as advocates for the children who are victims of abuse, neglect, and deprivation in our society. They are lovable, sympathetic young people who clearly need and want help. It is a lot harder for us to feel nurturing and protective about the children I just described to you, the children I see as a juvenile court judge every day. But let me tell you that almost all of those children were the ones who three or four years ago were the abused, neglected, and deprived children. It was easier to love and to care about them then, but they are still the same children. They still need our care and concern. Without it, they will be lost. With it, they may be able to change the direction of their lives.

You may think, None of my children will ever be like this. Or, the children I know are not criminals; they don't do these things. But the shocking truth is that even in the state of Utah, one of every three children will come to the juvenile court at some time before turning eighteen. The odds say that it may be one of your children, or at least someone you know. It is not only possible but probable that you will experience some of these problems in your own families, and if not in your own families, then on your street, or in your ward, or in your town or city. As you already know, your children are going to school with these children. Your children are walking the streets with them, talking with them, playing with them. They exist within the same community, so it's very important for us to advocate for these delinquent children as well as for the ones who are neglected and abused. More often than not, they are one and the same. They are often still experiencing abuse and neglect; they are simply reacting in different, more dangerous ways.

Let me tell you about what kind of advocacy exists for these children within the legal system. First, let me say that the court system is not the best place to solve problems, because by the time these children get to my courtroom, their problems and patterns of behavior are already deeply ingrained. In these cases, the old saying about an ounce of prevention is true. Prevention is far preferable to the cure, because by the time we get to the cure, many people have already been hurt. Nevertheless, although court services may not be the best place, for many it may be the *only* place someone tries to intervene in the direction these children's lives seem to be taking. The courts are the last resort, and they *must* respond. Thankfully, we do still see a lot of success with children who reach the courts. They are *not* beyond hope or help.

The United States Supreme Court and juvenile court judges around the country uniformly agree that no child should appear in juvenile court without a legal advocate. If a child is charged with a crime, that child should not have to come to court without a lawyer. Nonetheless, most children still come to juvenile court, admit to felony offenses, and are punished for those offenses without lawyers. That happens primarily because many parents, and also the counties who have to pay for court-appointed legal counsel, do not believe that children need lawyers. They are wrong. It is very important for each child in a courtroom to have a lawyer. These lawyers are not appointed to help the guilty get away with committing a crime. They are there to make sure the charges are accurate and to explain the legal process to the family and child. Whatever is determined in court becomes a permanent part of that child's record. Consequences for future employment, court involvement as an adult, and even religious participation are long-range and serious. Our resources, public and private, need to be sufficient to assure that good lawyers are available to every child in juvenile court.

In addition to those charged with criminal violations, children who are victims of abuse, neglect, or dependency also need a legal advocate in court. Federal and state law require that the court appoint a guardian ad litem to represent the interests of the child in every case of abuse or neglect. Again, although that's what the law says, too often lack of resources prevents a guardian ad litem from being appointed. In most states, guardians ad litem are lawyers, who often are assisted by lay volunteers who have been specially trained to advocate for children. That is one way you as concerned individuals may assist victimized children in the legal system: Volunteer to be a court-appointed special advocate or a volunteer guardian ad litem. Most states use one of those systems and will use your services to assist children through the court system, both in juvenile and criminal court. Call the juvenile court in your city or county for information.

Another program that is understaffed is foster care. There are now only about half as many foster parents in the country as there were ten years ago. Meanwhile, the number of children entering the foster care system has continued to grow. A lot of people stomp their feet and demand that the state provide better foster care services to children, and yet the foster care services that can be provided are directly related to the quality of foster parents who are willing to take children into their homes. It's often very hard for parents to deal with children needing foster care. They have a whole host of special problems and difficult behaviors. They are sometimes not very loveable. Despite the great need for foster homes, most of us and most of our neighbors are not foster parents. Stomping our collective foot and saying the states must do a better job of providing foster care is pointless. A state can provide foster care only through those people who are willing to be foster parents. If you believe you want to try, contact your local child welfare or human services agency.

Besides building a reservoir of foster parents, it is equally important for us to support and empower natural parents. Often people who are child advocates believe that the legal system ought to provide the best possible parents to every child. Now, if you think about it, on a given day any of us may not be the best possible parents. We wouldn't want to lose our children because of our off-day mistakes or even our more serious failings at parenting. Ideally, the legal system is intended to help a child's natural parents be the best possible parents for their own children, not to shuffle children around to find a better match or a better set of parents. Parents have the right to raise their own children. Even more important, children have the right to be raised by their natural parents.

Admittedly, many people I see in court are terrible parents. But the answer isn't always to take their children away and place them for adoption. Let me tell you about some of the children who come before me in court. I had a whole family in last Monday. The children who were being tried were the last four of a very large family that, in my ten years at the juvenile court, I have just about raised. We're getting there; these are the last four. The father, who died a year ago, was responsible for some serious abuse and neglect in this family. The mother simply cannot keep a house that is adequate for children to live in. Hers is not like what you'd see if you visited my dirty house this afternoon, or your house on any bad day; this is a house where mice wouldn't live. And she just cannot, even with all the assistance in the world, seem to do anything about it. She also cannot seem to set limits for or discipline her children. She just can't manage to give any structure to their family life. She lacks the personal ability and resources to do it. Her children are thriving in foster care. They're growing, learning, succeeding. These children are quite happy in foster care, and they're never going to go home to live with their mother. She doesn't want them to, and they don't want to. We will continue to raise them in the public system.

So why don't we terminate the mother's parental rights and let the children be adopted? You should ask every one of those children why we don't. She's their mom. They don't want to be adopted by someone else. And I can guarantee you that if we terminated her parental rights and told them she wasn't their mom anymore, they would all leave their foster homes and go straight home to mom. Many studies show that approximately 90 percent of all children in foster care—abused, neglected, chemically dependent, and delinquent—do eventually return home. So if they're going to go home, then our jobs ought to be to make their homes the best possible places they can be, instead of trying to replace them with other homes. That's a hard thing for some child advocates to accept. We must all understand: Rather than replace inadequate parents with foster care, we really need to help all parents, including not very good ones, make their natural homes safe, healthy places to be.

So what can we do? I spent an hour on the telephone today with a friend who is a juvenile court judge in Indianapolis. We were both bemoaning our lot, specifically our frustrations that things don't seem to be getting any better. In fact, especially for children, things seem to be getting worse. People ask us when we give speeches, "Well, what can we do? What can be done?" We don't really have the answers, except that each one of you individually may make a difference in one child's life. If each of us makes a difference for just one child, hundreds of children will be helped. How can we make a difference? A good model to follow is that of the ideal LDS ward. Somebody visits us in our homes at least once a month. Somebody checks on us to make sure we're okay, and if we're not okay, they offer assistance to us. Do you know how many kids never have that kind of neighborly assistance from anybody? If we treated more of our neighbors the way we treat ward members, we could make a difference. And when I say neighbors, I may mean neighbors farther away than the two streets next to yours. But if we all adopted one street or even one house in our cities and treated them as we do our visiting teaching assignments, we would make a difference. And we can support community organizations with similar aims. Look for Big Brother, Big Sister, foster grandparents, or other mentoring organizations. Your local juvenile courts should be able to refer you to such organizations.

Where else could we help? Consider being shelter parents or foster parents. It is a hard thing to do, but giving foster care is an incredible service to these children. Volunteer to assist a guardian ad litem or a court-appointed special advocate. Volunteer to be a tracker, which means you're going to help some child get out of bed and to school every morning, to check to make sure he or she stayed there, and then maybe to help that child get home. There are a lot of elementary and middle-school-aged children who don't have a parent to do that. Volunteer to be a mentor. Take a child with you to a Jazz game—or a Bulls' game, or Lakers', or whatever team or sport you support. Take a child in your neighborhood who would never get to go any other way. Help a child or two with their schoolwork; help them with their Cub Scout projects. Could you help a boy build one of those wooden race cars? Just look for those opportunities because, honestly, the more of those opportunities you take, the fewer of those children I'll see. That would make my life a lot easier, but more important, it would make at least one child's life a lot happier. Remember, every *one*—even just *one*—is important:

"As the old man walked the beach at dawn, he noticed a young man ahead of him carefully picking up starfish from the sand and placing them back into the sea. Finally, catching up to the youth, the old man asked him why he was doing this.

"'Because the stranded starfish will die if they are left in the morning sun,' he replied.

"'But the beach goes on for miles and there are millions of starfish everywhere!' scoffed the old man. 'How can your efforts possibly make any difference?'

"For a moment the young man contemplated the starfish in his hand before he tossed it gently into the waves.

"'It makes a difference to this one,' he said."[4]

NOTES

1. J. Michael McWilliams, remarks delivered at National Conference of Juvenile Justice, 2 Mar. 1993, Seattle, Washington. Copy of typescript in my possession.
2. Marian Wright Edelman, *The Measure of Our Success* (Boston: Beacon Press, 1992), p. 29.
3. Ibid., pp. 30–31.
4. "The Starfish Story," distributed by the Utah Chapter of the National Committee for the Prevention of Child Abuse.

Side by Side, Desk by Desk: Gender Equity in the Schools

EILEEN D. BUNDERSON

Doctrine and Covenants 88 reminds us to seek words of wisdom "out of the best books," and to learn, "even by study, . . . things both in heaven and in the earth, and under the earth; . . . and a knowledge also of countries and of last kingdoms." These instructions are given to all who are "laborers in this last kingdom," the last dispensation. (Vv. 118, 79, 74.) The Prophet Joseph himself was a voracious, eclectic learner who believed in educated discipleship for all members. He invited Eliza R. Snow to Kirtland to teach a "select school for young ladies." He started the School of the Prophets, which soon divided into "the Elder's School for Theological training and the Kirtland School for temporal education," including courses on arithmetic, grammar, and geography.[1]

Most adults in the United States and in many other areas of the world began their educations in a schoolroom. It may have been a public school, a private school, or a home school, but each of us likely started early and dutifully worked our way toward graduation. Consequently, we reminisce over football games and proms. We attend high school reunions. We understand and commiserate when our children complain of "unreasonable" homework and "mystery food" at school lunch. Underlying our conversations is the unspoken assumption that we have all shared a common experience: we have "been to school."

As we muddled through and mastered our math, science, history, reading, and social studies, we labored under another assumption: because we were all sitting in the same classrooms, studying from the same books, and listening to the same lessons, we all had equal access

Eileen D. Bunderson teaches gender equity issues in the natural sciences at Brigham Young University. The parents of six children, she and her husband, C. Victor Bunderson, coordinate the Blazer Scout program in their stake.

to the knowledge and skill of our teachers and administrators as we moved through the educational process. Actually, a great many studies conducted in classrooms throughout the world spell out in repetitive detail that the educational experience may be quite different for the boys in the class than for the girls sitting next to them.

Consider the following: A group of parents were asked to view the infants in the newborn nursery. As the parents gazed through the window, a nurse presented each baby in turn and asked the parents to note whether they thought the infant was male or female. The infants were clothed in identical hospital sleepers. As the mother of six children, I admit that I have had difficulty identifying the sex of my own newborns without a good look at the plumbing. Nevertheless, the parents in the experiment proved to be remarkably astute. They were guessing correctly approximately 90 percent of the time. The researchers were puzzled, because they related more to my difficulties in identifying gender, even of my own children, than to the results of this intuitive group of parents. They tried another group of parents and tallied the same percentage of accurate guesses. This time, however, when the nurse presented the children to the parents at the window, the researchers noticed an interesting pattern. As the nurse presented Baby A, she held up the baby for all to see, and the parents made their choice. When the nurse presented Baby B, she cuddled it tenderly in her arms. Baby after baby was presented in either "A" or "B" fashion. The parents quickly caught on that the proud presentation of infants A suggested males and the gentle presentation of infants B, females.

Differential treatment of males and females starts very early in life. In another study young mothers were asked to entertain a two-year-old named "John" in a simulated day-nursery situation. When "John" cried, "mother" usually handed him a truck, encouraged him to read a story with her, or tried to turn his attention to something fun and interesting. These same mothers, asked to entertain two-year-old "Mary," were more likely to pick her up, sing to her, cuddle and soothe her when she cried. The mother's actions were geared to what she thought was appropriate to the sex of the child.[2]

By the time children enter school (whether preschool, kindergarten, or first grade), their gender identity is firmly in place. Even "enlightened" parents, who would never purposefully give their child a toy gun, watch in astonishment as their five-year-old son picks up a broomstick and rat-a-tat-tats at the cat. Little girls with working mothers and "house fathers" will go to the dollhouse in the free-play corner of the kinder-garten room and promptly put the mother doll in the kitchen.

How does the reality of gender differences and gender roles affect the educational process for children? In a gender symposium at Utah Valley Community College in 1992, educational psychologist David Sadker asserted that the most critical asset in the modern schoolroom is not the new computer, the modern textbooks, or the eye-catching bulletin boards. The single most important contributor to the quality of education received by each individual student is the amount of atten-tion that child gets from the teacher. A careful analysis of classroom interactions reveals some unexpected variations in how and to whom teachers give attention. A teacher can interact with students in four basic ways:

1. Teachers can praise. "Peter, that was an excellent solution to that problem." "Janice, you turned in a perfect paper." "Kurt, that was another perceptive comment."

2. Teachers can criticize. "Laura, that handwriting was pretty sloppy." "Cut out the nonsense, Jim. You know better than that." "You are not thinking very clearly."

3. Teachers can help or remediate. "Why don't you try it this way, Nancy?" "How do you think the situation would improve if you tried it this way, Tom?" "Barry, your long-division problems will be easier to solve if you line your numbers up more carefully."

4. Teachers can also respond with nonjudgmental, neutral comments. "Uh huh." "All right." "Go on." "Okay."

Many studies have tabulated classroom interactions.[3] Researchers have consistently found that boys receive most of the praise, most of the criticism, and most of the help and/or remediation. Girls receive most of the "Uh huh's." What effect does this have on the educational expe-rience of boys and girls?

Teachers tend to ask boys more questions. If you have ever taught a class of active children, you may be saying, "Yes, but that's how I man-age my class. When the boy over in the corner starts to act up, I catch his attention and bring him back by asking him a question." What is the effect of that question, that manifestation of teacher attention, on that child?

The important factor is the *attention*. Oddly enough, it doesn't par-ticularly matter whether that attention is positive or negative. The child has been noticed. The teacher has demonstrated that he or she recognizes the personhood and presence of the child in the classroom.

In addition to asking boys more questions, teachers tend to ask them different types of questions. Note the following exchange:

Teacher: "Nathan, what is the longest river in the United States?"

Nathan: "The Mississippi."

Teacher: "No, Nathan, it isn't the Mississippi. Think! Remember Lewis and Clark?"

Nathan: "Oh, yeah. The Missouri River."

Teacher: "Very good, Nathan! Jane, what is the widest river in the world?"

Jane: "The Nile."

Teacher: "Mary?"

Mary: "The Amazon."

Teacher: "All right. Let's move on to mountain ranges."

What subtle interactions are going on here? When Nathan answered incorrectly, the teacher pressed him to "Think!" and supplied a clue, "Remember Lewis and Clark?" She didn't let him off the hook, so to speak, by calling on another student as she did when Jane answered incorrectly. Putting Nathan on the spot, pressing him to think, may not be something a student enjoys, but it conveys the teacher's respect for his intelligence even when his first answer is wrong and, more important, it encourages him to solve problems and earn that "Very good!" response. Mary's correct answer got a mere nod, "All right. Let's move on." Though the exchange was definitely a gender-based interaction, teachers are seldom conscious of either the behavior or the inequities such gender-based interactions create.

Let me add a few more research facts not illustrated in this last example. Teachers are more likely with boys to (1) ask higher order questions (how or why instead of who or what); (2) ask follow-up questions that encourage deeper understanding ("Why do you think the cure for anthrax was so important for the people of Pasteur's time?"); (3) wait longer for boys to remember or to formulate an answer. Does the time a teacher waits for an answer from a student make a difference? It certainly does! The student gets a chance to think and organize his thoughts. He realizes the teacher has confidence that he really can come up with an answer—and he is more likely to do so.

A related problem, especially prevalent in such subject areas as science and math, appears in the following contrasted interactions:

Sam: "Teacher, why doesn't my osmosis experiment work?"

Teacher: "Look at your experimental diagram. Let's follow it through together. Can you reconstruct your apparatus so it matches the diagram more closely?"

Sally: "Teacher, my osmosis experiment won't work. What's the matter with it?"

Teacher: "It's a simple error. I see what you've done wrong. Scoot over and I'll fix it."

This teacher's interaction with Sally illustrates a phenomenon called "learned helplessness." Students, especially girls, learn very quickly that you needn't figure the problem out for yourself if you can get someone else to do it for you. Besides, you really didn't think you could do it for yourself, anyway. If you could, the teacher would surely expect you to puzzle out the answer for yourself. Our culture encourages learned helplessness in subtle ways. The teacher is willing to be tough with a Nathan or a Sam, to press them to puzzle out solutions to their problems or questions. We are habitually gentler with girls, because—according to our cultural stereotypes—the delicate, emotional female lacks the mental stamina to try again and again to solve the problem herself. The teacher is demonstrating "chivalry" and protectiveness by relieving her of unnecessary and painful mental effort. Unfortunately, the teacher is also robbing her of the opportunity to experience the mental growth required to solve the problem on her own.

Other cultural factors contribute to differences in classroom performance. A group of students had just finished taking a test. As they were leaving the classroom, the teacher stood by the door and asked them how they thought they'd done on the test. In chorus, the girls moaned, "Oooh! It was so hard! We know we failed!" The boys laughed it off. "It was easy, a real snap!" When the tests were corrected and returned, there were no differences in average scores of girls and boys. Although a self-deprecating attitude regarding one's accomplishments is part of our culture, especially for females, girls tend to be more anxious about taking tests, more uneasy about the results, and much more negatively affected by poor scores. Boys manage to rationalize poor test scores by attributing the result to bad luck, a poorly written test, a teacher "who hates him," or (if pressed) an admission of not having studied. Girls are more likely to internalize the test results and interpret the poor score as a confirmation that they don't have the ability or brains to do better.

Teachers underestimate the power of their comments to confirm those feelings. Mrs. Braithwaite handed back a physics test to her eleventh-grade class. She was very understanding when discussing the grades of students who had not done very well. She handed the top paper in the class to Jennifer. "Congratulations, Jennifer. You did very well on this test." "Oh, Mrs. Braithwaite, it's just because you're such a good teacher. I could never have passed without your help." "Why thank you, Jennifer. It's very nice of you to say that." What's wrong with this polite exchange? Person to person: nothing; teacher to student: a lot. Jennifer's confidence in her own abilities is undermined. It didn't occur to Mrs. Braithwaite that she should have said to Jennifer, "You did very well because you knew and understood the mechanics of Boyle's law." Such a comment would enable Jennifer to take responsibility, and credit, for mastering difficult material. Could that happen to a boy? Yes, but boys are less likely to respond to praise by being self-deprecating or complimenting a teacher in return.

Other cultural and social expectations for girls and boys carry over into the classroom. For example, teachers are much more likely to accept a comment or question called out by a boy who has failed to raise his hand. When a girl calls out a comment, she is more likely to be told to please raise her hand first. Studies show that teachers are more likely to stand closer to boys and to call on boys more often, although most teachers will say, in truth, that that is just classroom survival management. They are more likely to remember boys' names, more likely to look a boy in the eye while he is answering or commenting, and more likely to ask follow-up questions.

The quantity and quality of the teacher's attention is a crucial resource in the educational process.[4] The volumes of research carried out during the past twenty years have fairly conclusively established that student-teacher interactions are not the same for girls as they are for boys. Boys are given more than their share of this ever more limited resource and, as a result, their classroom years produce different kinds of learning experiences. For girls, the experience can foster confusion, a lack of direction, and a loss of self-esteem.[5] It is difficult for girls to maintain an upbeat, confident opinion of their intellectual prowess and personal worth. Although girls are routinely expected to excel in some areas, these are more likely to be neatness, organization, social expertise, and deportment.[6] Ironically, they excel in the areas that allow them to be ignored.

Studies continue to show that the self-esteem of girls begins a steady and sometimes rapid decline as they enter their teenage years.[7] What other evidence do we have that the learning environment in our schools may not be as friendly a place for girls as it is for boys?

Utah students routinely take the Stanford Achievement Test of Basic Skills in the fifth, eighth, and eleventh grades. Scores are reported as a percentile rank; for instance, a score of 65 percent indicates that the student scored higher than 65 percent of all other students nationwide who took the same test. In Utah Valley, fifth-grade boys and girls scored basically the same in areas such as reading, language, study skills, science, math, and social studies. As students move into junior high and high school, however, patterns change. On a test administered in October 1992, eleventh-grade boys in Utah Valley high schools outscored the girls by 17 percentile points in social studies, 17 percentile points in science, and 16 percentile points in math. In some schools, boys also outscored girls in reading and language arts, areas in which girls are traditionally thought to shine.

Curiously, girls received higher course grades in classes they shared with boys, although they scored lower on the SAT tests. A group of high school teachers was asked to offer explanations of why boys consistently score higher on standardized tests and yet girls receive higher grades in class. When one teacher volunteered that girls were much better behaved in class, another teacher expressed surprise: "I thought behavior was reported in the separate citizenship grade!" A third teacher noted that the girls were more conscientious about handing in their homework assignments. A fourth wondered, "If the girls are doing more of the homework we assign than the boys are and still are getting lower test scores on the standardized tests, what does that say about the relevance of our homework assignments?" All these comments reinforce the assumption that girls excel in behavior and deportment. No one addressed the hard problem of the disparity in test scores. No one went beyond surface issues to wonder how the system may be failing to challenge and educate girls.

Nevertheless, all the responsibility cannot be placed with the schools. Gender identities are formed early and are constantly being reinforced at home, in peer groups, in social and religious groups, and in the media. Gender identity defines what it means to be male or female in our world; only part of that definition results from student/teacher/peer interactions in our schools.

How can we help the schools challenge and better educate our daughters? We can't afford to compromise the education of 50 percent of our young people. How can we, as parents, grandparents, relatives, associates, and teachers of young women, extend educational opportunities to all students? Fortunately, the educational process need not place boys and girls on opposite ends of a seesaw. Raising the quality of the educational process for girls does not necessarily lower its quality for boys. We can ensure an equitable education for all.

So what do we do? We become involved. We can watch for the subtle inequities that work against girls. We can introduce young children, both boys and girls, to such toys as Legos and Erector sets, which develop spatial skills essential to learning science and math. We can encourage both boys and girls to use and love computers. We can consult with the school counselor who says about our daughter, "I've recommended that Julie not take math because I feel she shouldn't have to work that hard." We can tell the counselor (and Julie) that for every math class she takes after eighth grade her average salary, if and when she should need or desire to enter the work force, will go up by an average of three thousand dollars per year. You can remind the science teacher that your daughter is a whiz with equipment and you expect that she will participate fully and well in the laboratory work. You can suggest to the social studies teacher that there is more to history than wars and rumors of wars. Girls enjoy learning about the daily lives and contributions of great (and not-so-great) women. Suggest that the schools read about women, provide significant female role models, and validate the experiences and lives of women.

Sensitize people to the issues created by the inequities in the test scores. Perhaps the teachers are not aware that the average percentile scores are available by gender. Do you know what the scores are for your school? Discuss with your child's teacher the gender distributions of scores for his or her class. How is your child doing? What can you do to help?

Provide good books in your home and read them yourself as well as with others in the family. Read the newspaper and discuss more than just the sports page and the horror stories about wars, earthquakes, taxes, or gangs. Listen to your children when they report their day at school. "I never get called on, even when I know the answer." "I don't know why I even try in science. The scholarship nominees were all boys." "I hate math! I'm so stupid." "I can't read *Jane Eyre*. That's a girl's book!"

"Our class gets to do Ireland in the social studies fair next month. Will you help me find a project?" Get involved in the educational process of both your daughters and your sons.

Most teachers are eager to do whatever they can to improve their teaching curriculum and style to benefit their students. Gender-equitable behavior can be learned. More and more schools are inviting teachers and interested parents to training workshops and symposia dealing with equity problems in the classroom. As a parent-teacher organization leader, you might initiate such activities. Watch your own interaction patterns in the many settings where you teach youth: Sunday School, Primary, Young Women, school volunteers, and cooperative preschool. Informed teachers, working with informed parents, can improve the educational experience for everyone.

The future of our homes, our families, our community, and our Church depends on how well we educate all of our children. Brigham Young instructed: "Cultivate [your children's] mental powers from childhood up. When they are old enough, place within their reach the advantages and benefits of a scientific education. Let them study the formation of the earth, the organization of the human system, and other sciences; such a system of mental culture and discipline in early years is of incalculable benefit to its possessor in mature years. Take . . . the young ladies now before me, as well as the young men, . . . and do not confine their studies to theory only, but let them put in practice what they learn from books. . . . It is the duty of the Latter-day Saints, according to the revelations, to give their children the best education that can be procured, both from the books of the world and the revelations of the Lord."[8]

Men and women are equal in the eyes of God, and his sons and daughters are equally deserving of the best educational opportunities we can provide for them. "And I, God, said unto mine Only Begotten, which was with me from the beginning: Let us make man in our image, after our likeness; and it was so. And I, God, said: Let them have dominion . . . over all the earth." (Moses 2:26.) God was speaking to *them*, male and female, as he gave to *them* the directive to exercise knowledgeable and faithful dominion. In the face of mounting evidence of subtle and not so subtle inequities in the education of our young men and women, we need to "give [our] children the best education that can be procured." We need to hear Alissa say, "Mom! I got a 94 on my chemistry test. Science is really interesting!" or Julie exclaim, "Dad! I learned in my math class how to tell by triangulation how tall our pine tree is. Let me show you! Let's go measure it!" With knowledge and determination, we can move toward the goal of a quality education for *all* our children.

NOTES

1. Eliza R. Snow, "Sketch of My Life," in *Eliza R. Snow, An Immortal: Selected Writings* (Salt Lake City: Nicholas G. Morgan, Sr., Foundation, 1957), p. 7; James B. Allen and Glen M. Leonard, *The Story of the Latter-day Saints* (Salt Lake City: Deseret Book Co., 1976), pp. 95–96.

2. S. Askew and C. Ross, *Boys Don't Cry: Boys and Sexism in Education* (Philadelphia: Open University Press, 1988).

3. Jane Butler Kahle, "Why Girls Don't Know," *What Research Says to the Science Teacher: The Process of Knowing*, ed. M. B. Rowe (Washington, D.C.: National Science Teachers Association, 1990), pp. 55–67; Alison Kelly, "Why Girls Don't Do Science," *Science for Girls?* ed. Alison Kelly (Philadelphia: Open University Press, 1987), pp. 12–17; Myra Sadker and David Sadker, "Sexism in the Classroom: From Grade School to Graduate School," *Phi Delta Kappan* (March 1986): 512–15.

4. Sadker and Sadker, "Sexism in the Classroom," p. 514.

5. American Association of University Women, *The AAUW Report: How Schools Shortchange Girls* (Wellesley: AAUW Educational Foundation and National Education Association, 1992).

6. Margaret Goddard Spear, "The Biasing Influence of Pupil Sex in a Science Marking Exercise," *Science for Girls?* pp. 46–51.

7. American Association of University Women, *AAUW Report*, pp. 10–15.

8. Brigham Young, in *Journal of Discourses*, 26 vols. (London: Latter-day Saints Book Depot, 1854–86), 17:45; discourse delivered 18 Apr. 1874.

Family Ties

LUCILE JENSEN

My mother wanted excellence from me
(I thought perfection).
She was always instructing me what to
And not to do.
It was tough to find approval
Between her rules—
It was always too much or too little
Too soon or too late,
Never enough.
She still tries improving me
(Goodness knows I need it).
She thinks it makes no difference
Now I'm gone from home,
But her apron strings can still tie knots
In me—
I still peel the potato skins too shallow
Or too deep,
Then wash the rebellion down the sink.

Lucile Jensen, the third of nine children, is a human resources educator and published poet. She has received awards for original verse and poetry reading. She and her husband, Keith V. Jensen, are the parents of six sons and one daughter.

Within the Walls of Our Own Homes: The Father's Involvement in Child Care

ALAN J. HAWKINS
KATHRYN POND SARGENT

The process of nurturing life is the most profoundly
transforming experience in the range of human possibilities. Because women have this experience and
men generally don't, we live and think and love
across a great gap of understanding.[1]

Fatherhood is one of the hot topics of the 1990s. On the down side,
we read a lot about "deadbeat dads," fathers who neglect their family
responsibilities. On the up side, considerable evidence promotes the
importance of full-fledged fathers in children's lives, and many fathers
are choosing to be more involved with child-rearing.[2] Little, however,
is said about the reverse relationship: the importance of children in
fathers' lives. We believe that a father's involvement with his children
is essential to his own psychological development and that, equally
important, his participation in child care profoundly affects the quality
of the marital relationship.

ADULT DEVELOPMENT: THE TASK OF GENERATIVITY

As their children grow up, parents watch a process of systematic
change as a child, if all goes well, develops into an increasingly func-
tional, adaptive, and mature individual. We tend to think that the
processes of systematic development stop when a person reaches adulthood because the external process of physical growth is largely complete.

*Alan J. Hawkins is an assistant professor of family sciences at Brigham Young
University. He and his wife, Lisa Bolin Hawkins, are the parents of two children.*

*Kathryn Pond Sargent received her master's degree in family life education from
Brigham Young University. A homemaker, she and her husband, Steve Sargent, are the
parents of one daughter. She serves in her ward Young Women organization.*

Yet as adults we experience important changes throughout our lives. Psychologist Erik Erikson describes a set of three essential "developmental tasks" that individuals should accomplish during life to become morally and emotionally mature adults.[3] His theory about healthy adult development helps us understand the importance of men's involvement in children's lives for men's sake.

Erikson divides the life span into three general developmental stages in normal, healthy mental and social growth. Specific developmental tasks characterize each stage of growth. The first general stage is childhood. The primary developmental task of childhood is gaining a sense of hope about the world, a feeling that the world is a safe place where our needs can be met. In other words, to develop normally, children must feel secure and learn to trust. Obviously, early caregivers play a primary role in helping children develop this sense of security and hope.

Erikson's second general stage of human development is adolescence. The sense of hope and security they gained in childhood allows adolescents to focus their emotional energies on a second major developmental task: achieving faith in themselves and in their abilities. Adolescents strive to answer such transcendent questions as Who am I? Am I a good person? Am I competent? What will I do when I grow up? This necessarily self-centered period of development is a normal part of striving for identity. Even though it can be exasperating to parents and teachers, this challenging developmental phase generally leads to changes that are healthy and necessary.

Unlike many theories of human development, Erikson's model does not end with adolescence. He believed that adulthood is also a period of major growth with a critical developmental task to accomplish: learning to care for others and, more specifically, learning to nurture the next generation, our children. According to Erikson, the vital, overarching developmental task of adulthood—which he labels *generativity*—requires a person to emerge from the self-centered stage of adolescence and to achieve an identity that includes a concern for the well-being of others, particularly children. Achieving generativity means to invest in, to commit to, and to care deeply for others—to become fully human. The family is not the only context in which to learn generativity, but it is the most common and for many the most effective one.

Erikson points out that the three basic developmental tasks—hope, faith in self, and caring or generativity—correspond with the three religious values of faith, hope, and charity, spoken of in the New Testament. "And now abideth faith, hope, charity, these three; but the greatest of these is charity." (1 Corinthians 13:13.) Generativity, then, may be best understood as charity, the ability to love and care for others on a level commensurate with "the pure love of Christ." The capacity to love in ways that are committed, unselfish, and without condition doesn't just happen. This capacity to love beyond self-interest develops as a person takes on the tasks of generativity in the adult stage of human development.

Mormon, who defined charity as "the pure love of Christ," added that "whoso is found possessed of it at the last day, it shall be well with him." (Moroni 7:47.) We take that to mean that achieving generativity is necessary for our salvation. It is also crucial to our moral and psychological well-being in adulthood. According to Erikson, men and women who fail to learn to care for the next generation regress "from generativity to an obsessive need for pseudo intimacy . . . often with a pervading sense of stagnation and interpersonal impoverishment. Individuals who do not develop generativity often begin to indulge themselves as if they were their one and only child."[4] Erikson had observed that parents who failed to expand their identity and sense of self to value their children's well-being as much as their own actually regressed psychologically into adolescence or childhood, becoming self-indulgent and self-absorbed.

Adults who involve themselves deeply in the process of nurturing children usually develop generativity, but because fathers are significantly less involved than mothers in caring for dependent children, men face greater struggles to achieve generativity than women. That is especially true if a man's primary activity—his profession—is not an effective context for learning to care for and nurture others in a generative way. And if mothers are achieving generativity but fathers are not, that can seriously strain the marital relationship. The beginnings of these strains frequently can be found during the transition to parenthood.

TRANSITION TO PARENTHOOD

The birth of a child initiates a crucial transition in the life cycle of most people. Research shows that in the early stages of marriage, before the first child is born, couples' lives tend to be fairly synchronous; that is, husbands and wives are involved in similar activities, mainly work and school. In addition, their family functions tend to overlap or even to be carried out side by side. Young husbands and wives begin to build a world together by sharing laundry, cooking, and cleaning. This stage of marriage is a wonderful time of life. As a result of sharing so many activities and overlapping responsibilities, wives and husbands in this honeymoon phase are often in similar developmental phases. The transition to parenthood, however, may alter husbands' and wives' developmental directions in ways that eventually result in significant developmental differences.

Even though many couples intend to share parental responsibilities, studies reveal that after the first baby is born, men and women often begin to divide family role responsibilities along more traditional lines.[5] Surprisingly, even the increased number of women in the labor force has not significantly changed the traditional allocation of family roles at the transition to parenthood.[6] Mothers employed outside the home usually take a leave of absence to adjust to the new baby. During her time at home, a mother learns to care for her dependent child. That intense investment of time and psychological energy in an infant is a powerful force that bonds mother and child. The baby's needs and a mother's early commitment to nurturing push a mother towards generativity.

What happens to fathers as this powerful psychological bond is being formed between mother and child? Usually mom's income has been lost, at least temporarily. Consequently, a tremendous feeling of financial responsibility often weighs on men as they confront the pressures of providing for a family that now includes a dependent child. Work or school or both take on new urgency; now a steady, healthy income is necessary for the survival of the family. Thus, while mom is shifting time and energy to the new baby, dad is increasing his temporal and psychological investment in work and/or school.

What about the time when dad is at home? Can't he use this time to nurture the new baby? As parents of newborns will attest, besides crying, new babies do only three things: eat, sleep, and soil their diapers. Breast-feeding, although wonderful for baby and mother, limits a father's opportunity to feed, cuddle, and nurture a contented baby. And changing all the diapers may not be the best way to promote a psychological bond between father and child. In addition, the time when dads are usually home (after 5 P.M.) tends to be a child's most fussy time. What happens when the child fusses and dad's efforts to comfort the child are unsuccessful? Often mom takes over and "magically" calms the child. Of course, mom has no magical maternal powers; she acquired her skills gradually through daily care of the child. In fact, women who remember the transition to motherhood may recall their anxiety during the first few days of caring for a newborn. By trial and error, they become more confident and competent. Because the baby only nurses, fusses, messes, and sleeps, dads have little to do early in the child's life. As a result, dads may view themselves as relatively inadequate caregivers compared to moms and shy away from daily caregiving. Ironically, the tasks that a new father could do, such as changing diapers, bathing the baby, cooking, and household work, are often done by a visiting grandmother who lovingly steps in to help her daughter adjust to a first baby.

A common portrait of the transition to parenthood, then, is of mothers leaving the workplace (at least temporarily) and focusing on their new babies. Meanwhile, fathers focus on the workplace and are edged out of the new household routine. This division of tasks, although a practical response to the new situation, tends to send men and women in different developmental directions.

The transition to parenthood, we believe, represents a critical crossroads for the developmental paths of adult men and women. Beginning with nine months of pregnancy followed by the steady, intense demands of caring for a newborn, a mother is quickly and deeply challenged to develop a strong generative commitment to her dependent infant. For fathers, however, the transition to parenthood is usually quite different. Whereas women are expected to actively participate in their infant's daily care, men are not. Their involvement is still viewed as a nicety, not a necessity, thus impeding their ability to achieve generativity. As Daniels and Weingarten, the authors of *Sooner or Later: The Timing of Parenthood in Adult Lives,* explain, "Mothers are expected to become parents instantly, but fathers are not. The translation of paternal identity into parental generativity, as we have seen it, has been optional."[7]

Thus, the transition to parenthood in the developmental sense of enlarging one's identity to include a child differs greatly for fathers and mothers. Some women find motherhood easier than others, but almost all women accept this mandatory role. Because fathers generally don't have primary responsibility for child care, parenthood in the fuller sense of generativity may occur later, or never, for a man. "The striking feature of men's parenthood experience is the variation in the timing of

. . . the turn to hands-on fathering," observe Daniels and Weingarten. "Biologically, men become fathers and women become mothers at the moment of their first child's birth. But only through daily care, and in sustained emotional engagement in their children's lives, do fathers and mothers become parents in the generative sense."[8]

Even as their children grow older, dads tend to be playmates or baby-sitters who act as substitute caregivers until mom gets home. As a result of this lack of ultimate parental responsibility, the transition to parenthood tends to find women on their way towards the important developmental task of generativity while men lag behind or even regress to a more egocentric stage of life. For example, new fathers often complain that their wives no longer pay attention to them. Although a new mother is, indeed, less focused on her spouse, the husband's complaint may signal not merely his discomfort with their newly diverging roles but also be an early sign of his regression to becoming more focused on himself than others. His wife, struggling with the demands of the new baby and accustomed to his sharing tasks with her, may be puzzled by her spouse's sudden insensitivity to her exhaustion and need for his support.

In theory, role specialization seems to be a logical response to the realities of contemporary family life. Babies need mothers to nourish them when they are first born. Mothers need time to recover from pregnancy and childbirth. Economic pressures are real. Men earn more per hour than women do. While a husband devotes his time and effort to providing for the family, his wife can devote her time and effort to nurturing the new baby. Although that arrangement may be economically rational, it often constricts men's opportunities for personal growth in the adult task of developing generativity.

Furthermore, most married couples count on more from each other than just economic and physical survival. They want psychological satisfaction and intimacy. But if women have progressed further along the developmental path of generativity than men, marital relationships may be at risk. Couples with developmentally different partners are likely to experience more barriers to building close relationships than couples who have matured to similar points in the life cycle. If a wife is moving towards generativity while her husband is not, they may come to see the world in qualitatively different ways. Different perspectives soon lead to different priorities and interests. In short, because the transition to parenthood tends to push women, but not men, toward the achievement of generativity, husbands and wives often end up feeling psychologically separated from each other. Under such circumstances, marital intimacy may be elusive. Simply developing better communication skills is not the solution. Instead, fathers need to become more involved in the generative work of nurturing children.

WHAT CAN WE DO?

Because the transition to parenthood is such a pivotal time, how can a couple deal with the forces that push men and women in different directions at that critical juncture? The syndicated comic strip "Cathy" offers one possible solution. Andrea and Luke, the parents of twins, are arguing about who should stay home with the babies.

Andrea says: "I can't leave my babies to work full-time, Luke!"

Luke replies: "I had to leave my babies to work full-time the day after they were born, Andrea!"

Andrea: "But I'm their mother. I can't leave them!"

Luke: "And I'm their father. I'm tired of leaving them!"

Soon they're both shouting, "Why should I spend my life at a stupid job while someone else raises my family?"

In the last frame Andrea relents, "Oh, go ahead and make the call." Luke dials the phone and says, "Would you please send over two people to take care of our careers while we stay home and pursue our children." It's a great thought—hiring somebody to tend the careers so that both parents can care for their children full time. Realistically, however, what can be done to allow and encourage men to be more fully involved in the care of their children? The following suggestions may be helpful.

Planning for early involvement. The father's participation early in child care establishes a pattern for involvement. As wonderful and valuable as the assistance of grandmothers and grandmothers-in-law can be, a father's involvement in the early weeks is vital. Dad's involvement becomes a necessity rather than an option if mom relies on him instead of her own mother. Dad should be at home so that he can learn to care for the child at the same time and in the same way that mom does—feeling scared to death the first time he picks up the baby but learning that he can do it. Syndicated columnist Bob Greene described his feelings at the birth of his daughter: "People talk about the emotions that come when a baby is born: exuberance, relief, giddiness, pure ecstasy. . . . But the dominant emotion inside me was a more basic one. I was scared; scared of what I knew was sure to come, and more scared about what I didn't know. I am of a generation that has made self-indulgence a kind of secular religion. I looked down at that baby, and suddenly I felt that a whole part of my life had just ended, been cut off, and I was beginning something for which I had no preparation."[9] These feelings of disequilibrium mark the transition to a new stage of life for both women and men—a stage of connectedness and personal growth. By devoting himself to his child's care, a father can develop a wonderful psychological bond with his child.

That early involvement is difficult to achieve. Finances as well as family traditions stand in the way. Only 1 percent of corporations in the United States offer paternal leave. Virtually none offer paid paternal leave. Under the new Family and Medical Leave Act, U.S. businesses with fifty or more employees must allow their employees to take up to twelve weeks' unpaid leave to care for their families.[10] Although this law helps some fathers, it is still unpaid leave. So if paternal leave can be taken, parents must plan, anticipate, and save for the time after the baby is born.

A delayed career start is another way to foster the father's early participation in child care. Some fathers choose to stay home a year or two while mom finishes her education or gets some experience in a profession. That kind of early involvement pays high dividends down the road. Once dad is back at work full-time, he knows how to relate to his children when he is home, and his children are used to his parenting style as well as mom's.

Even if those suggestions are not feasible at the birth of a first child, the birth of a second child can be a valuable change-point for fathers. In fact, some family researchers humorously suggest that it takes only one child to make a mother, but two to make a father.[11] The birth of a second child can sometimes pull dad into greater involvement with the first child because mom is necessarily focused on the new baby. Thus, instead of experiencing the birth of a sibling as a loss, a first child can experience it as gaining another primary parent—dad.

Also, although birth is an important time to establish connections, it is not the only time. A good friend of ours intermittently phases out of the work force and focuses on his family. Of course, he has a job that allows him to do that, and he works very hard and earns a substantial salary. Also the family lives frugally, so he can take time off. For example, he once arranged an educational leave from his company to go to graduate school. Most people don't think of graduate school as a vacation. But he left his sixty-hour-a-week job and thirty-hour-a-week bishopric responsibilities to study for only forty hours a week, reserving the rest of the time for his family. After his leave he returned to work, but later when his wife was overwhelmed with the approaching birth of their sixth child, he arranged a six-month unpaid paternity leave from his company.[12] (Of course, six months won't be an option for everyone, but a month or two may be an option for some.) During the months that he stayed home, this hardworking provider really got to know his children and became part of what was happening at home. Those six months significantly changed his life and improved his relationship with his children and his wife.

Preparental agreements. The vast majority of young men in our culture approach the transition to parenthood wanting to be involved fathers.[13] Indeed, if the "Cosby Show" father, Cliff Huxtable, is the prototype, fatherhood is in style. When the reality of parenthood hits, however, men often fall short of their own high expectations. One possible solution to this problem is for expectant parents to anticipate and discuss the issues involved in the transition and then write up a "preparental agreement." For example, couples could delineate the tasks involved in a typical parental day—bathing, dressing, feeding, taking the child to the sitter, packing the diaper bag, etc.—and decide how these tasks will be divided. Obviously, the agreement should be flexible, friendly, and open-ended because not all tasks involved in child care can be anticipated. The intent of a written agreement should be to open the lines of communication about father involvement, not close them. A contract can help a couple brainstorm and map out how a new father can be involved in more nurturing ways when the baby is born.

In addition to conferring about child-care tasks, prospective parents should also articulate and discuss the potential stresses that will occur at the transition to parenthood. Couples can examine increased financial pressures and dad's lack of time and opportunity to be with the baby. The couple might then discuss how to combat those specific stresses. A couple might, for example, plan to use occasionally either formula or pumped breast milk to allow dad opportunities to feed the baby. Another idea might be to use vacation time and money on new-baby leave instead. Saving enough money so that dad can take some time off work when the baby is born would probably mean a wonderful memory as well as a push toward generativity. Even small adjustments can benefit the relationship. Alternating who takes the baby's middle-of-the-night shift, for instance, can extend the shared-tasks phase of marriage. That may seem obvious to you, but you would be surprised how rare such communication is and how helpful just talking about problems can be, even if the "solutions" are far from ideal.[14] If dialogue about a father's involvement starts before the baby's birth, it is much easier to continue discussing such issues later on; however, dialogue is better late than never. Second child or sixth, it's never too late for a father to discover what he's been missing. The path of generativity is demanding but infinitely worthwhile.

Responsibility versus helping. Research shows that the amount of time fathers have *sole* responsibility for their children's care is critical to pulling men into the nurturing role. Sometimes dad may "help" with the children, but if he can hand the child off to mom for comforting or changing, he may not be changing psychologically. Taking sole responsibility—"I'm in charge here, and if something goes wrong I have to solve it"—is the attitude that leads to generativity. Prolonged, sustained interaction must occur and be coupled with "the-buck-stops-here" responsibility for a child's welfare from food to clean clothes to schoolwork.

As fathers increase their involvement, they tend to take on the more pleasant tasks: bathing the baby or taking the children outside to play. Although that kind of involvement from dad offers relief to mom, it tends to leave her with the more tedious responsibilities. Furthermore, when dad "helps" mom, he tends to view himself as the substitute caregiver or baby-sitter, rather than a primary parent. Dads often say, "I'm babysitting the kids tonight" or "I'm tending the kids for my wife today." Generative parents do not babysit or tend their children; instead, generative parenting is a frame of mind or a way of being. Sometimes fathers are lax because they know that mom will pick up the slack. For example, a popular book about couples' struggles with sharing domestic labor, *The Second Shift: Working Parents and the Revolution at Home*, describes a father who let his kids eat ice cream and cookies for dinner when he was home because he knew his wife would feed them balanced meals the rest of the week.[15] In contrast, when dads have sole responsibility for their children for long periods they are forced to think harder about their children's needs. That kind of experience for fathers is generative. A wife who goes on retreats or to women's conferences with her friends gives her husband a gift as well: the time he needs to be alone with his children. She is not effecting a temporary escape from the responsibilities of child care that unfairly burdens her spouse. Instead, she should view her retreat as an opportunity for her husband—her children's father—to enter his children's daily lives and to become a more generative, nurturing human being.

Gatekeeping. Ironically, wives often block husbands from becoming more involved in the lives of their children. Researchers call this phenomenon "gatekeeping." Because moms as primary caregivers control dads' entry into the family sphere, they are gatekeepers. They determine how much and in what ways dads get involved. Paradoxically, even a mom who longs to have dad participate more in the home often unconsciously hinders him from doing so. Why does this happen? A father's involvement can sometimes be very challenging. Dad is too rambunctious with the young children; he doesn't put the right clothes on the baby; he even stacks the dishes wrong in the dishwasher! While it probably doesn't matter whether the baby goes to church in overalls or the cute, frilly dress Aunt Maude sent, dad's failure to do things the "right" way, namely mom's way, often frustrates mom. Thus, rather than have dad do it wrong, mom does the task herself. Or, some women avoid this conflict by, for instance, laying out the clothes and then asking dad to dress the baby. What message does this send? "Dad is a good helper but he can't do things on his own." Perpetuating the "helping" role prevents the psychological investment, or sense of responsibility, that develops generativity.

Dad's involvement can be even more deeply challenging. When a father becomes competent at caring for the children, sometimes a mother feels psychologically threatened. Even for working women, the role of mother is central to a woman's core identity. It is a powerful psychological reward to know that you are the only one who can comfort your child. But wives have to be willing to share such rewards with their husbands. Children do not have a finite amount of love. If they begin to love dad more, they will not love mom less. Instead, children's boundaries will expand and their capacity for love will increase as they gain another primary parent.

REFRAMING THE ISSUE

Research consistently confirms that wives do more than twice as much domestic work as their husbands, even when they are employed full-time outside the home.[16] Although that division of labor may be unfair to mothers, in the long run the situation is detrimental to fathers as well. Without investing time and effort, they will be at a serious disadvantage in their struggle to be involved, nurturant fathers and to develop the rich, personal relationships that facilitate maturation into generativity. Failing to share the tasks of generativity also harms marital relationships, as we have already noted, because wives are soon at a different developmental level than husbands. That situation impedes psychological intimacy.

Although unfairness is indeed irksome, reframing a father's under-involvement as a developmental issue rather than a struggle for "domestic democracy" is crucial. Arguing from a domestic-democracy perspective encourages power struggles and emphasizes differences rather than our common goals as men and women in relationships. This domestic-democracy perspective casts women in the role of critics who point out injustices for which their husbands are responsible. In contrast, a developmental perspective accentuates the necessary connections between men and women. Wives can assume a mentoring role as their husbands go through the challenging process of achieving generativity, a process mothers are usually forced to learn first and at a faster pace.

In addition, encouraging a father's increased involvement in child care from a developmental perspective makes more sense because it focuses on what is really at stake: what fathers gain, rather than the leisure they sacrifice, by greater participation in the daily work of the home. Strong maternal instincts and societal expectations push women toward generativity. Since men are not pushed into caregiving in the same way, they may need to be drawn into greater participation by being shown the benefits of intimate involvement in child care.

The challenge, then, is to enhance men's development by expanding their involvement as fathers. The result will benefit children, mothers, and fathers. In addition, we're convinced that marital relationships will be stronger if couples are on the same developmental track on the way towards generativity as they care for and nurture the next generation. Most family scholars acknowledge that adult men's under-involvement in children's lives is an important social problem, one that affects the quality of life for women and children. We maintain that it hurts men also. Accordingly, in the words of Malachi, we believe it is time to "turn the heart of the fathers to the children, and the heart of the children to their fathers." (Malachi 4:6.)

NOTES

1. Dorothy Dinnerstein, *The Mermaid and the Minotaur* (New York: Harper and Row, 1976), paraphrased in Mary Kay Blakely, "Executive Mothers: A Cautionary Tale," *Working Mother*, Aug. 1983, p. 73.

2. Henry B. Biller, *Fathers and Families: Paternal Factors in Child Development* (Westport, Conn.: Auburn House, 1993).

3. Erik H. Erikson, *The Life Cycle Completed: A Review* (New York: W. W. Norton, 1982).

4. Erik H. Erikson, *Identity and the Life Cycle* (New York: W. W. Norton, 1980), p. 103.

5. Carolyn Pape Cowan and Philip A. Cowan, *When Partners Become Parents: The Big Life Change for Couples* (New York: Basic Books, 1992).

6. David H. Demo and Alan C. Acock, "Family Diversity and the Division of Domestic Labor: How Much Have Things Really Changed?" *Family Relations* 42 (July 1993): 323–31.

7. Pamela Daniels and Kathy Weingarten, *Sooner or Later: The Timing of Parenthood in Adult Lives* (New York: W. W. Norton, 1982), p. 161.

8. Ibid.

9. Bob Greene, *Good Morning, Merry Sunshine* (New York: Atheneum, 1984), p. 7.

10. S. Alexander, "Fears for Careers Curb Paternity Leaves," *Wall Street Journal*, 24 Aug. 1990, p. B1.

11. Robert B. Stewart, *The Second Child: Family Transition and Adjustment* (Newbury Park, Calif.: Sage Publications, 1990), p. 213.

12. Jeff Hill, "Full-time Dad," *Good Housekeeping*, June 1991, pp. 54–57.

13. Ralph LaRossa, "Fatherhood and Social Change," *Family Relations* 37 (October 1988): 451–57.

14. See Cowan and Cowan, *When Partners Become Parents.*

15. Arlie Hochschild, *The Second Shift: Working Parents and the Revolution at Home* (New York: Viking Press, 1989).

16. See Demo and Acock, "Family Diversity and the Division of Domestic Labor."

"Precious Children": Responding to a Disclosure of Abuse

RUTH B. WRIGHT

Late one night as my husband and I were snuggled on the couch watching television, we saw what we thought was a short advertisement. A small girl in a darkened bedroom was crying in her bed. She glanced nervously at the clock on her night table. It read 12:30. The next scene seemed to be the same. The little girl was still crying in her bed, and the camera once again focused on the clock. It now read 1:30. Suddenly a door opened, a light went on in the room, and the camera focused on this little girl's face, which was filled with terror. She clutched her covers, pulling them tightly to her body, and then turned over, whimpering. In a chilling instant we knew that this child was a victim of repeated abuse.

That thirty-second spot changed me. It was jarring, startling, horrible. I could not sleep all that night. I tossed and turned and finally got up and prayed for all children who suffer from abuse of any kind. We know there are many. Child abuse is increasing in frequency and intensity throughout the world, even in the Church. The Lord knows and has counseled, "But whoso shall offend one of these little ones which believe in me, it were better for him that a millstone were hanged about his neck, and that he were drowned in the depth of the sea." (Matthew 18:6.)

President Thomas S. Monson has said, "If only all children had loving parents, safe homes, and caring friends, what a wonderful world would be theirs. Unfortunately, not all children are so bounteously blessed. Some children witness their fathers savagely beating their mothers, while others are on the receiving end of such abuse. What

Ruth B. Wright graduated from the University of Utah in elementary education and has taught fifth grade in Utah and California. She and her husband, Gary E. Wright, are the parents of five children. She serves as second counselor in the general presidency of the Primary of The Church of Jesus Christ of Latter-day Saints.

cowardice, what depravity, what shame! Local hospitals everywhere receive these little ones, bruised and battered, accompanied by bald-faced lies that the child 'ran into the door' or 'fell down the stairs.' Liars, bullies who abuse children, they will one day reap the whirlwind of their foul deeds. The quiet, the hurt, the offended child victim of abuse, and at times incest, must receive help."

President Monson then cites a letter from a district court judge notifying him of " 'an alarming increase of reported physical, psychological, and sexual abuse of children.'" He states emphatically, "The Church does not condone such heinous and vile conduct. Rather, we condemn in the harshest of terms such treatment of God's precious children. Let the child be rescued, nurtured, loved, and healed. Let the offender be brought to justice, to accountability, for his actions and receive professional treatment to curtail such wicked and devilish conduct. When you and I know of such conduct and fail to take action to eradicate it, we become part of the problem. We share part of the guilt. We experience part of the punishment."[1]

President Howard W. Hunter, in a letter to Church leaders that accompanied information to educate them about abuse, said, "Those who abuse children or other family members violate the laws of God and man. Every effort should be made to protect individuals from abuse and to help those guilty of abusive behavior to repent."[2] In April 1989 general conference, President Ezra Taft Benson's closing message was to the children of the Church. After helping them understand that they were children of God with great potential, he added, "Now, I want to say something to you children who do not feel safe and who are frightened or hurt and do not know what to do. Sometimes you may feel all alone. You need to know that even when it seems that no one else cares, your Heavenly Father does. He will always love you. He wants you to be protected and safe. If you are not, please talk to someone who can help you—a parent, a teacher, your bishop, or a friend. They will help you."[3]

If a child told you of his or her abuse, how could you help? First, we need to understand that disclosure is the beginning of the healing process. The child must identify the abuse. We must be prepared to respond to such a disclosure in a positive way, to reinforce the child's courage and encourage talking. How you react to a child's disclosure is a very important part of the child's ability to trust another person and feel safe. I was told of a child who approached her Primary teacher many years ago with such a disclosure. Instead of finding comfort, she was told, "Your father is a wonderful man. He wouldn't do that." This child never again sought help, continued for years to suffer the abuse, and finally came to terms with her pain only in her early forties.

Perhaps by mentally rehearsing some responses, we can prepare ourselves to help rather than harm. Remember the child is frightened, confused, uncomfortable about the experience, and uncertain what to do. Act, don't react. Keep your own feelings under control. Be calm and nonjudgmental. Do not express emotions such as shock, embarrassment, anger, or disgust. Do not criticize or belittle the child's family. Children are most often abused by someone they know and trust—a father, an uncle, a neighbor. Their feelings toward that person will remain mixed—protective as well as fearful. They will not understand your feelings of outrage and anger.

Respect the child's privacy. Find a private place to talk, and don't share the disclosure with others. Know that the child has come to you in confidence. You need to keep that confidence, but take care not to make promises you can't keep. You may need to talk to someone you trust to help you evaluate your options. Unless you are willing to let the abuse continue or happen to some other child, you need to report it. Children seldom lie about being assaulted or sexually abused.

Support the child's decision to tell the story. Make it clear that telling you was the right thing to do. Remember, a person who molests a child fears exposure and might have threatened the child with loss of love or with physical harm. A small child may have been told, "If you tell anyone, your mom and dad won't love you anymore," or "People will be disgusted, and no one will ever play with you again." Express your love and confidence with words and gestures. Give positive messages: "Thank you for telling me this," or "You've made the right decision." Avoid challenges starting with "Why?" such as, "Why didn't you tell me that before?" or "Why did you let that happen?" Decide ahead of time what you might say so that you will be calm when handling the problem. "Thank you for telling me. You are not at fault, and I will try to help you."

It is vitally important to explain to the child that she or he is not responsible and has done no wrong. The child may have feelings of guilt and assume blame for what has happened. In cases of physical assault, many times children will have been told that they *deserved* to be beaten or battered for misbehaving. Children may not even realize they are *victims* of abuse. They almost always feel responsible for what has happened to them.

Your assistance and support can help a child through a difficult time. Make sure the child feels that you believe what you have heard. Communicate with the child. Respond to the child's questions and feelings in a calm, matter-of-fact manner. Do not push the child to share more than he or she is willing to share. The child needs warmth and acceptance, not curiosity or interrogation. Your sympathy, understanding, support, and optimism will encourage any necessary additional disclosures and discussion.

One of the worst things you can do is to express anger at the child for having violated previous warnings or instructions. A grandmother was preparing a bath for her three-year-old granddaughter whom she was tending. She was disturbed that the little girl kept touching her genital area and said, "Oh, don't touch yourself there." The child answered, "But Bill hurt me there," and the grandmother responded, "Don't talk like that! That's not a nice thing to say. Bill wouldn't hurt you!" Once the child was in the bathtub, the grandmother saw obvious evidence that she had been abused. She took her to the hospital, where they were asked what had happened. The little girl wouldn't repeat the story. The time for disclosure had passed. How might the grandmother have handled this differently? She could have responded, "I'm glad you told me about this. You are not responsible for what happened. Let's see what Grandma can do to help you." Without asking unnecessary questions or prying into the details of the abuse, she could have offered support.

Remember when responding to a child's disclosure that you should not promise that the abuse will not happen again unless you can make sure that it will not. If you promise to prevent future abuse and it does happen again, then the child's trust will be broken a second time. Finally, you should report the abuse to your local social services agency.

The pamphlet *Preventing and Responding to Child Abuse,* prepared by the Church and available through Church distribution centers, instructs: "If you are not sure whether a child needs help, call the social services agency in your community that deals with child abuse. Its staff will determine whether a child has been abused. Remember, a prompt report is better than a late report, and a late report is better than no report at all. Reporting allows professionals to assist the child and his parents or family, minimizing unnecessary emotional and physical injury."[4]

In conclusion, above all please remember that the Lord loves that precious child who has come to you, and he is aware of the problems of child abuse. As you carefully listen and respond, assure the child that Heavenly Father and our Savior Jesus Christ love and care. You might say, "Our Heavenly Father and Jesus love you and care about you. You are not to blame for what has happened to you. You are an important person. You are a child of God." When the Savior was on the earth, he called the children to him and blessed them. We need to go to him in earnest prayer for guidance. I believe he wants all children to feel safe and at peace. We follow his example when we respond to their cries for help.

NOTES

1. Thomas S. Monson, "Precious Children—A Gift from God," *Ensign*, Nov. 1991, p. 69.

2. Howard W. Hunter, Reporting of Child Abuse, letter from the Council of the Twelve Apostles to priesthood leaders, 4 Jan. 1990.

3. Ezra Taft Benson, "To the Children of the Church," *Ensign*, May 1989, p. 82.

4. *Preventing and Responding to Child Abuse* (Salt Lake City: The Church of Jesus Christ of Latter-day Saints, 1991), p. 11.

When You Can't Really Fix It: The Courage to Listen and Love

D. CRAIG CONDER
MARJORIE DRAPER CONDER

Introduction by Virginia H. Pearce, first counselor in the Young Women General Presidency

About eighteen years ago, my husband, Jim, came home from work one night deeply distressed. He had been in practice as a doctor of internal medicine for only a few months, yet he already had several parents in his practice who were literally destroying their own health as they worried and suffered over the behavior of their children. That very day a good man—a conscientious, loving father—had come into the office complaining of severe insomnia. He had hardly slept in the last two weeks. As they talked, trying to determine causes and treatment, he told my husband about his son, a moody and sensitive young man whom he described as having fought against life from the time he was born. Two weeks earlier, this man and his wife had been sitting at the kitchen table when they heard a loud explosion in the basement. They rushed down to find that this son had shot himself. Jim paused to look at our four adorable, innocent, and fairly manageable little girls. The oldest was seven. Who could guess what lay ahead for them—for us? My husband, his voice full of foreboding and fear, asked, "What have we done?" And when I thought of the capacity and the

D. Craig Conder received his bachelor's degree in computer science from Brigham Young University. He and his wife, Karen Spilker Conder, are the parents of a son. Brother Conder filled a mission to Tokyo, Japan, and serves in his ward as membership clerk.

Marjorie Draper Conder received her master's degree in sociology from the University of Utah and is employed as a curator at the Museum of Church History and Art. She and her husband, Darrell Conder, are the parents of six children and the grandparents of seven. Sister Conder is a teacher in her ward Primary.

possibilities for pain, the certainty of sorrow, when we bring a child into the world, I too wondered at our great rashness. What had we done?

That conversation so many years ago was my first glimpse of the principle of "opposition in all things" applied to parenthood. When children are young, mothers are usually successful at relieving pain and frustration. They fix them with hugs, cookies, or at most, a visit to the kindergarten teacher to see if she can manipulate the situation a little. As our children grow, fixing the hurts becomes more and more difficult. Their troubles get bigger, and the possibilities for self-destructive behavior and subsequent pain become greater. When eternal consequences are at stake, this process becomes almost unbearable for a mother to watch. At the peak of the pain and the frustration, some of us disengage or abdicate. We say, "I can't stand this any more; I can't afford to care. I'm backing out of this. Don't tell me anything; don't let me see it. I can't do anything right anyway." Others, at the other end of the pendulum, take the opposite tack: "I will make this work. I'll fix this. I'll talk to this person, and I'll talk to that person. The bishop will fix this. Somebody's got to fix this!" Many of us, faced with insoluble, painful parenting problems, swing from one end to the other: from "fix-it" to abandonment and back again, perhaps over and over.

There is, however, a balancing place on that pendulum between the two extremes, although it is hard to get our souls to stay put when life continues in rapid motion. Such words and phrases as "support," "long-suffering," "patience," "faith," "unconditional love," "prayer," "promptings of the Spirit," "listening," "confidence," "respect," and "agency" describe a place of loving engagement between the two extremes of fixing or abandoning a child with a complex problem. Let me give you a small example, a minor stress compared to Marjorie and Craig Conder's experience and to some of the trials in your lives. Several years ago, our oldest daughter, then in seventh grade, came home with a tearful litany of discouragement. She sobbed out all the sad distortions of junior high life: "I don't have any friends. No one likes me. I don't even know why I'm crying." As we sat on the sofa and her description of her failings and frustrations went on and on, I remember how hard it was for me just to sit and hold her and allow her to keep crying. My mind raced along thinking, How can I fix this? You're wrong, you *are* cute! You do too have friends! I wanted to pile up evidence to prove that she had no right to be sad. My mind moved on—maybe I could invite one of her friends over, maybe two. They could have a sleepover this Friday. But as I mentally anticipated her resistance, I felt myself swinging the other way. I thought, "Okay, you've cried enough. Quit now; it's over." Those feelings of impatience were a type of abandonment. Translated, they were, *"I* don't want to feel this way anymore, so *you* can't be upset anymore. At one point, I heard the noise in the other room of my younger children arriving home, and I remember feeling relieved and thinking, In a minute somebody's going to call me and then I can get up and leave and this will be over. But no one called and I stayed with my distraught teenager, saying nothing but floating back and forth between those two poles of feeling. Gradually, my need to intervene faded.

I vividly recall how long it took just to listen, to hold her and let her spill it all out. Initially it was painful, but when it was over, she stood up, blew her nose, and went on with her life. My confidence in her took a leap forward. And as the weeks went by—some sunny, some sad—I gained new respect for her ability to last it out, if nothing else, and I saw clearly that she was growing into a person who would be able to manage her own life successfully. And after all, I thought, I guess that's what's going to happen eventually. I'm not always going to be here.

My final example comes from a heated discussion we were having one night with a sixteen-year-old daughter over her failure to follow our advice. Not only was our advice excellent and wise but it was, in fact, advice she had solicited—and then ignored. Believing that we had suggested a better solution than she had chosen and feeling frustrated that we couldn't force her, her dad said, "Okay, we get the message; we're out of your life. Just don't ask us again." That's abandonment, isn't it? Just don't ask us for help again! But with an understanding beyond her years, she said, "No, you're not getting it. I want to be able to come to you and talk to you about what I think. And I want to know what you think, but that isn't an agreement that I'm going to do everything your way."

It's tough being a parent. It's tough striking a balance even in the little hurts and less consequential choices. And when life brings trials we did not imagine or deserve, and as Craig and Marjorie describe, situations we simply cannot begin to fix, it takes not only patience but prayerful, relentless courage to listen and love.

* * * * *

Craig: I am the eldest of six children in an active Latter-day Saint family. Both my parents are rock-solid Church members. Growing up, I went to all my meetings and was even knowledgeable and precocious enough to correct my teachers when I thought they were wrong. I went to seminary, graduated from high school, attended Brigham Young University for a year, and then served a mission in Japan. In short, I was a typical LDS young man. After my two-year mission, I went back to BYU for another year and married in the temple a young woman I had known in high school. Cyndie and I had dated in high school and before my mission. I enjoyed her company and hoped she would be there when I got back, but I didn't want to force any promises that would have to last two years. When I did get back, she was still there, and we still enjoyed each other's company. Since I was now a returned missionary, I felt I could now admit to loving someone. We got married about a year after I got home from my mission.

Marjorie: At that point in our lives I was probably feeling fairly self-righteous and smug. My family wasn't perfect, but we were on track, according to plan. Also, my son Craig and I were close. We often talked for hours on end. In fact, my husband would sometimes come out and say, "Aren't you people ever going to bed?" And the answer was usually no. Life was very good. But a big change was about to unfold.

Craig: Getting married seemed to be the beginning of the end. I knew going into the marriage that Cyndie was diabetic, but I wasn't prepared for the extent or the suddenness of her health problems. And I didn't know that her problems would be compounded by bulimic behavior that started in the weeks before we got married and ultimately was a disaster for a person whose health required a steady control of her blood glucose. Less than a month after we were married, she had to be hospitalized, and over the next few months we went in twice more.

We'd been married about nine months when we found out that Cyndie was pregnant. At first I was really excited. We hadn't planned on having children until I graduated from college, but I liked the idea of being a dad. Plenty of young couples struggle through and make it, and I figured that we could too. But it was not to be. Cyndie's body couldn't adjust to the hormonal changes of pregnancy. Even in the hospital she continued to vomit, and her glucose levels fluctuated dangerously. She got sicker and sicker, and it soon became obvious that our only real alternative was abortion. Considering our backgrounds, abortion was a very distasteful option. But as I saw it, I could either lose my baby, or I could lose my wife and my baby. The choice was pretty obvious. I still believe that if we hadn't decided to have the abortion, Cyndie would have died within three weeks.

I also believe now that Cyndie never really recovered, either physically or emotionally, from pregnancy and from the abortion. Her body had been terribly weakened, and the slightest sickness escalated into a trip to the emergency room. It also seemed that she began to use the hospital as an escape. Her physical and psychological problems became so intertwined that I could not tell how much of these sicknesses was physical and how much was psychological. During the next three years, we averaged a trip a month to the emergency room.

I was a student when all our troubles began, and we didn't have any insurance to begin with. Even after I graduated and had insurance, it wouldn't cover preexisting conditions. When I talked to the hospital financial adviser about the twelve thousand dollars we owed, he said the hospital would be willing to work with me—I could take up to three months to pay if I needed to. Three months! Eventually, when we owed about twenty thousand dollars, I was forced to take out a Chapter 13 bankruptcy. I eventually paid back a lot of the debt, but I needed the bankruptcy as a stop.

During that time Cyndie and I became more and more distant. We never really had a chance to bond properly to each other as husband and wife. Instead of a wife, I felt that I had a sick child. I can say honestly that I tried to make the marriage work and to help her get better. I was not a perfect husband, but my mistakes were made out of ignorance. I tried as hard as I could, but it wasn't enough.

Cyndie began to sleep during the day and stay awake at night. I felt, and I still feel, that this was to avoid facing me. After two fairly serious suicide attempts, she finally left me to live with her parents in New Mexico. On our fourth anniversary, we decided it would be better for both of us if we got a divorce. The divorce became final about five months later, and about three months after that she died of complications of bulimia and diabetes.

Until the last part of my marriage, I'd stayed fairly active in the Church. Sunday had always been a good day to recharge my batteries and help me face the rest of week. Near the end of my marriage, I required the week to recover from Sunday. When Cyndie and I had moved into a new ward, we told the bishop about our situation, about Cyndie's health and the abortion, and that we might need some help.

He tried to reassure us, saying, "Well, don't worry. Just know that all things are in the Lord's hands, and that you can be forgiven." Now, like anybody else, I have a lot to be forgiven for. But I didn't, and I still don't, think that the decision to have that abortion was something to be forgiven for. It was necessary.

In that ward, I attended church, usually by myself, and listened to too many inspirational stories. Speakers often talked about somebody in a difficult situation with a difficult decision to make. Sometimes the decision was righteous, and good consequences *always* followed. Sometimes the person made unrighteous decisions, and bad consequences followed. There were never any stories about people who struggled to make righteous decisions, and their lives still fell apart. I sometimes felt like standing up on the back row in sacrament meeting and shouting at the speaker that he didn't know what he was talking about. Instead I came home week after week so uptight that I finally decided the extra grief in my life was not worth it, and I quit going to church. I also quit paying tithing, unsure how landing in bankruptcy court qualified as the windows of heaven. The emotion I felt most of the time was betrayal. I'd really tried to do everything right, and my whole world had come crashing down around me. The day of Cyndie's funeral was the low point in my life, even lower than the day of the abortion. I had really loved the "old" Cyndie. As time went on, I felt the woman I loved slipping away from me. I couldn't understand why, or what I could do to prevent it. During the last several months of her life, I had only very minimal contact with her. When she died, I felt that any opportunity to resolve things and reach some closure was now gone forever.

Through all this trauma and disillusionment, my family, and especially my parents, were usually helpful. They were very frustrated that one of their children was struggling with so much grief and they couldn't make it better. My deepening cynicism must have been painful for them. I felt no qualms about challenging them, asking them questions that I knew they couldn't answer. The few times they did try to talk religious doctrine with me made matters worse. I always found holes in their arguments, and I did not hesitate to point them out. To their credit, my parents finally backed off. I usually played basketball with my brothers at their house on Saturdays, so I continued to see them often. We talked, but we did not discuss religion, which was really for the best at that time.

Marjorie: We knew Cyndie was diabetic when Craig married her. That did not seem to be an impossible problem. What we didn't know was that she was also bulimic: I don't think I'd even heard the word in 1982. Diabetes and bulimia are a very bad combination. As Cyndie got sicker and the problems mounted, I felt a widening gulf between Craig and me. We had always talked about everything and anything: now I had to watch every word I said. Like Craig, I would say that the day of Cyndie's funeral was the worst day of my life. No other day comes close. It was the oddest, most surreal funeral I have ever attended. There was no closure, no peace, no hope. We walked from the mortuary a short distance to the graveside for a service. Our family literally held Craig up on that short walk. At the graveside, he physically collapsed. No one had offered him a chair. I looked across that open grave to ward members on the other side and saw no judgment in their eyes, only questions. They knew that they were not seeing an ordinary event. Craig's physical collapse at that moment also symbolized to me his emotional, financial, and, especially, his spiritual collapse. I did not think he would ever be all right again. What a great tragedy, a great waste, and an unjust burden that had brought us to this! As did Craig, I felt forsaken.

My husband, Darrell, and I were going through some other problems during this time. We had two children on missions, which was fairly daunting financially. The car broke down, the refrigerator broke down, the washer broke down, and so on. We also had serious health problems to deal with in both our extended families. Our whole world seemed to be falling apart. I too began wondering about the windows of heaven. I had paid tithing as far back as I ever had any money, and I had paid it with a good attitude. I never thought the windows of heaven necessarily dispensed cash, though I've heard stories of that happening. But I thought, comfort, peace, knowledge, *something* . . . I was trying in every way I had ever heard to get spiritual knowledge and enlightenment, but the heavens seemed as brass. I felt that I could peel my prayers off the ceiling. I felt nothing was being heard.

It seemed the harder I prayed and tried, the worse things got. One day I read in Malachi the tithing promise—the windows of heaven. I continued to the next verse, "And I will rebuke the devourer for your sakes, and he shall not destroy the fruits of your ground; neither shall your vine cast her fruit before the time in the field, saith the Lord of hosts." (Malachi 3:11.) Well, I thought, I don't have any fields, and I don't have any vines. My crop is children, and the devourer is literally destroying one of them. What I did next is pretty audacious, but I was desperate. I opened my scriptures right to that page, laid them down on my bed, knelt down, and pointed out that verse to the Lord. "I have obeyed this commandment probably as perfectly as I've obeyed any commandment in my entire life," I said. "I'm not asking for cash; I'm asking that the devourer be rebuked."

Nothing changed immediately, but I felt heard for the first time in a long time. A few things in our life seemed to improve, but the thing we were most concerned with, Craig, did not visibly change. If we'd had to go forever without a washing machine, life would have been bearable. But the pain of watching what appeared to be the unjust destruction of a beloved child was more than I could handle. Craig deliberately challenged our faith, baiting us with questions that he knew we couldn't answer. We didn't have the final theological answers. All we had was our faith and our feelings. Perhaps he just wanted to hear us say, "We don't know."

Craig: Over the next two years, I seldom attended church, but I did mellow. I felt I had arrived at a flat, green plateau after a tough, rocky climb. I could finally relax. I buried myself in my work and didn't worry about church. I was living with friends and kept in touch with my family. That was my life: "All very nice, but not very good," as a Barry Manilow song puts it. I needed that plateau time—and the perspective it gave me—in order to heal. As the months went by, my calm turned to boredom. Nothing was really happening in my life. I was twenty-six years old and hoped only that by the time I retired in forty years I would have done something besides bury my face in a computer terminal. I didn't want to become a hermit. I began looking around and thinking about life.

About this time, the bishopric changed. The new bishop invited me in to talk to him. I had nothing against talking. After I'd given him a two-hour version of my story, he sat back, shook his head, and said, "One of my counselors is a therapist. Would you mind if I talked to him about this? I won't mention your name." I responded, "Mention my name. I'm not hiding this." I began meeting weekly with the bishop's counselor as my therapist. He pointed out to me that I had no right to feel betrayed, because bad things happen to everyone. Just because you're doing good things doesn't mean that good things happen to you; just because you're doing bad things doesn't mean that bad things happen to you. I was ready to listen.

My parents, who had taken a beating from me, still cared about me. I began to feel that I was coming in for a landing. That landing took me about two years. During those two years, I began dating a friend I had known thirteen years before. Karen and I are now married, and I am active again, serving as ward clerk. Bringing Karen into my life helped me, but I did not come back to the Church and become active again for her. My relationship with her undoubtedly gave me more reason to look at the Church, but my decision to come back was my own.

Marjorie: My husband, Darrell, and I consistently and specifically prayed for Craig. We kept his name on temple prayer rolls. Many times I would wake up in the morning and, just lying in bed, feel that I should fast for Craig that day. I could not go back and trace what was going on in his life on those days, but those feelings were there at times and I acted on them. I could see that talking did not help. In fact, Craig let me know that he needed space, and I gave it to him. I started being quiet, but I didn't think I should be quiet all the time, so I prayed to know when to be silent and when to speak. I prayed for courage and for guidance so that when I did speak I would know what to say. I received many more messages to be silent than to speak. I was walking a line, feeling the Spirit but still uncertain and even afraid. Walking by faith when I cared so much was hard.

The day after Cyndie's funeral happened to be Easter Sunday. As I sat trying to sort out all this pain, in a very tender spiritual experience I understood the Atonement in a new way. In a way that I cannot explain, I knew that someday Craig would be all right. Patience has never been one of my stronger virtues, but I accepted that message. I even thought, Maybe by the time he's forty or fifty, he'll be okay. But the road back looked so far, and I knew I couldn't fix this hurt. In fact, I felt I had been told that I couldn't fix it, that God would somehow heal Craig. I came to know that I probably could not even be a visible player in repairing the situation. Whatever I did had to be behind the scenes. I could pray for him, fast for him, and pray for others—even for the "chance encounter" or word that would touch his soul.

Several times during these years, Darrell had asked Craig to help him give blessings to various people, and Craig had declined. He didn't feel right about participating. Some time after that Easter day, Darrell himself was very sick and wanted a blessing. Our youngest son was too new an elder to know what to do alone. I approached Craig, who hemmed and hawed. I knew he wouldn't participate unless he felt right about it, but I also knew the great love and respect he had for his dad. If he could possibly push himself off the line, I knew he would do so. After some thought, he decided to help his younger brother give his dad a blessing. To me that decision was like the dove Noah sent out from the ark that returned with an olive leaf in its mouth. I couldn't see dry land yet, but I felt hope.

When Craig was talking with the counselor in the bishopric, and again when Karen came into his life, he seemed calmer, happier. I loved Karen then and I love her now for the happiness and calmness I see in Craig when he is with her. I came to trust that God knew what Craig needed to hear and when he would be receptive to hearing it. To this day, I don't know all the help Craig received, and perhaps he doesn't either.

Craig and Karen came over to tell us the day they became engaged. Of course, I hoped for a temple marriage, but I didn't want to offend him by asking. Craig knew what I wanted to know, but "Well, we're getting married" was all he said and then told us the date. Of course, I had to ask, "Where?" When he told me the Salt Lake Temple, it was for me closure and joy.

Craig and I realize that our story has a happy ending and that the happy ending came within two years of the absolutely worst day of both of our lives. Yet neither of us feels that we can say, "Go thou and do likewise," and guarantee a happy ending. Life has so many variables. So much is in God's hands. But even if Craig hadn't found happiness, this experience taught us as parents to walk that fine line between feeling personally responsible to fix whatever goes wrong and throwing up our hands and abandoning the situation. It was a lesson I would not have asked for, but one worth learning.

Firstborn

MARGIE G. HOLMES

I write this essay because of Brian, his life and his death. Brian was our firstborn child. My husband and I received our master's degrees in June and our baby in August. I vividly remember our driving home from the hospital very slowly and carefully, Blair at the wheel, Brian cradled in my arms. We were filled with the desire to protect this child from harm and raise him well. In Colorado, Blair and I were far enough from extended family members to feel as if we were venturing alone into the unknown. I had grown up the oldest daughter in a family of ten children, so I was surprised at how overwhelming the responsibility of a completely dependent child was to me. Still, I was confident that my strong desire to be a good parent and our love would be enough to sustain his healthy development.

Brian grew to be a beautiful child—affectionate, sensitive, social, and intelligent. He was somewhat small of stature, and his muscle development was a little slow. As a result, his music, writing, and art were full of feeling but were not as technically proficient as he would have liked. He was also very independent—or should I say, headstrong—but he came by that naturally. Avoiding power struggles was one of our challenges in parenting, and we did so with varying degrees of success.

By the time he reached high school, Brian was doing excellent academic work and had a small circle of good friends. At the beginning of his junior year, however, all of that changed. He kept his old friends but acquired others, many of whose influence I worried about. His manner of dress, his study habits, and his sleep patterns changed as well. We knew he had some involvement with alcohol, tobacco,

Margie G. Holmes is a research associate in the Research Information Department of the Church. She and her husband, Blair R. Holmes, are the parents of six children. Sister Holmes serves as teacher development coordinator in her ward.

drugs, and the occult. To this day we're not sure how deep that involvement was or to what degree he suffered from depression or other emotional illnesses that went undiagnosed and untreated. Mostly he was angry, and nothing we did to try to help him seemed to work. Our lives were full of conflict, and our family was torn apart.

A month after his eighteenth birthday, Brian died in his sleep after drinking into the night with friends and taking some sleeping pills that an acquaintance had given him. I don't know if Brian intended to die and knew what amounts in combination would kill him or if he wasn't thinking very clearly and made a fatal mistake. There is evidence to support either conclusion, and the uncertainty surrounding his behavior and his death made coming to terms with the situation very difficult.

My reaction to his death involved a complex interplay of feelings. At first there was a kind of numbness, shock, bewilderment, and disbelief. There was a sense of unreality, of watching myself go through the motions of making funeral arrangements, dealing with the police, letting friends and family know what had happened, and noting, "Oh, look, I'm living through this." The numbness was interspersed with intense feelings of anguish. My chest and stomach would fill with a dark purple, tight pain, and I would sob and groan, especially in the shower where the warm water on my body helped release emotion. I also felt a great deal of shame, an overwhelming sense of failure at not providing Brian with what he needed to survive. On the day of the funeral, however, the music, prayers, and gentle words of friends filled me with peace, calmness, and comfort, and I felt sustained by the Spirit of the Lord.

As time went on and the reality of Brian's death became clearer, feelings of longing became very strong. I would have given anything to see Brian again, to touch him, to talk to him. I was filled with regrets about our conflicts and our inability to get the help he needed. I could remember clearly every mistake I had made with him, but I couldn't give myself credit for the years of devotion I had lavished on him—the stories read, the costumes made, the chauffeuring, the hugs, the praise, the birthday parties. I carried a lot of guilt, and although I wasn't angry at the woman who gave him the pills or the acquaintances who encouraged his destructive choices, I couldn't forgive myself or my husband for what we saw as our failures. We had a tremendous drive to make sense of all of this, to understand it, to find out what had happened and why. Placing blame and feeling guilt were a part of trying to make sense of a senseless act.

I also experienced a loss of ambition. The professional identity that I had clung to so fiercely to prevent being devoured by my roles as wife and mother became much less important. My work was helpful as a respite from grieving, but for several years my efforts were channeled primarily into restoring my sense of myself as a decent human being. Mostly that meant allowing myself time with good friends who loved me and time to read and think.

Another emotion that surprised me was a deadening of feeling toward my five other children. I had read with disbelief accounts of parents in earlier centuries whose attachment to surviving children was blunted by repeated losses of young children to disease. Now I understood how that could be. So much of my energy was tied up in mourning Brian's loss, even wanting to join him, that enjoying my other children was difficult. Ironically, the events that taught me with great clarity the worth of a soul, even a troubled, difficult soul, were blunting my feelings toward other precious souls. For a long time, I felt I had a foot in both worlds, this one and the next. Eventually that phase ended, however, and I was left with the exquisite awareness of the goodness of my children, an appreciation for the very ordinary things that they did, and the ability to love them for who they are rather than for what I had hoped they would be. That is Brian's legacy to his younger siblings: wiser, more patient and appreciative parents. Small things that had annoyed us before seemed very insignificant now. A missed piano lesson, an imperfect household chore, a B instead of an A grade—what did they matter? Our children were alive and learning and growing. They were good citizens and would grow up to marry, have children, hold down a job. Mundane things that we had assumed happened to everyone now seemed like great blessings. Enhanced gratitude for ordinary things is another aspect of Brian's legacy.

As the months and years passed, I felt a lot of concern for Brian's well-being. It's hard being a mother when there's nothing you can do for your child and you can't even get a letter to let you know how he's doing. I wondered if he was suffering, if he had been healed, if he was experiencing joy, if he was in the company of those who loved him. I worried about his spiritual well-being. I alternated between thinking, on the one hand, that he was suffering for his sins, that he was in Satan's clutches and would never be free, and on the other hand, that he wouldn't be punished for his choices because he had suffered enough in this life to pay for them, and that I and others were largely responsible for his problems anyway. My grieving was prolonged by my desires to take upon myself any suffering owed by my son, so that he wouldn't have to endure it.

I was reexamining my own relationship to God as well. When I allowed myself to be aware of it, I felt I had been abandoned in my time of greatest need. I'd followed the rules to the best of my ability, but it just hadn't worked out the way I'd been led to expect. Deep down I'd really thought that Mormons were special. If we tried hard enough to do what was right, terrible things wouldn't happen to us. What I learned was that none of us can do it all right. All of us sin and fall short of the glory of God—even Mormons who try very hard. And why should I be special? When Ethiopian children were starving to death and Jews by the millions had died in the gas chambers, why did I think I should be spared suffering? God loves the Muslim woman pregnant through rape just as much as he loves me. I developed a kinship with suffering people everywhere. The prisoner serving time for dealing drugs has a mother who weeps for him, too. The homeless, the mentally ill, the criminal are not from a different race. They're someone's sons and daughters. They are my brothers and my sisters, and we are all wounded by life. We are all in need of God's grace, his love, and his mercy.

Eventually I came to understand that Christ's atonement applies to me, to my son, to my husband—not just to other good people. I did everything I knew how, and it wasn't enough. Nothing we do will ever be enough. That's why we have our Savior. What a relief that has been to me. I don't have to do it by myself. I can love others because I am so grateful for the love that has been extended to me and I want to return it. I can hold the hands of my fellow sufferers. Most of the time I can't fix anything. But I can love, I can accept, I can understand, I can withhold judgment, I can cry with my friends. I can offer my heart, which truly is broken and softened, and my spirit, which truly is contrite. I don't worry about my image any more. When I failed at the most important task of my life and found myself acceptable before God and loved by my friends, it freed me to be more authentically who I am.

I don't worry much about Brian now. I trust that our heavenly parents love Brian much more than even I am capable of loving him. Surely they will provide him with the experiences he needs to become the righteous, magnificent son of God that is his potential. Surely he has been healed by experiencing the pure love of Christ upon leaving this life. If he is in prison, surely he has been taught by those who love him, and he will be able to choose the light, if he has not already done so. For me, this life is not so much a test as a school where we learn the good from the evil by our own experience. The suffering we endure here serves to turn our hearts to God and to one another, to prepare us for further growth in the life to come where Jesus Christ waits with open arms to embrace us, heal us, and lead us to the next stage of our growth.

Obsessive Scavenger

MARILYN VAN KEIZERSWAARD

For my birthday my sister gave me a card that read, "I found the absolutely perfect birthday gift for you. I mean, it was one-of-a-kind. It was you! Then, I turned my back for just a second, and someone else snatched it up! Geez, those garage sales can be vicious." For Bosses' Day last year, the clerks in my unit gave me a gift certificate to the secondhand store up the street. I was ecstatic! In 1991, our family went on summer vacation to Montana. We don't know a soul in Montana, but I had read an article in *Architectural Digest* about a designer who goes back to her home state to buy items for clients in those wonderful antique and secondhand stores. Well, I had to see for myself. For Christmas a few years ago, my husband surprised me with a Jeep Cherokee. The first thing I said when I saw it was, "This will be great for yard sales."

I am, I confess, an obsessive scavenger. I take great pleasure in poking into thrift shops and rummaging through attics and basements. I find a yard sale irresistible. I've skidded to a halt at the mere glimpse of a wardrobe standing at the back of a driveway, a possible fulfillment of that little wish list I always carry in the back of my mind. I leap from my car, repeating rapidly, please don't be sold, please don't be sold, please don't be sold. I walk straight to it, my eyes searching for a sold sign. There is nothing. "How much?" I ask. "$150," she says.

The adrenaline is flowing fast. I keep my wits about me. "Will you take $125?"

"Sure," she says. She tells me that it used to be painted pink and she stripped it. I am grateful. I would have paid $300.

In Manti, my family stopped at a small antique store, at my request,

Marilyn Van Keizerswaard is a supervisor for Surety Life Insurance Company. She and her husband, Neil Van Keizerswaard, are the parents of three children. Sister Van Keizerswaard is the Young Women's president in her ward.

of course. We all moseyed in. My oldest daughter, Lisa, and I went one direction, and the other two kids followed their dad on another path. My eyes were scanning numerous shelves of glassware and dishes. I reached up and pulled down a yellow, purled creamer. I carefully turned it over to read the bottom and, more important, to find the price: $4. Warmly I brought it to my chest and held onto it tightly. We finished our looking and met up with the other half of the family.

"I see you found something," Neil, my husband, said, a teasing glint in his eye.

Lisa said, "It was love at first sight."

My friend Gail and I stopped in at Deseret Industries one afternoon to scope out any possible treasures. In the furniture department we each laid claim to a chair. I found charm in a slipper chair, a small, upholstered chair with no arms and a large ruffle around the bottom. It was covered in a dark, royal-blue velvet with a big slit in the seat. The cotton guts were spewing out. I could picture it in the corner of my bedroom. The price was $1. Gail's chair was a wood-framed armchair with a worn leather-like seat and back. It was $2. A clerk walked by and announced that today all furniture was half price. We immediately divided by two in our minds. We put our chairs next to each other and debated on the purchase. Can we get them home? Will we really fix them up, or will they just sit in the basement? Will there be much sewing in order to re-cover them? Will we do it? We laughed at ourselves for debating about $1.50's worth of chairs. We could give them away or throw them away at that price.

Now the slipper chair, with a new, crisp chintz cover, sits with dignity in my bedroom. It is a one-of-a-kind piece with a story—and those are the pieces I value the most in the decorating of my home. I've put something of myself into them. They make my home different, unusual, unique.

The lure of decorating with orphaned furniture and discarded items is the challenge of making something out of nothing. It's my passion. Scavenging unlocks a creative excitement, a friendly sort of frenzy. It forces me to look at objects, to be inventive and resourceful. It keeps me open to the unexpected. And when I find myself bored with an item or desiring a change, I recycle it: I take the unwanted piece to a consignment store, or I trade it in for credit at my favorite secondhand store.

I have found that I am consistently attracted to certain treasures.

They are like magnets. I now have many minicollections: bowls, colorful plates, creamers and pitchers, baskets, rugs, and Levi's 501 button-up jeans. Why jeans? Because they pay. Let me give you an example. This is a list of items I bought one Saturday last April:

4 pairs Levi's, $3.50
AT&T cordless phone, $5.00
2 pairs women's shoes, $1.50
1 new curling iron, $.75
2 pairs kids' Levi's, $4.00
1 pair boy's Docker's, $1.00
1 brand-new boy's Polo dress shirt, $1.00
1 pair Cole Haan ankle boots for girls, $5.00
1 pair Forenza pants, $2.00
1 Bundt pan, $1.00
1 yellow bowl, $1.00
1 dishtowel, $.50

I spent $26.25, but then I turned in the Levi's for cash at one of those places that says, "Will pay cash for Levi's," and received a check for $26.50 for my wares. I actually made $.25 that day.

I do not require the shine of the all-new. I am warmed by the gently worn and still affordable. Joe Ruggiero says in his book, *Found Objects:* "There is something of the scavenger, the historian, the child, the archaeologist, the functionalist, the resourceful treasure hunter, the collector, the recycler, the poet, and the artist in us all—and finding an object and reusing it in our homes is a way to give expression to these facets of our personalities."[1]

I am an obsessive scavenger. I delight in poking into thrift shops and rummaging through attics and basements. I find a yard sale irresistible.

NOTE

1. Quoted in JoAnn Barwick, "Thinking Aloud," *House Beautiful,* Mar. 1987, p. 10.

Miss Titled

NATALIE CURTIS McCULLOUGH

The summer I was thirteen, I was invited to participate in the Miss Oak Hills Neighborhood Beauty Pageant. I was not beautiful. I had no discernible talent. I did not need both pieces of my two-piece swimsuit. For all of these reasons, I was accepted by my dozen or so girlfriends. I had some wonderful friends who enjoyed being together. We laughed at jokes we didn't understand for their humor but which we knew would be funny had we understood them. We sang Brighton camp songs plus "When You Walk through a Storm, Hold Your Head Up High" in creative harmonies. And we were all contestants in the Miss Oak Hills Neighborhood Beauty Pageant. I don't know exactly whose idea the pageant was, but some older neighborhood girls chose to flourish their creative abilities for glamour and entertainment on the grass roots level at my group of a dozen or so girlfriends. I was delighted.

Each of us had been assigned a judge who rated in strictest secrecy a week's worth of projects, which ranged from making something hand-sewn to cooking from scratch. I went happily through the week as though being sent on a treasure hunt for my talents. Then the big night of performing in the pageant came, and all our families and neighbors were invited. One of the pageant producers scored a big coup by getting the Foothill Gas Station to donate free bags of popcorn. My friends and I dressed in our Sunday dresses, and I wore my first pair of nylons.

I did not have a Talent to perform. I remember being anxious about that from the beginning. My mother, however, was a very talented dramatist and an idealist. She found a dramatic reading for me to learn and had me memorize her interpretation of a story about a very

Natalie Curtis McCullough earned her bachelor's degree in English from the University of Utah. She and her husband, James R. McCullough, are the parents of four children. Sister McCullough serves as Relief Society president in her ward and is the solitary recipient of the coveted "Ms. Understood" award.

old-fashioned schoolmarm trying to get through a commencement exercise. Mother loved it. It was naive humor I understood and didn't think was funny because I understood it. That night I performed the dramatic reading, feeling that I was making people uncomfortable to show such naked emotional extravagance. But I could render the reading only as I had been taught, so I gave myself to my interpretation of Mother's performance.

Finally the contest was over. We were all sent to a back bedroom to dress and come out for the awards. It had been much harder work than any of us had anticipated. It had not been as much fun for us as it had been for the pageant promoters, who talked about us, compared our virtues, assessed our talents, and assigned our status. I wondered if our friendships would ever be the same. We went out, not saying much, to ride out the momentum and, of course, to see who won.

It was lovely, really. Each contestant received a beautiful pearl pendant and a title to go with it—"Miss Music," "Miss Seamstress," "Miss Dance," and so forth—until there were only two girls left without titles and jewelry: Lynn and I. I was relieved to think that I must not have humiliated myself as badly as I had thought by my reading. I guessed that my private projects of the week before must have gone well. I felt that First Runner-Up or Queen were equally respectable titles, and I made a mental note to hug Lynn no matter what the verdict was.

They called out Lynn's name as the first Miss Oak Hills, gave her a bouquet of flowers, and put a rhinestone tiara on her head. They played music and made her walk out in front of the audience while everyone clapped and she held back tears.

I never got a chance to hug her. I never got a pearl pendant. I was never granted a title . . . any title, not even "Miss Imitation Talent." I was completely forgotten. Not only was I not runner-up to the neighborhood title but I was going to have to run away from the neighborhood in disgrace. (Not to be confused with "Miss Grace," a title I would have dearly cherished.) My worst beliefs about myself had been validated. They were compassionate to pretend they hadn't heard my dramatic reading. There was no malice or judicial favoritism. The plain fact was—I was not worthy of a title.

Two weeks later, several of the pageant producers stopped me in the hallway at Mutual. They thrust into my hand an open box bearing a necklace on cotton and said they had meant to give it to me at the pageant but had just forgotten. The necklace was not like the other contestants'. It was not terrible, but it was clearly an afterthought. I did not know whose mother had pointed out their oversight but hoped it had not been mine. I was not gracious. I told them, "No, thank you. I do not wear much jewelry." They followed me down the hall toward my classroom, begging me to take it. I was three years younger than they were. I was embarrassed. I was proud and shy and grateful and hurt. I took it without thanks and never wore it. No title was offered.

I have told this tender, trifling tragedy because it has had a greater effect on my life than I could have anticipated. It seared the fleshy tablets of my heart with the belief that I would always be titleless and wear jewelry as an afterthought.

I was asked to speak at Women's Conference because I have no name recognition and no special title. I am the person that conference participants unwittingly requested on their feedback forms as the "common woman." That information from conference planners caused me no small uneasiness in coming here to speak. But it is a good circle to complete, really. Now I am chosen for having no title. When contemplating letters to put behind my name in the printed program, I thought of offering H.R.M., not for Her Royal Majesty but for Home Room Mother.

While I was in my twenties, raising small children, I wondered at painful length what I would be when I grew up. I graduated from college, pregnant with my third child, and still I had no answers. In my early thirties, I went into severe panic over medical complications with my fourth baby that prevented my having any more children. I sincerely wanted more children. But along with that loss came the frightening prospect of facing myself alone, sooner, and I was no nearer knowing what I could become, what I would call myself when the title "Mother" dimmed. I thrashed about. While I worried, I volunteered in my children's classrooms, got sick, taught a couple of literature seminars for school districts. I took nonmatriculated graduate hours, got sick, visit taught, entertained friends, and built a cabin out of a dream. I traveled. Loaded and unloaded cars, coolers, and clothes. I loved my husband, loved my children. I hated my husband and my children, ran away, repented, loved them again . . . this, many times. I made lunches, cooked dinner, taught adult scripture classes, drove carpools. I worshipped. I canned and dried fruit, did laundry, napped, delivered dinners to neighbors, sewed disastrous dance costumes, helped children write historical fiction novels, substituted at my children's high school, wallpapered, put on spook alleys and carnivals, gardened, skied, joined a tennis team, prayed, read, got sick. A friend accused me of being Domestic. That sounded like something that could be written on a résumé, and I felt severely complimented. I envied my talented and titled friends. I worried about being asked what I do.

I helped my children develop talents: drove them to sewing lessons, gyms, tracks, and soccer fields, violin studios, piano and saxophone teachers, orchestra and theater tryouts, art classes, wrestling camps, tennis courts, reading and math tutoring, and even—once—because of my insecurity, I guess, tried to interest them in ant farming. I did what some of you do. I lived a scattered, scared, and sacred life.

For my thirty-fifth birthday, I went all alone to Snowbird for a day to ski and recite poetry to myself on the lift. In contemplating the joy I felt in living my life, I realized that the elusive thing I have always wanted to become, I already am. And I am who I am by the grace of God, who is the Great "I AM."[1] How large a gift, this gentle revelation, though there is still no pearl pendant or "Miss Title" to rescue me from questions about myself.

I read a lovely Japanese folk story, *The Crane Wife,* about a poor farmer who rescues a wounded crane from death. The farmer is then visited by a strange and beautiful woman who becomes his wife. The woman offers to help financially by taking up weaving, but after she sets up her loom, she hides behind sliding paper doors and tells her husband that he must never look in on her when she is working. She weaves without thread for three days and nights, and when she is finished, she looks thin and pale, but her cloth is exquisite and sells in town for a very high price. Three times, as they come to the end of their resources, she closets herself with her loom. Each time she weaves, she grows weaker and more pathetic, but her cloth grows more iridescent and remarkable. Eventually, of course, the husband becomes both greedy for the wealth her work could bring and curious about the mysterious manner wherein she creates fabric without using thread. When he can bear it no longer, he opens the doors to look in on his wife's creation. What he sees is a "crane, smeared with blood, for with its beak it had plucked out its own feathers to place in the loom."[2] His initial rescue of the beautiful crane and her sacrificial attempt to reciprocate his kindness have been in vain. Their love is forfeited for her final bolt of beautiful cloth, stained with a single strand of crimson, her blood.

This story haunts me. I, too, believe that I must create behind paper doors, where no one can see the price I pay to weave the fabric of my life. Also, I have believed that I must weave alone, as if any of us were inexhaustible resources working by ourselves. It is a long lesson to learn that we do not strengthen the kingdom by single-handedly being the blanket that covers all who are cold and shelters all who swelter in the heat. Many of us grow threadbare in this belief and, not unlike the Crane Wife, destroy ourselves in the process of our own creation.

Perhaps the Relief Society organization has come of age as the great loom upon which we are all invited to participate in weaving the fabric of our self-esteem and sisterhood. It is the collective blanket of strength that serves the kingdom in ever more glorious and unusual patterns. Here a strand of wool, coarse and thick and warm, shuttled against a strand of shimmering, refined silk, back again with warm bread and a casserole, woven through and pushed taut against a court brief, a day spent skiing, a child cared for, a note of appreciation or acknowledgment sent. We are the warp and woof of our tapestry. Our talents and interests anchor the threads of service, friendship, and spiritual gifts. This is grace to grace—all our solitary threads shuttled into the greater whole. Our losses and mistakes right next to our successes and repentance. All of it shown with love and gratitude for the whole experience.

We do not need to make fabric so exquisite, so flawless, that beside our achievements our souls are emptied. Like the Crane Wife, we are all indebted for our ultimate rescue. Unlike her, our Redeemer does not require us to pluck out our own feathers, to diminish ourselves to the point of extinction, in weaving our souls. Grace is the act of filling our souls, sharing the creative processes by which our souls are enlarged. The Savior's grace to us may not be represented in the confines of a completed tapestry, of a title. He already made the ultimate sacrifice. Perhaps what he wants for us is our willingness to accept the flaws and limitations in our own patterns, which teach us to reach for the grander pattern in the larger tapestry of his atonement. It is not by sacrificing our*selves* but by learning how to cherish and value his grace and his sacrifice that his rescue will not have been in vain.

I am useful here, dependent there, compassionate today, unwise tomorrow. Each is its own gift. Each is a title but with the first letter uncapitalized. Perhaps our titles lie about us, anyway. And the lies separate us. What shared title could be holier or happier than "sister in Christ," each sister a thread in the fabric whole? I strengthen the fabric by both my creative solvency and my undisciplined darkness. Grace to grace has been all my journey from unclaimed contestant in the Beauty Pageant of Life to unknown speaker in the Marriott Center. The title never was important. It is by the grace of God that I am what I am, not that I am called what I am called. Whereas we contest for titles, we participate in grace.

Anyway, things could have been worse. I could have been titled "Miss Guided" or "Miss Taken."

I feel it a great privilege to have stood where any of you could have stood to share this portion of my heart, to unravel the little thread of what I am because what I am involves all of you. I salute each of you in your myriad good choices and thank you for the honor I feel it is to be woven alongside you in the broadly textured Relief Society tapestry.

NOTES

1. See 1 Corinthians 15:10; Exodus 3:13–14.
2. Sumiko Yagawa, *The Crane Wife*, trans. Katherine Paterson (New York: Mulberry Books, 1981), p. 24.

My Hat Dance

ELISA PULIDO

Josefina, mi maestra, taught me the wild
stomping and tapping of Mexican dances,
Josefina, maestra bonita, had raven braids
coiled at the nape of her neck, almond skin,
crimson lips, long silver bangles
from her ears, lace petticoats
that peeked from under ruffled skirts,
fringed silken serape
and high red heels.
At the fiesta, Josefina's partner
was tall and dark
in a white shirt and red sash,
slender hips in tight pants.
He teased her with the boyish
bounce of his dancing.
But then, at once, both his moustache
and his sweet hot breath
brushed the cheek
of Josefina as he took a rose
from her red lips
in his own white teeth.

I wore the skirt my mama bought,
coarse and heavy, woven by Indians,
and a cotton blusa

*Elisa Pulido received her bachelor's degree in German from Brigham Young University.
She and her husband, Timothy Jay Pulido, are the parents of three children. Sister
Pulido served a mission to Switzerland, and she conducts the choir in her Pennsylvania
ward.*

embroidered with pink roses.
My short brown hair
was clean and combed.
I danced with a muchacho muy gordo,
and when the sweet sound of mariachi violins,
guitars strumming, and brassy trumpets
sang from the phonograph,
I dragged three left feet
around and around the sombrero.

You Tell Me Your Dreams, and I'll Tell You Mine: Bridging the Gap

EMMA LOU THAYNE

COOKIES IN THE AIRPORT

Cookies. Pepperidge Farm Milanos. Just a few. Perfect for between flights. Buy a bag to put down with your belongings on the seat between you and the man also waiting down the row. Pick up your mystery novel, get absorbed, pass the forty-five-minute layover with no anxieties.

Fine. But then . . . what? That man. What's he doing? Reaching for your bag of cookies? Opening it? Taking a cookie out! Surely not. You look his way, try to be nonchalant, wonder what in the world . . . ?

So you reach into the bag, take one yourself, looking intently at your book. Let him know just whose bag of cookies that is. But then . . . surely not again. He's taking another cookie. Two! Eating them as if he'd done nothing wrong. The nerve, the very nerve. And he looks like such a nice man, smiling the whole time, not at you, but at the newspaper he's reading. Or pretending to. Like you with your book, now far from your focus but a great prop.

He reaches for the bag, takes two more cookies. You do the same, neither looking at the other but seeing it all. Again him. Again you. Finally, the end. He reaches in, rustles his hand around in the bottom of the bag, and takes the last cookie! Oh come on! Do you accuse him? Give him a vampire look? Tip the empty bag over in his face? Make him somehow aware? At least let him know that you know?

He's standing up now, picking up his carry-on, and smiling. Smiling right at you, nodding as if he were the most pleasant man in the airport. Really? Not a word, not an apology?

Emma Lou Thayne, a lifelong resident of Salt Lake City, Utah, has twelve published books of fiction, nonfiction, and poetry and is a member of the board of directors of the Deseret News. She contributes regularly to a variety of publications. She and her husband, Melvin E. Thayne, have five daughters and eighteen grandchildren.

You stand to gather your coat, your purse, your own carry-on. You fumble for your ticket as you head for the line-up to the flight. He's now gone off to another gate. May his destination be jail!

You keep fumbling, watching him go. Then . . . oh, come on. Not really. In your purse, a bag of cookies.[1]

What little bit of talk could have cleared up whose cookies were being eaten? How much just plain interest instead of indignation could have suggested a simple question, some reaching across the chasm of misunderstanding? Might that exchange, any exchange, have turned the encounter into something worthwhile? Instead, two people went their ways the less for being reluctant, afraid, too proud or shy to find the truth.

Meantime, in the real world, in the Church, too often we know each other and our intentions by what we read in the papers or see on television or hear about in isolation from each other. The media generally tell the truth but often tell it with a slant. What "hearings" we have with each other are too often via preconceived assumptions, as with the cookies, focused on who really owns which.

What can such dividing bring about but divisiveness? We become victims of our own distancing. But bridging the distances can be difficult even among those who care about the same people and concerns. About a year ago, a meeting was going overtime inside the room at 47 East South Temple where the First Presidency and the Twelve meet. Our monthly meeting of the *Deseret News* board of directors always started at three sharp in that same room with President Thomas Monson and Elder James Faust presiding, with Bishop Victor Brown, Elder Neal Maxwell, BYU presidents Dallin Oaks and then Jeff Holland, advertising executive and former newsman Glen Snarr, bank president Bob Bischoff, and me.

For sixteen years I'd dangled or slumped to occupy the too-large leather armchair between the publisher and the editor of the newspaper and across from Bob Bischoff. He and I had laughed about being "token" on the board, he the one nonmember, I the lone woman. Those had been eventful years of budgets and bottom lines, advertising and circulation reports, attention to editorial and page makeup, news holes, news, and the price of newsprint, all recorded by Arthur Haycock, secretary to maybe five presidents of the Church, and then Lynn Cannegieter, secretary to President Monson. We had toured newsrooms and presses, watched writers move from the clatter of rooms full of type-writers to the muted ticking of computers as stories and artwork appeared on screens to be paginated, printed, and tossed on porches like fields of energy with information packaged for perusal.

I had loved and respected the whole process, and the people who made it happen. Yes, and also those men in the twelve chairs surrounding the table under the paintings of Joseph Smith and President Benson, who preside in our meetings as surely as if they were holding forth in person. Doors at either end opened into offices of, during my time, President Kimball and then President Benson, and at the other end, President Monson. At our assigned places, always the same, Russ Gallegos, comptroller, had positioned our black ring binders with tabbed agendas, minutes, reports, and checks we discreetly pocketed—or for me, pursed—before the prayer we took turns offering.

In those nearly seventeen years, we'd had more than two hundred meetings together in that room, plus as many other meetings in offices in that building or at the paper, plus dinners and lunches with and without spouses, Christmas cards and parties, summer cookouts, and the weddings and funerals of each other's loved ones. We'd shared pulpits and publishings, jokes and concerns. We were friends. And we were engaged in a common cause.

Now on our regular Wednesday at 3:00 P.M., those of us not General Authorities waited on the huge blue Oriental rug under the light of brass and mother-of-pearl sconces of the inner entry as those who daily occupied that pillared building finished their business inside. When the great brown door opened, we of the newspaper board automatically formed a line to go in. Out streamed two of the Church presidency, all the apostles, the heads of Relief Society, Young Women, and Primary, and the president of BYU, cordial as at a wedding, shaking hands as they passed. Only a few had the grab-and-move-along-as-fast-as-possible handshake acquired in too many confrontations with thronging.

I knew well all but the newest apostle, Elder Richard G. Scott. I'd been schoolmates with many; my husband, with others. I'd served on other boards, played tennis, been on civic and university committees, exchanged letters, and formulated plans, eaten with, laughed with, and been easy in each other's company over many more than those seventeen years on the *Deseret News* board. They now asked about my latest poem or a move of one of our children and said to say hello to Mel. I asked them about a wife with phlebitis or commented on a recent talk or book or act of goodwill, so many beyond our immediate family of concerns. Our exchange was first-name, warm, real.

That night I thought and have since, What good men and women, called to give their all to run this gigantic organization of a church. How I would hate to have their job, especially being subject to the kind of scrutiny that would beleaguer a microbe under a microscope. I felt the burden of their callings and the potential for misunderstanding between their deliberations and even the doings of the next meeting in the room they had just left—let alone between them and the millions who see them only on television or in the *Church News,* the millions whose stories they can never be privy to in the making of their worldwide decisions any more than those millions can know those decision makers and the backgrounds and personalities that have shaped them. How can the hundreds, thousands, now millions like me interpret and internalize every word and move in terms of our own unique findings and flounderings, securities and struggles, all of it as personal as the connection by media is distant?

Add to this the bludgeonings of opinion, misinformation, out-of-context assumptions, time pressures, overcommitment for most of us and certainly for them—and how do we expect to hear, let alone understand, each other's stories? And it is that hearing that can make all the difference.

I grew up in a church as personal and approachable as that lineup outside the door in the Church Administration Building. I believe still in the private exchange. I believe, too, that we need each other, those on either end of a handshake and genuine "How are you?"

I know that those men and women in authority offer different kinds of goodness for us to respond to, just as the others of us in our various callings and commitments would like to offer in return. And I know that we're wanting the same things for people of good faith and willingness to work for good causes. I know this because I could turn to other gatherings and receive the same cordiality and sincere concern as among those in the Church Administration Building, including those gracious women who work there daily to free the men for other things. Each of us is different, each of us trying our level best to paddle well and stay afloat in our seas of dailiness and demands and wanting to do better.

Why then the divisiveness? Why the labeling, the "us" and the "them," the questioning, the suspicion of each other's motives, the

defining in and out of the gospel mainstream by judgments and surface evaluations? Across the board, alliances regarding the labels are
formed and charges are made. When will we be able just to recognize
that we do need each other? We need not agree with everyone's point
of view, but we need to respect each person's right to have it without
being suspected of being on the road to apostasy or dismissed as being
too conservative. We need to hear each other's stories and to understand, not fear or ostracize or condemn each other. Are we delivered
or doomed by our history of persecution? If the Church was a haven
back in Joseph Smith's time, why not now? For all of us believers at
the various stages of our questing as well as following?

Twenty years ago as part of the general board of the YWMIA,
Joleen Meredith and I wrote a hymn, "Where Can I Turn for Peace?"[2]
As part of the 1985 hymnbook, it has been sung in many languages,
several times by the Tabernacle Choir, and in various arrangements
both recorded and live. Perhaps its wide acceptance has been because
all of us feel sometimes under siege, asking,

> Where can I turn for peace?
> Where is my solace
> When other sources cease to make me whole?
> When with a wounded heart, anger, or malice,
> I draw myself apart,
> Searching my soul?
> Where, when my aching grows,
> Where when I languish,
> Where, in my need to know, where can I run?
> Where is the quiet hand to calm my anguish?
> Who, who can understand?
> He, only One.
> He answers privately,
> Reaches my reaching
> In my Gethsemane, Savior and Friend.
> Gentle the peace he finds for my beseeching.
> Constant he is and kind,
> Love without end.

No, those in authority whose hands I shook and whose warmth I
felt that day coming out of their meeting cannot be there for each of
us to turn to. But like Christ, they can offer solace through listening to

honest concerns of faithful members. In that comforting exchange we can send love to each other. In our prayers we can do the same. We must not push each other away at the very time when we need each other most. We must listen and talk and try to understand rather than judge and label.

More than anything, we must trust each other. Trust that our dreams can be told and that they likely will, in the big picture, be surprisingly alike.

In two recent conferences of LDS women from the East and the Midwest, I felt, instead of a sense of oppression, a sense of hope—hope for the power of prayer and the reality of answers to it. One woman suggested we circle on our calendars the last day of every month and set it aside for special prayers for women in Somalia, men in the UN armed forces, children in the streets, babies born and unborn, and for those in authority in our LDS faith to feel our longing to shake their hands and wish them well and offer the very best we have to the causes and dreams we share. This we can do, through the divine connections we know are as real as any handshake in any coming together anywhere.

Meanwhile, when the storms crash about me, I know that the ultimate turning for peace is inward. Like a lightning rod in a thunderstorm, I can stay grounded in what I know is true and let the threat of being harmed become instead the power through which I operate. I can trust in the love beyond end to supply the grounding, even as I return light for light, like a sparkler in the dark, saying, You are, I am, and we are eligible for any reaching our reaching might persuade.

Bless us all to see that light in each other and to let it bring us peace, not conflict, dreams, not nightmares, and hope, not despair, because we are willing to hear and see and care about each other, no matter what rooms we occupy or dreams we dare to dream. After all, it was Joseph's daring to ask and then to dream that started our meeting together in the first place.

NOTES

1. This story must be of the urban folktale variety. Nearly six months after I'd written up the story as I'd heard from a friend who had heard it in a church meeting, another version surfaced at a gathering in New Hampshire. This time the source was British, the cookies tea biscuits, and the setting a pub.

2. *Hymns of The Church of Jesus Christ of Latter-day Saints* (Salt Lake City: The Church of Jesus Christ of Latter-day Saints, 1985), no. 129.

Armies of Light:
A Report on Troop Morale

CHERYL B. PRESTON

In the world's "most profound, comprehensive, and systematic examination of war,"[1] Carl von Clausewitz, a nineteenth-century military philosopher, observes: "There is no higher and simpler law of strategy than that of *keeping one's forces concentrated.* No force should ever be detached from the main body. . . . Incredible though it sounds, it is a fact that armies have been divided and separated countless times."[2] Divide-and-conquer is an age-old tool of military strategy; it is also the tool of the enemies of righteousness. President Gordon B. Hinckley warned, "We live in a society that feeds on criticism. . . . The enemy of truth would divide us and cultivate within us attitudes of criticism which, if permitted to prevail, will only deter us in the pursuit of our great divinely given goal."[3]

Given such warnings, I have watched with concern an unnecessary divisiveness among sisters in the gospel. I am not searching for sameness in thought or action, but I long for greater harmony, cooperation, cohesive support, and mutual respect for our widely diverse thoughts and actions. As a teacher at Brigham Young University, I am in a position to read about, listen to, and watch women, especially Latter-day Saint women. Like war correspondent Lowell Thomas, who followed Colonel T. E. Lawrence during the Arabian Revolution,[4] I can report on the condition of the troops.

Harmony among all members of the Church, women and men, is, of course, of critical importance. I focus here on unity among sisters because enormous cultural upheavals and the widening of opportunities and alternatives for women have fueled profound questions, first,

Cheryl B. Preston, an associate professor of law at the J. Reuben Clark Law School, Brigham Young University, teaches banking and finance and women's issues in law. She and her husband, Stan Preston, are the parents of three children. Sister Preston serves as a Compassionate Service/Social Relations teacher in Relief Society.

about determining our own choices, and second, about accepting each other's varied choices.[5]

TIME OF FOCUS ON WOMEN

We are at a critical juncture for women. As future generations chronicle our time, they will identify it by its focus on women. In the last few years, the world of scholarship has been inundated with material written by and about women in every field of study.[6] Much of the writing about women is a celebration of women's thinking and experience, a previously undervalued contribution now recognized in all human endeavors. For instance, psychoanalytic sociologist Nancy Chodorow suggests that women's tendencies to be empathetic, relationship oriented, nonhierarchical, and consensus building will have a dramatic effect on the workplace. Carol Gilligan, professor of education at Harvard, identifies through psychological studies a feminine approach to moral reasoning. Christine A. Littleton, professor of law at UCLA, promotes equal legal recognition of "culturally female" choices, such as child rearing, rather than measuring women's worth against a male status quo.[7] What a wonderful time this is to be a woman, when the study of women and women's ways is itself so rich!

Being watched evokes responsibility—and accountability. In the limelight, we have a chance to demonstrate that women's contribution to public life, as well as private life, will make the world a better place. How we treat each other in these unique times will matter.

Unfortunately, in this era of great opportunity, we are not always cohesive as women. There are fissures and cracks in the body of sisterhood. Through the cracks hiss themes that divide and alienate us. Consider some of these themes. Current popular magazines and newspapers contain a host of articles on "mommy wars," the inability of some women who work outside the home and some women who work inside the home to join forces in cooperative efforts. Titles such as "Working or Nonworking, Moms on the Defensive" from *The Cleveland Plain Dealer* or "Mommy Vs. Mommy" in *Newsweek* indicate that unrest is widespread.[8] A July 1993 *Wall Street Journal* article reports an interesting swing of the pendulum: the stay-at-home mom is becoming a status symbol, similar, says the article, to a BMW, an economic luxury very few can afford. Those who are not "M.C." (maternally correct) are excluded from the clubs of fashionably wealthy at-home moms.[9]

Current news articles also discuss the "queen bee syndrome," in which women who get a toehold on certain opportunities push back other women as though there is enough room only for one.[10] A queen bee can also be the woman who "chooses female friends who are a little less attractive. She complains about women drivers while considering herself the next [Mario] Andretti. She treats male co-workers with respect while sharpening her claws on female colleagues."[11]

Some women seek to dissociate themselves from females generally. They see other women as part of a "pink ghetto" of less significant people.[12] Sociologists have also identified a "Not-Me Syndrome" including, for instance, elderly "women uncomfortable with their own aging [who] try to distance themselves from the notion" of aging by criticizing and belittling other old people.[13]

REASONS FOR THE CONFLICT

Why are we frequently harder on those with whom we have the most in common, those who should be our natural allies? Maybe it is because we consider ourselves "experts," better able to judge female behavior than male. Maybe we project our own insecurities and negative self-images on other women. Maybe the jealousies born of comparisons and competition sometimes plague us as women. We live in a world that cannot seem to acknowledge "different" without thinking "better" or "worse." Yet making others feel "unimportant, unspecial, wrong" is Satan's method of achieving counterfeit self-esteem.[14] Maybe it is part of Satan's plan to separate us from those with whom our alliance would be most critical. In C. S. Lewis's *The Screwtape Letters*, the tempters try to convince the Christian to "direct [his] malice to his immediate neighbors whom he meets every day and to thrust his benevolence out to the remote circumference, to people he does not know."[15] Then he can *believe* himself benevolent without ever having to practice benevolence. It is the real day-to-day cases that test us, not the theoretical and abstract ones.

I too am guilty. I remember, ten years ago, being so defensive about being a working mother (and so exhausted) that I allowed myself to construct attitudes, under the guise of self-defense, that unwittingly devalued my sisters who chose not to work outside the home. I realized that my feelings of hurt and exclusion prevented me from seeing that they too might be hurting and struggling to feel valued. One day a new sister moved into my neighborhood. She offered to help with my children's needs when I had to work late. I first heard in this offer not her tender concern for my well-being but a judgment that she would just have to take over for me because I was a bad mother. I have come, over time, to love her dearly and to know that she is filled with compassion, not judgment.

I have also come to admire my neighbor's considerable talent as a homemaker and companion to children—her own, mine, and others. The current focus on the voices of women is an opportunity for us to redefine greatness. We can celebrate and reinforce the value of those women—the achievers, champions, and geniuses—whose accomplishments are not reflected by official titles, degrees, trophies, or paychecks.

Laurel Thatcher Ulrich's *A Midwife's Tale* celebrates the life of a late eighteenth-century homemaker and midwife, Martha Ballard. Is it the distance in time that makes Martha Ballard's life of interest and value? What about the twentieth-century homemaker, school volunteer, and Cub Scout den mother? What about the Pulitzer-prize-winning scholar herself, who took nine years to obtain her doctorate, at a pace that allowed her time for commitment to family and the Church as well as to history?[16] We should celebrate each other's chosen paths to and areas of excellence.

EXAMPLES FROM BYU LAW STUDENTS

Instead of women championing women, I see defensive attitudes wedge themselves between sisters with much in common, much to share, and much need for each other's support. My particular path in life has heavily involved me with the women students at BYU's law school. Last semester, several of those women came to me in pain about what they perceived to be the negative judgments of other women.

One of those women has been exceptionally successful in law school. She has been offered a prestigious and high-paying job in a legal market so tight many have no jobs at all. She told a group of other women in her class that she had chosen to decline employment to stay home after law school with the baby she was expecting. Some of her classmates responded with disapproval and dismay. They suggested that she was letting them down and wasting herself.

Another student has struggled for years with the intense personal anguish of infertility. Recently, she asked me how she might respond to two well-meaning women in her Relief Society who had made the assumption that she had "chosen" to pursue a career in law *instead* of having children.

A third student spoke of her deep love and respect for her mother. Then she confessed that her mother's apparent admiration of her daughter's success in law school had become a source of discord and confusion. The mother, at age fifty, had begun to question the worth of her own life, to ask whether raising a family paled against her own daughter's academic achievements. The mother wondered whether encouraging her daughter's efforts would ultimately diminish her own value. My confused student was afraid that a recent dramatic drop in her grades might be a subconscious effort to please her mother by reducing the threat that her success seemed to pose.

DEHUMANIZING WITH LABELS

Unlike those examples, most of the woman-to-woman combat I observe is fought at a distance, not among immediate friends and family. We find it easier to attack a faceless enemy. Rather than focusing on how we are similar as sisters, some focus only on the ways we are different. We put other women in broad categories of disapproval; and once we reduce a human being to a label, it is simple to criticize and condemn.[17]

Like divide-and-conquer theory, the strategy of dehumanization is time-honored and well practiced. In war, soldiers must be taught to kill. Modern military leaders know that killing is made easier when the soldier can avoid thinking of the enemy as a human being. Soldiers are told again and again that the enemy "is not really a full human being like themselves; it is permissible and praiseworthy to kill him."[18] In training, they persuade "gunners [to] fire at grid references they cannot see; submarine crews [to] fire torpedoes at 'ships' (and not, somehow, at the people in the ships); pilots [to] launch their missile at 'targets.'"[19] Once we objectify our sisters as "things"—philosophies, activities, habits, or choices—we can sneak our condemnations past the place in our heart where our training in Christian love resides.

I have only one sister by birth. We are very close, notwithstanding great distance in miles and a thirteen-year gap in ages. I know her particular strengths and her weaknesses; I know the beauty of her soul and her occasional missteps; I know her complexities and her contradictions. Even so, I recognize that our heavenly parents know and love her in dimensions far beyond my ability to comprehend.

I occasionally find people who have met us both at different times. Some have not immediately recognized the connection, even though the minute we open our mouths my sister and I are virtually indistinguishable. What if such a stranger were to say to me, "I met a woman in Portland, Oregon, who looks something like you, but she was just a house frau, a cookie-baker type"? (Believe it or not, "house frau" and "cookie baker" are, I'm told, popular slang for deriding full-time homemakers and mothers.) How would I feel about this summary of the significance of my sister's existence? How dare someone reduce her to a one-dimensional label, even if it may reflect some portion of her activities.

I have recently heard a number of labels pinned on other women. Think of the face of your own sister and replace her name with one of these labels, which dismiss her as

just a spinster
just a divorcee
just a feminist
just a libber
just a house frau
just a doormat
just an old maid
just a dried-up prune
just a blue-hair
just a weirdo.

To this list could be added an array of ethnic terms and unflattering adjectives.

While you are holding the image in your mind of your biological sister belittled under such a label, think again about who is your sister. In reality I have at least 3.4 million sisters who are the members of Relief Society around the world. Am I less alarmed when one of these sisters becomes the target of an effort to reduce her to a one-dimensional caricature rather than a multifaceted, brilliantly shining daughter of God? Perhaps the divisiveness of labels is part of what the prophet Nephi had in mind when he defined a righteous generation as being without "any manner of -ites." (4 Nephi 1:17.)

Our leaders in the war against evil have warned us repeatedly of the dangers of infighting. Elder Loren C. Dunn, for instance, asks us to "allow the qualities of mutual respect, mingled with charity and forgiveness, to influence our actions with one another; to be able to disagree without becoming disagreeable."[20] Infighting saps our energy and distracts us from our common goals.

DIRECTION FROM THE COMMANDER-IN-CHIEF

Our code as Christian soldiers, our handbook of instructions, is the scriptures. They reverberate with pleas for solidarity and refraining from judgment. They urge us to seek the unity that underlies a Zion society. (4 Nephi 1:17; Moses 7:18.) They remind, "Every [sisterhood] divided against itself is brought to desolation; and a house divided against a house falleth." (Luke 11:17; see also Mark 3:24–25; Matthew 12:25.) As sisters in the gospel, we have promised to bear one another's burdens, not increase them. (Mosiah 18:8; Galatians 6:2.) Moreover, we have been told by "Christ, the royal Master, / [who] Leads against the foe"[21] that, if we are not one, we are not his. (D&C 38:27.)

Women's particular criticism of other women is addressed in the scriptures. Jesus found it necessary to gently reprimand Martha for her efforts to require her sister Mary to conform to Martha's vision of proper behavior. (Luke 10:40–43.) Perhaps the message of the story of Mary and Martha was particularly aimed to our day. Martha's contribution in being "careful and troubled about many [good and important] things" is valuable. But it is "needful" also to allow Mary the "good part" she has chosen, which does not diminish Martha's contribution.

FORMING A LASTING ALLIANCE

As a law student in the 1970s, I had no women teachers; as a young lawyer in training, I had no women mentors. Now, I have been given a second chance. I learn more than I ever teach from the women who sit in my classrooms and who seek with me to find answers to the complexities of both life and law. Their insights and aspirations inspire me. I happened upon this declaration of personal commitment written this spring by one of my sister-students, Alison W. Brady: "Women are moral agents capable of choosing to recognize their similarities and affiliations with one another. I choose to do that. No other worldly association can benefit as much by my acknowledgment and preference to ally myself with it. I consider it a cherished obligation to stand with women of the world to eradicate injustice and promote righteousness."

The strength we need to resist evil and to find joy in these troubled times can be had only in unity with good and righteous women everywhere—our sisters—standing hand in hand encircling the world. Imagine the beauty and the power of a harmonious chorus of women's voices, in every language, and from every corner of the universe, singing boldly the third verse of the hymn "Onward, Christian Soldiers":

> Like a mighty army
> Moves the Church of God;
> [Sisters], we are treading
> Where the Saints have trod.
> *We are not divided;*
> *All one body we:*
> *One in hope and doctrine,*
> *One in charity.*
> Onward, Christian soldiers!
> Marching as to war,
> With the cross of Jesus
> Going on before.[22]

NOTES

1. Herbert Rosinski, as quoted in "The Continuing Relevance of *On War*," in Carl Von Clausewitz, *On War*, ed. and trans. Michael Howard and Peter Paret (Princeton: Princeton University Press, 1976), p. 45.

2. Ibid., p. 204.

3. Gordon B. Hinckley, "Five Million Members—A Milestone and Not a Summit," *Ensign*, May 1982, p. 46.

4. See Lowell Thomas, *With Lawrence in Arabia* (New York: Doubleday, 1967).

5. See Gordon B. Hinckley, "Rise to the Stature of the Divine Within You," *Ensign*, Nov. 1989, p. 96.

6. When I entered law school, only one major scholarly review focused on women and law; when I graduated there were two; and since 1987 at least two more have begun publication in each year. The first women's studies program was formally approved at San Diego State University in 1970. Women's studies courses are now offered at most major universities. The primary challenge facing the effort to compile a bibliography for women's studies in 1978 was to find enough legitimate reading material to use. The biggest challenge in redoing the bibliography in 1985 was winnowing down with ruthless selectivity the mass of literature worthy of inclusion. Catherine R. Loeb, Susan E. Searing, and Esther F. Stineman, *Women's Studies: A Recommended Core Bibliography, 1980–1985* (Littleton, Colo.: Libraries Unlimited, 1987), pp. xi–xii.

7. Nancy Chodorow, *The Reproduction of Mothering* (Berkeley: University of California Press, 1978); Carol Gilligan, *In a Different Voice* (Cambridge, Mass.: Harvard University Press, 1982); Christine A. Littleton, "Reconstructing Sexual Equality," 75 *California Law Review* (1987): 1279. See also Mary Field Belenky, et al., *Women's Ways of Knowing: The Development of Self, Voice, and Mind* (New York: Basic Books, 1986).

8. See, for example, Nina Darnton, "Mommy Vs. Mommy," *Newsweek*, 4 June 1990, p. 64; Judy Ernest, "Working or Nonworking, Moms on Defensive," *The Cleveland Plain Dealer*, 8 Aug. 1993, 5-H; Lynda Richardson, "Mommy Wars: On the Front Lines in Battle between Work-at-Homes vs. Career Mothers," *Chicago Tribune*, 11 Oct. 1992, p. 5.

9. Alecia Swasy, "Stay-at-Home Moms Are Fashionable Again in Many Communities," *Wall Street Journal*, 23 July 1993, A–8.

10. See, for example, Vincent Bozzi, "Assertiveness Breeds Contempt: Assertive Women Managers," *Psychology Today*, Sept. 1987, p. 15; Judy Klemesrud, "Special Relationship of Women and Their Mentors," *New York Times*, 11 Apr. 1983, A–22; Carol Krucoff, "Careers: 'Banking on Women,'" *Washington Post*, 14 Oct. 1980, B–5.

11. See Karen Schwartz, "Hating One's Own Kind: Bias or Human Nature?" *Los Angeles Times*, 29 Nov. 1992, A–3.

12. See, for example, Tom Campbell, "Out of the Pink," *Business First of Buffalo*, 19 Oct. 1987, sec. 1, p. 19; Shawn McCarthy, "Women Now Nearly Half of Work Force," *Toronto Star*, 3 Mar. 1993, A–12.

13. Schwartz, "Hating One's Own Kind," A–3.

14. Chieko N. Okazaki, *Lighten Up!* (Salt Lake City: Deseret Book Co., 1993), p. 137.

15. C. S. Lewis, *The Screwtape Letters*, rev. ed. (New York: American Reprint Co., 1961), p. 31.

16. See Laurel Thatcher Ulrich, "A Phi Beta Kappa Key and a Safety Pin," commencement address, University of Utah, Salt Lake City, Utah, 1992. Typescript in my possession.

17. See Ann N. Madsen, "Differences . . . Allow All Men the Same Privilege,'" in *BYU 1981–82 Fireside and Devotional Speeches* (Provo, Utah: Brigham Young University, 1982), pp. 183–88.

18. Gwynne Dyer, *WAR* (New York: Crown Publishers, 1985), p. 121.

19. Ibid., p. 119.

20. Loren C. Dunn, "Before I Build a Wall," *Ensign*, May 1991, p. 82.

21. *Hymns of The Church of Jesus Christ of Latter-day Saints* (Salt Lake City: The Church of Jesus Christ of Latter-day Saints, 1985), no. 246.

22. Ibid.; emphasis added.

A Valentine for Mel

EMMA LOU THAYNE

How much difference that we love?
Do you, knotted with concerns, need me
More for a head rub or for turning down the furnace
Or for explaining silence and its offering
Or for playfulness, the unbelievably enormous attractions
Or for seeing that things happen?

Waiting as we are today for four more days before we
Know why blood tests highlight a prostate like your
Yellow felt tip on a page of scripture,
Much as love would like, I cannot be with you on the
Inside any more than from this little distance
You can feel the spring that wakes in me,
Your wife watching the snow melt in the rain
And listening for your sweet whistle of arrival
Cradling me as I would cradle you
In the well-supported shape you have worried
And loved into our life.

My one hand holding tight to yours
I will come celebrate with you
That so far what has tried to kill us, either one,
Has not succeeded. And that for each other
Nothing ever will.

Emma Lou Thayne, a native of Salt Lake City, Utah, has twelve published books of fiction, nonfiction, and poetry and is a member of the board of directors of the Deseret News. *She contributes regularly to a variety of publications. She and her husband, Melvin E. Thayne, have five daughters and eighteen grandchildren.*

Punctuation of the Divine

LINDA HOFFMAN KIMBALL

As a writer I get a chuckle out of this song that Garrison Keillor, the radio celebrity, sings:

> Come along boys and have a glass a cider
> I'll tell you what it's like to be a freelance writer . . .
> Writing is easy and the money is great
> But it's hard to know how to punctuate . . .
> Comma ti yi yippie yippie yay yippie yay
> Comma ti yi yippie semicolon.[1]

I can't say I share his experience with the pay scale, but I do agree with him that learning to punctuate is tricky. When you work with words, it is sometimes hard to know when, for best effect, something should be a question or a statement or a declaration or a phrase. I think grappling with parts of speech and punctuation provides some interesting metaphors for our relationship with God.

Take the exclamation point, for example. We need a few of these in our lives. We need some givens—some core, unembellished, irrefutable YESes to anchor our beings. We need to recognize them and be thankful for them and celebrate them.

One of my favorite passages of scripture is in the book of Exodus, in which Moses talks to God in the burning bush. Moses asks what name God goes by so that he can know how to introduce God and explain this experience to the children of Israel waiting at the base of Mount Sinai. Exodus 3:14 gives God's response: "I AM THAT I AM." The point is clear. God just *is*. God describes himself as a verb, a state of being.

Linda Hoffman Kimball received a bachelor of arts degree from Wellesley College and a master of fine arts degree from Boston University. A homemaker, writer, poet, artist, Cub Scout den leader, genealogy buff, Relief Society counselor, and mom, she thinks of herself, therefore, as a juggler. She and her husband, Christian E. Kimball, have three children.

He is not preoccupied with defining himself. Succinct, to the point, vital and vibrant—God is the ultimate given.

The restored gospel provides other exclamation points for me. These are things that I treasure as revealed truths, seared into my own heart by the Holy Spirit. These are the reference points by which I judge everything else. These exclamation points are the things that, in Mormon parlance, I have a testimony of. Some aspects—like life beyond this, or the power of prayer, or the confirmation that a specific calling is God's idea and not just the bishop's—are brilliant, beautiful sparks flashing from and orbiting around these precious exclamation points. Though I wish I were surer about some things, apparently I have enough to go on for the moment. I would prefer more, but I have been granted what I have been granted and more will come as the Lord sees fit.

I am increasingly comfortable with this minimalist view. Partly this comfort comes from remembering the great and first commandment—to love the Lord with my whole being—and its companion pledge—to love my neighbor as myself. Partly this comfort comes from studying the eleventh chapter of Third Nephi, in which Christ gives over and over and over again a profoundly simple explanation of the gospel. And partly this comfort comes from learning the difference between exclamation points and other punctuation marks.

Take the period, for example—the full stop. I do not like them very much. During the course of my twenty-two years in the Church, I have heard a number of things presented as statements of fact, neat and complete with a full stop at the end. I weigh those things against my personal givens—my exclamation points. Sometimes I accept such sentences, and they help me in my life, in my relationships, in my communion with God. "Visiting teaching bonds sisters." "The Sabbath should be a separate kind of day." "Offer thanks for the food you eat." These are just a few sentences that I find really work.

There are others that I scratch my head about but go along with. Some examples of this type might be "Little children should be present during sacrament meeting," "Men should bounce babies when blessing them," or "Knowing how to brandish a glue gun is a vital homemaking skill."

There are other statements, made usually by well-meaning people who take complex issues, analyze them, sum them up, codify them, and lay them to rest. Period. Such statements are not limited to matters of faith. It is part and parcel of life in our Western civilization to want to define and resolve things. We as a society are uncomfortable with too much open-endedness. A *Time* magazine article about statistics gives a good example of this mind-set: "Mitch Snyder, the late activist for the homeless, once admitted that his figures on people without shelter were essentially meaningless. 'We have tried to satisfy your gnawing curiosity for a number,' he told a congressional hearing, 'because we are Americans with Western little minds that have to quantify everything in sight, whether we can or not.'"[2]

But when it comes to my spiritual life, putting periods where they don't belong can be dangerous to my spiritual health and well-being. I am wary of them. An example of that would be the proliferation years ago of explanations of why blacks could not hold the priesthood. I never heard an explanation that didn't make my heart ache or make me feel diminished as a sister. The only answer that fit at all was "We don't know." And HALLELUJAH! God hit the delete key, got rid of that period, got rid of that whole sentence, and set us to the work of widening our margins and getting ready for more.

Ours is a gospel that teaches believers to seek for further light and knowledge. That means that some sentences that seem to have periods on the end really need ellipses. Dot Dot Dot . . . Stay tuned! More to come! To be continued!

This ellipses aspect of the gospel is evidence of something alive, growing, dynamic. It is the hallmark of that marvelous concept of "continuing revelation." I am reminded of the time when I made bread dough with Rapid Rise yeast, snapped a plastic lid on the bowl, and put it in the refrigerator. A few hours later I opened the fridge and saw a huge, billowing, beige goo that had muscled its way up and over the Tupperware, casting the puny lid aside, and edging its way toward a terrified bunch of broccoli. Where there is life, nothing as ineffectual as a plastic lid—or a poorly placed period—can stop the flow.

Joseph Smith used a more poetic description: "What power shall stay the heavens? As well might [people] stretch forth [their] puny arm[s] to stop the Missouri river in its decreed course, or to turn it up stream, as to hinder the Almighty from pouring down knowledge from heaven upon the heads of the Latter-day Saints." (D&C 121:33.)

There is much I don't understand about Joseph Smith, but I believe he understood the life, the robustness, the fluid dynamics of God's gracious outpouring to seekers of truth. Think of what we now understand better because as a boy he asked a question in a grove of trees; because

his wife—fed up with a nasty clean-up job after tobacco-spitting men—
prodded him to ask more; because with a friend he asked for insight
into what heaven is like. I believe Joseph Smith was a champion of questions and ellipses and exclamation points. I believe that in those early
years there was such a flood coming in that there was neither the desire
nor the time to put a period down. It isn't surprising to me that the Book
of Mormon punctuation was put in after the fact.

In our lives now we ask God questions. They come in all shapes
and sizes from "Where did I put my keys?" to "What is the meaning of
life?"

Some are not really questions that have answers but realities that
defy analysis. For example, why is it that only by admitting my weaknesses I can become strong? Why is it that by letting go I gain control?
How is it that when I take on his yoke, my burden is light? These all
fall into the category I like to call "The Spiritual 'Huh?'"

As I mentioned, our Western approach to life gets a little twitchy
with this kind of thing. Oriental philosophy thrives on it. As we know,
anything that is true—regardless of where it is found—is part of our
gospel. I hear truth humming in this proverb from the Tao Te Ching
by Chinese philosopher Lao Tsu:

> Under heaven nothing is more soft and yielding than water.
> Yet for attacking the solid and strong, nothing is better.
> It has no equal.
> The weak can overcome the strong.
> The supple can overcome the stiff. . . .
> He who takes upon himself the humiliation of the people is
>   fit to rule them. . . .
> The truth often sounds paradoxical.[3]

In my own life I have plenty of questions. Sometimes my assessment of where they fit on the "lost keys to the meaning of life" scale
does not mesh with God's assessment. Take, for example, the odd
interweaving of our dog with my husband's career plans.

Last summer our big, goofy, wonderful eighteen-month-old puppy
got sick. Very sick. After three months of watching this poor pooch
dwindle despite considerable efforts by specialist veterinarians and considerable expense on our part, we had to have him put down. We were
all heartsick. I felt as if some major organ had been removed from me.
The autopsy revealed the dog had an inoperable brain tumor. The

breeder, who was also saddened by the news, promised us another puppy, although she said she would not likely have a litter for another year.

Meanwhile, my husband, Chris, decided to shift careers. Last fall he began interviewing for teaching jobs at various places around the country. Weighing all the pros and cons was exhausting. God seemed not to have a preference, and we were left to sort things out without any particular divine nudge. I pleaded for some direction.

During the final month of interviewing, I began to get what most people would call "baby hungry," although in my case it was "dog hungry." It even seemed something worth mentioning in my prayers. I told friends I had the odd sensation that when we finally made a decision about my husband's professional life, the breeder would call and say her dog was pregnant. There was something cosmic—something in the vibes—about a dog for us, and it had something to do with the job.

While Chris was at his last interview, the breeder called. She had an eight-month-old puppy whose owners could no longer give it the attention it needed. Were we interested in owning him?

We didn't need to think twice. We went out the next day and brought home our beautiful, obedient, *housebroken* puppy, whom we named Worthy.

We still didn't know which job to take. Nothing seemed resolved in that department. I asked myself, Why doesn't God answer my weighty prayers about something as important as our professional future, my children's social, educational, and spiritual environment, my own network of friends and loved ones? With all of these questions bombarding him all my waking hours, why does he brush them aside and send us a dog?

I believe it was God's way of giving me a Bart Simpson kind of message: Don't have a cow . . . have a puppy!

I asked God about this one night at my bedside, and we had a most delightful conversation. I had the sense that God was saying, "What I really want to know is what kind of questions you will ask about this career shift. I want to see what things you think are important to consider as you face this decision. I want to see how you sort out things, weigh all the options, choose your priorities. And, Linda, you are doing just fine. You will be OK."

I felt good humor from the Lord. I felt acceptance. I felt embraced by a love I can't express adequately.

God knew the hole left inside me when our first dog died. He gave me this new dog as a gift to a grieving heart and as an evidence that he knows me intimately, knows my circumstances, and knows my questions. What he most wants me to know is that I am known and I am loved.

I also believe that he who knows when sparrows fall, heard the unbarked prayers of a dog and placed Worthy with us for protection and affection and for that creature's best welfare. (I have a dot, dot, dot after that one.)

Eventually we did come to a decision about where to go. We will be moving to Boston in a few months. I still haven't felt a burning confirmation that this was "the right" choice, but after my little bedside exchange, I'm not really expecting one. All things considered, the future looks bright indeed.

I want to tell you about another time involving my questions to the Lord, a time in the past that looked very gloomy. Some years ago a string of horrible things happened. My dear former boyfriend committed suicide. A Church leader I knew well was excommunicated for adultery. A very close family friend died in a plane crash, leaving a wife and two young children.

I was shaken to the core. Sentences that I had taken as facts crumbled into dust: Church leaders lead righteous lives. Life is good. Living a godly life can protect you.

Even my exclamation points disappeared in a fog. I wondered whether anything I had ever trusted was real. Though I kept doing the "iron rod" things—like going to Church, doing my visiting teaching, and showing all the external signs of faith—internally I was gutted. Nothing seemed real or true or trustworthy anymore.

It was also at this time that a relative started sending me articles about why the Book of Mormon couldn't possibly be divinely inspired. I remember kneeling night after night—in case there really was a God—following that admonition we always hear, "I would exhort you that ye would ask God . . . if these things be true . . . " You know the one.

One night in particular I knelt and prayed again for the bzillionth time, "Is the Book of Mormon true?" As I got up to brush my teeth, something communicated to me these precise words: "You're asking the wrong question. What you need to ask is 'where does the Lord want you?'" No sooner had the question been formed than the answer was clear: "God wants me here in The Church of Jesus Christ of Latter-day Saints."

To me that was evidence not only that there was a God out there but that this God knew me! He knew me so well that he, being my Editor as well as my Creator, not only heard my question but rephrased it for me. He knew my questions and my worries and my fears, and he accepted me, valued me, approved of me—and wanted me in this Church. He didn't answer my intellectual questions—there are still a lot of things I don't understand—but he gave me what I needed to move ahead out of that abyss of grief and confusion. He gave me faith to move despite unanswered questions.

I am impressed by God's creativity in communicating to me. Sometimes when I think I am doing things the right way—praying the proper prayers, asking the expected questions, reading the predictable sources—God will surprise me with insight from unexpected sources— a dog, a rephrased prayer, a spiritual impression from a Chinese philosopher or a cartoon character. God is so much more resourceful, so very expansive, so much bigger than I generally give him credit for.

One night when I was distraught about some other unresolved issue in my life, I picked up the Bible in the translation familiar to me from my childhood. I read a passage in Psalms and knew God was speaking directly to me. It sums up for me the mood I need to have in order to cope. This is Psalm 131: "O Lord, my heart is not lifted up, my eyes are not raised too high; I do not occupy myself with things too great and too marvelous for me. But I have calmed and quieted my soul, like a child quieted at its mother's breast; like a child that is quiet is my soul."[4]

I have fun exploring the symbolism of parts of speech and punctuation in my dealings with God. Of course, God is far beyond the limits of language, clauses, or tenses. I thank him for enveloping me in a nurturing love that quiets my sometimes troubled soul. I praise him for knowing me well enough to customize my answers—even my questions. I celebrate a living God who knows me intimately and who is not finished with me or with his work yet. I rejoice in the divine love evident in every answer, every question, every silence, every nuance of communion with my God.

NOTES

1. Garrison Keillor, "Freelance Writer," in *Prairie Home Comedy: Radio Songs and Sketches* (St. Paul: Minnesota Public Radio, 1988). Used by permission.

2. Anastasia Toufexis, "Damned Lies and Statistics," *Time*, 26 Apr. 1993, p. 28.

3. Lao Tsu, *Tao Te Ching*, trans. Gia-Fu Feng and Jane English (New York: Vintage Books, 1972), no. 78.

4. Psalm 131, Revised Standard Version. In this case, the King James Version did not have the same effect on me. KJV Psalm 131:2 reads: "I have behaved and quieted myself, as a child that is weaned of his mother: my soul is even as a weaned child." Having breast-fed children, I find that the image of a "weaned" child does not communicate the intimacy and nourishment that the phrase "a child quieted at its mother's breast" conjures. Also, in times of stress, being told to "behave" is just one more pressure and source of guilt. "Calming and quieting my soul" is for me a much more freeing, peaceful image.

Redeeming Reality:
Images of Women's Lives

SHARON LEE ESPLIN SWENSON

I believe there are connections on many levels between photographs and feelings. Something happens to us when we take photographs, when photographs are taken of us, and when we look at
photographs. My comments have a scholarly dimension based on several concepts currently important in the academic criticism of film and
photography,[1] but my comments are also very personal, involving
photographic images of me and my family. I'm using myself as an
example, you see, hoping that you will feel an irresistible temptation
to pull out your own family photo album and look at yourselves in a
new way.

Does that sound dangerous? Well, reality *is* dangerous, but we're
talking about redeeming reality, redeeming it from its inevitable fall
into distortion and despair, redeeming it into revelation. What I'm talking about is becoming seers in its broader meaning of "see-er," one who
sees. By profession, I'm a seer. I really love to look. It's been my blessing to find the ideal job. I get paid to look at movies and photographs
all day and then talk about them.

Seeing a photograph—looking at a photograph—seems like an
automatic action. It's something that occurs instinctively, naturally, physiologically: I look at you, you look at me. But seeing is really a social
act, one mediated and shaped by our culture. Our eyes register the image,
but what our brain registers is the *meaning* of the image. It assigns function, significance, even symbolism to the physical image that our eye
scans physiologically.

What is that meaning? It is identity. We construct our own identities,

Sharon Lee Esplin Swenson, an assistant professor of theater and film at Brigham Young
University has specialized in critical studies in film history and theory and is interested
in gender and family in film. Sister Swenson teaches the Gospel Doctrine class in her
Salt Lake City ward. She and her husband, Paul, are the parents of two children.

those of other people, and that of the world we inhabit by creating meaning for images as we identify and label them. This interaction is two-sided. Let me give you an example. I'm standing in front of you speaking. Although you assign meaning to what you see, I constructed this image that you're seeing. I thought about what I'd wear, how I wanted to look, how to do my hair, how much make-up to put on. I always wear nylons at BYU and never wear sandals, because I want to have the credibility that comes from a formal, take-charge, in-control image. It took a lot of time and energy to put myself together. I want to impress you. I want to be believed. (I'm revealing my vulnerability and insecurity on this issue because even though I know it's silly, a part of me actually believes I can create my identity by how I look. I can control what you think of me and even who I am by what physical image I present.)

So I drove this carefully, even artfully, constructed image of myself to BYU today, and one of my colleagues just told me I'd overdone my mascara. Well, of course I panicked. Was it true? Was I coming across as a circus clown instead of an impressive, professional professor? And *mascara!* My most vulnerable point!

You need to understand that mascara is important to me, very important. When I was learning what I should look like, I pored over pictures of women. (I still do.) I looked at pictures of women in magazines, in movies, on television, on book covers, and on the back of Kotex boxes. Every beautiful woman, every smart woman in every one of those images had eyelashes. But the awful truth I learned as a teenager was that my eyelashes are so pale that they look as if I was in some other line when they were handed out. So today I suppressed my moment of panic. I did *not* race to the restroom and scrub my face. I tilted my head a little to the left, batted those overdone eyelashes, cooed, "Oh, really?" and sailed off down the hall. I would rather trust the eyelash image I have in my head than the image in my colleague's head. And that's what you're seeing now: the constructed image of myself as a professional woman. With eyelashes.

Photographs show us our surfaces, how other people perhaps see us, but they can also show us ourselves if we learn to see. Photographs are links between the physical and spiritual worlds even though they seem to be renderings of physical experience—as nonspiritual as you can get. A light-sensitive, flexible medium (the film) must be exposed to a source of light within a machine that controls the exact amount of exposure. It's a mechanical and chemical process. What could be more physical? But photography is a metaphor for identity because that's the exact process required for us to grow spiritually. A light-sensitive, flexible medium (that's us) must be exposed to a source of light (the Spirit), under circumstances that create meaning (the gospel and our earthly experiences).

To me, these parallels are very profound. The vision required to look at photographs summons meaning into existence, in the same way that God's saying, "Let there be light," summoned into existence the illumination by which all the rest of creation became aware of itself. The creation of meaning, the creation of identity, can be godlike in the same way.

Now, let me explain some principles related to film theory that are important to understanding and reading photographs. First, photographs have the potential of making us see reality afresh. Siegfried Kracauer, a scholar of German films of the thirties, described the power of visual images to redeem physical reality.[2] Most of us have probably had the experience of looking at a photograph and suddenly being struck by something that is a common part of our world but that we have never really noticed before—the extraordinary beauty of ordinary leaves on an ordinary tree, which we see for the first time in close-up. A photograph has the potential of making us see a physical reality that is lost to us in our day-to-day life.

I'm convinced that even the most ordinary photographs are important. Sometimes when we look at snapshots, we discount the ones that do not record singular, important occasions such as baptisms, weddings, or anniversaries. More often, we simply didn't get the camera out for events we are likely to forget without a photo of them. The dailiness of life is dismissed as too ordinary. Laurel Thatcher Ulrich won the Pulitzer Prize for history for her book *A Midwife's Tale*, which is based on the journal of a New England woman named Martha Ballard in the late eighteenth and early nineteenth centuries. It was a diary that many other historians had overlooked or minimized because it was so ordinary, with such short entries about such very common events. "It is in the very dailiness, the exhaustive, repetitious dailiness, that the real power of Martha Ballard's book lies," Ulrich commented.[3] I suggest that Laurel's own life as the mother of five children, as a religious woman, as a housekeeper, a gardener, and a quilter uniquely prepared her, in a way that male historians had not been prepared, to perceive

Martha Ballard's reality and interpret it for an audience two hundred years later. Laurel redeemed Martha Ballard from obscurity by making us see the meaning of her everyday physical life. Photographs have the potential of making us see our own reality afresh.

Second, semiotics, or the science of signs, has made us aware that we see by interpreting signs that are part of encoded meaning, systems, or codes. Semioticians argue that no element or aspect exists independently from all others; rather, each aspect and its meaning exist only in relation to something else. Our reality, in other words, is a complex social act that is created by experience, image, and the meaning we assign to both. The relevance of this concept to reading photographs is obvious. Photographic images are always related to a reality that pre-existed and to our own feelings about it. My feelings about my eyelashes, for instance, cannot be understood separately from photographs of women with long, beautifully darkened and beautifully curving eyelashes. But I don't have that team of photographers and make-up people to sustain the eyelash reality I want, which probably accounts for my colleague's comment on my mascara.

A third relevant concept from film theory is that of "the gaze." Film theoreticians argue that the camera has a controlling gaze or point of view. It records whatever it is focused on, which means that it calls that chosen set of images into being in a specific way, emphasizing certain powerful relationships, while ignoring all else. This gives the camera immense force. But in addition to the physical objects it records, it simultaneously calls into being certain meanings, or subjective realities. Decades of Hollywood films have portrayed women as pretty and passive objects to be perceived or gazed at by active men. Film critics argue that one effect of years of film watching has been to objectify norms of female identity. Both women and men see men as acting subjects in a scene, women as objects inviting the viewer's appraisal. In other words, we as women think of ourselves more as objects when we see a photograph or image of ourselves than men think when they see photographs or images of themselves.

Fourth, in addition to recording reality, giving more privilege to some realities than to others, and creating meanings for those realities, photographs can actually replace reality. The social critic Susan Sontag talks about how photographs function as metaphors or substitutes for our experiences.[4] When we go on a trip, we're so busy taking photos and capturing images that we don't have the experience itself. On a vacation, have you ever been distracted from contemplating the view by the request to "Hold it there. Let me take a picture! Smile!" And after a while you want to ask the shutterbug to take a leap over the edge of the nearest historic landmark because you want to *have* the experience of the place, not take photographs of it.

Let me give you an example even closer to home. It's time for the family portrait. The children are being bratty, your husband isn't helping, the photographer is losing patience, and while you're trying to comb somebody's hair for the third time, you hiss under your breath, "I'll snatch you bald-headed if you move one more time!" Then you turn around, curve your arm lovingly around this child, and smile angelically for the camera. Now what's reality—your feelings at the moment or that image on film? The answer, of course, is both.

Fifth, interaction with a photograph has a spiritual quality to it because of the multiplicity of meaning that a photograph contains. Even though they are flat, two-dimensional surfaces, they contain history, a record of events and emotions. They activate memory. Looking at any family photograph or snapshot of yourself creates an interaction between the person you are now and the person you were then. A photograph moves you through time and space. I want to argue that this interaction is a spiritual one. When we understand reality from a different perspective, there is always an opportunity for the Holy Ghost to speak to us. I want to insist on the aspect of spirituality. The Spirit speaks to us through the dailiness of our lives, not just the Mount Sinais of them. Often the most ordinary photographs have the most to tell. Yet we frame the pictures of reunions, weddings, or graduations and file away the photos of the four-year-old with a milk moustache or the six-year-old playing with the kitten on the back lawn because they're so ordinary, so daily. When we see with our spiritual eyes, we can see reality more accurately and assign meanings of greater significance.

To summarize the academic part of this paper, then, there are five principles of film criticism that are useful in helping us view photographs. First, photographs can create reality afresh for us. Second, we see by decoding a system of signs and meanings that come from our past experience. Third, the gaze of the camera helps create that system of signs by what it focuses on, or privileges, and by what it excludes. Fourth, photographs can actually replace reality, with image becoming more important than reality. Fifth, there is a spiritual aspect of interacting with a photograph because it can be an invitation for revelation.

Let's consider for a moment the process of having a photograph taken of ourselves. I try in every way I can think of to arrange reality, and then I collaborate with the camera to arrange reality still further. But if you're like me, you always see only the flaws. Do I see my perfect mascara, my professional and elegant suit, my sophisticated yet feminine earrings? I do not. I see my double chin, the bags under my eyes, and those insidious gray hairs threading their way through my carefully constructed chignon.

Only once did I succeed in creating a flawless image. Five years ago, soon after I was hired at BYU, the Public Communications office took my photograph for a story. Well, it's going to be my obituary photograph thirty years from now. A student of mine who specialized in make-up did my face so I had cheekbones. I sat up tall, and the photographer said, "Now, turn your body this way. Twist your head this way. Now tilt your chin up." And my double chin disappeared! That was a miracle. This was the photograph that I want everybody to believe I was forever! In fact, my shameless fascination with that photograph may have been the genesis of my remarks today.

But that was the only time I managed to pull it off. Imogene Cunningham, a wonderful portrait photographer, was speaking from experience when she said, "No one really likes to have a picture of themselves. Anyone else. But we don't look good enough." I know exactly what she meant. For how many of us is the first look at a photograph a reflex of dangerous materialism? "If I just had better make-up!" "If I bought a new dress . . . ?" "After I lose five pounds . . ."

That perfect photograph of me was not me. In fact, it wasn't even a replication of the way I feel inside. It was an arrangement of an image. It showed me what I desperately wanted to be. But the real me is more complex. True, one layer is the image of that beautifully arranged woman; but another layer is the reality of the double chin, the bags under the eyes, and the gray hair. Yet another layer is someone who needs— and sometimes has—the gift of charity to the extent that she can accept and love both the vain and glossy image and the desperately insecure and self-critical woman. The Spirit tells me *that's* the right way to look at ourselves. We should look with the eyes of love.

Photographs of ourselves and others are wonderful tools for insight, if we look with the eyes of love. We can move beyond our past experiences, learn a new semiotics, change our gaze to a loving one, recreate, reinterpret, and redeem our reality. Photographs freeze a moment in time for us. They hold up a reality for us to look at. If we look at them with the eyes of love, we can redeem our inner reality from the outer image.

For example, I cherish a photograph of my daughter Caitlin, age eleven, holding her kitten, and standing next to my father on our front lawn. I took this photograph, admired it, and tucked it into the shoebox where we store mementoes. The kitten grew up, became a cat, and died. Caitlin also grew up and, at age fifteen, became so angry with me that she was threatening to leave home. When I thought she might actually start packing, I sneaked that photograph out of the shoebox in her room because I wanted something to remember her by. (If you have adolescent daughters, you know what I'm talking about.) It was important to me to have this image of my beautiful daughter at age eleven, standing with her grandfather, worried only about lifting up her kitten's face so the camera could get it. It comforted me when I had a daughter who hated me most of the time, and whom, to be honest, I hated part of the time, too. (It was certainly poor planning for God to schedule her adolescence and my midlife crisis at the same time.)

It was important during that time to look at photos of the eleven-year-old Caitlin and at Caitlin as a baby, a beautiful gift that God gave me and my husband, Paul, and Caitlin at age four, holding her baby brother. I could see her smiling at the world, smiling at me, and suddenly Caitlin was back with me. The daughter I loved was real to me. And I could think to myself, She'll be back. And guess what? Now she's almost sixteen, she didn't leave home, we've both survived, and we even have whole sequences of days when we get along and like each other. The eyes of love saw a truer image than our contemporary reality.

I dug deeper into my own photograph album and found a snapshot of a very skinny boy standing on the seat of a tricycle in a swim suit, every rib showing, holding up his arms with his fists clenched to show off his (nonexistent) weight-lifting muscles. Beside him stands a little blonde girl in a hula skirt. That is my brother Fred, age eight, and me, age nine, dressed up for a neighborhood circus in Cedar City, Utah. Fred was the strong man, I the exotic Hawaiian. I was only thirteen months older, but I felt like his mother, responsible, protective, utterly loving.

And then I remember how angry I was a few years later when I thought, "Why does he get all the breaks? He got to drive the car before I did, even though I'm a better driver and more responsible, just because he was a guy." Then I remember how frustrated my brother felt because all his schoolteachers had taught me the year before and expected him to excel at academics the way I did. And I felt equally unhappy as his appendage because he became the fabulous baseball and basketball player, and everybody said, "Oh, you're Freddy's sister." This mutually resentful stage of our lives lasted for about ten years.

But now Fred is six foot eight. He has a very impressive beard, and nobody talks to either one of us about sports or academics too much. When I defended my dissertation a few weeks ago, I was totally burned out, exhausted, and fed up with academics; but Fred was excited enough for both of us. He radiated pride and delight. When the committee told me I had passed and I staggered out of the examination room, Fred was bouncing up and down, all six-foot-eight of him, grinning from ear to ear, and asking, "Can I call Mom and Dad and tell them? Can I?"

Now, that's quite a bit of experience and emotion to be generated by a snapshot of a skinny little eight-year-old in a swim suit, posing like a circus strong man. But it was all there in the photograph for me when I looked at it.

Now let's consider that little blonde girl in the hula skirt. I can't really see her. *I* never looked like that. I was never that pretty. No matter what kind of skirt I was wearing, I was never that cute. I was a clumsy, awkward, "don't-know-what-to-do" girl who spent her whole adolescence wishing she were radically different. So who is this very pretty little blonde girl in the photograph? Well, according to the camera, that's how I looked. Why can I look at my brother and see all of our relationship— love, frustration, pride, pulling together—and then look at that little blonde and not recognize her at all? When I look with the eyes of love, I redeem a reality that I spent most of my life denying because I saw myself so differently, because I put so much energy into wishing I were different, denying what I really looked like.

Photography can allow us to reenter moments that are part of our past. We can be there again with all the sights and smells. A photograph of my grandmother standing next to her Peace rosebush in front of her red-brick house in Orderville lets me step back into summer with her, taste the V-8 juice she kept cold in her refrigerator, hear the tick of the clock on the mantle, smell the cedar shavings from my grandfather's workshop, finger Grandmother's old-fashioned, flowered apron, and love her. All this happens to me when I look at the photograph. I see with the eyes of love. I become a seer. I know her love for me. Those memories of time past become real to me when I see an image of my grandmother, now dead these thirty years.

Truly seeing photographs can help us see ourselves and our experiences in their redeemed reality. We can rethink our past selves and our present identities. We see multiple perspectives, understand more than one meaning. There is a depth, a dimensionality in our daily lives that its very dailiness hides from us. Such moments of revelation, of transcendence may come in prayer, in song, in caressing the hand of a loved one. Images, rather than being artificial arrangements of reality, can become truer visions of what the world is and of who we are. Redeemed from the blindness that normally covers our eyes, we become seers.

NOTES

1. I thank Billy Plunkett, archivist and curator of photography at BYU's Harold B. Lee Library, and Kay Egan, associate professor of communications at BYU, for sharing their insights on the photographic work of Elfie Huntington and Edith Irvine, two women who recorded images of Utah and California around the turn of the century and whose work stimulated this presentation.

2. Siegfried Kracauer, "Basic Concepts" and *"The Cabinet of Dr. Caligari"* in *Film Theory and Criticism*, ed. Gerald Mast, Marshall Cohen, and Leo Braudy (New York and Oxford: Oxford University Press, 1992), pp. 9–33.

3. Laurel Thatcher Ulrich, *A Midwife's Tale: The Life of Martha Ballard, Based on Her Diary, 1785–1812* (New York: Knopf, Vantage Books, 1991), p. 9.

4. Susan Sontag, *On Photography* (New York: Farrar, Straus and Giroux, 1977), pp. 1–24.

When My Mother Visits

NEIDY MESSER

This time I don't react
to her comments
about how I'd look younger
with a new hairstyle.
When she waves her hand around
this room and that one, listing
ideas for making them livable,
I'm not offended.

I notice instead the slight
tremor of her hand
as she lifts the teacup,
the way her fingers no longer straighten
when she sets the cup on the saucer.
At night I bring her a blanket,
sit by the bed. While she retells
the crimps and pleats of her life,
I remember us, how every morning
she'd pull my hair into long ribbons and curls,
and how, just outside the door,
I'd pull the ribbons out,
shake the curls loose.

Neidy Messer lives in Boise, Idaho, with her husband, Bill Messer, and their two sons. She teaches English at Boise State College and was the Idaho Writer-in-Residence, 1990–91. A book of her poems, In Far Corners, has been published, and she is working on another volume. Sister Messer serves in her ward Relief Society.

Recording Women's Lives

JESSIE L. EMBRY

Women have always recorded their life experiences but in a variety of ways. Some kept journals. Laurel Thatcher Ulrich showed how valuable these can be in her *Midwife's Tale,* which is based on the diary of Martha Ballard, a midwife in eighteenth-century New England.[1] Other women expressed hopes and dreams in poetry. We sing the stories of Eliza R. Snow in "O My Father" and of Emmeline B. Wells in "Our Mountain Home So Dear." Others used autobiographies and letters, such as Ida Hunt Udall's family letters or her compassionate story of her life on the underground during the polygamy raids. Her autobiography and letters are included in Maria Ellsworth's *Mormon Odyssey.*[2]

But some women will never write their stories, and their experiences will be lost both to their posterity and to others. Fortunately, tape recorders can capture narratives without all the pain of struggling over words. A woman can tell her life story to an interested person and a machine and preserve it for the future.

What makes a good interview? For a moment imagine that you are being interviewed. What are you going to tell the interviewer sitting across from you?

I have been conducting oral history interviews since 1973, and I have interviewed a variety of women. My most successful exchanges have been with those who have been open and willing to share. These narrators were not afraid to tell what they felt, to reveal themselves as they really are. When I worked for the James Moyle Oral History Program at the Church's Historical Department, I was given the delightful assignment of interviewing Camilla Eyring Kimball. Although I had already

Jessie L. Embry is the director of the Oral History Program of the Charles Redd Center for Western Studies and an instructor of history at Brigham Young University. She is the author of Mormon Polygamous Families: Life in the Principle *and the forthcoming* Black Saints in a White Church: Contemporary African-American Mormons. *She serves in her ward Primary.*

talked to her brother about his experiences in a polygamous family, I was worried about asking the prophet's wife, "Tell me about growing up in a polygamous family." But I didn't have to do that. As we discussed the purpose of the interviews, Sister Kimball said to me, "I came from a polygamous family. I think we should recount that story." Those of you who have read her autobiography know of her honesty. She recalls, for example, that she was so unhappy when she found out that her father had married her mother's sister that when she was to set the table for dinner she gave Aunt Emma the oldest silverware.[3]

Sometimes honesty can be painful. I interviewed Esther Jarvis Young and Pearl Jarvis Augustus, for example, about their experiences in a polygamous family. The family was splintered with the death of the second wife and then the father. Pearl was "farmed out" to various families as, essentially, a maid. Although she had felt the first family was treated better, she had overcome her feelings of resentment years afterward when I interviewed her. She had learned to love her half-brothers and half-sisters.

Esther was one of those half-sisters. She recognized some of the inequities in her father's family and felt sorry for them. She had also been married and divorced several times and felt her former husbands had turned her children against her. I talked to Esther for about an hour, and she cried the entire time. But when I left, she gave me roses and thanked me for coming. It had been therapeutic for her to express her feelings.

I have also interviewed minority members of the Church, and they have been very honest. Natalie Palmer-Taylor, an African American, talked about a painful incident of discrimination that she experienced when she moved to Utah. She forthrightly declared that she did not think it was possible for her to be very close to white Latter-day Saints because her cultural experiences were so different.[4] Others told of the pain they felt when they were not accepted, and yet at the same time they spoke of experiences they had shared with white Latter-day Saints.

In their honesty, these minority members suggested ways that Mormons can improve their relationships with people whose backgrounds are different from their own. Helen Kennedy, a black Latter-day Saint from Ogden, Utah, wanted Mormons to be less "cliquish. I don't like them to just do everything for LDS people."[5] Donna Fifita, a Sioux married to a Tongan, felt she had to prove to other Mormons she was not "an Indian that would be inactive, an alcoholic, or whatever stereotype they had towards Native Americans."[6] Imelda Lom, a Latina, wanted North American Mormons to stop feeling superior to members from other countries.[7]

I have, of course, conducted interviews in which the narrators were less than honest. Although I have found far fewer problems in polygamous families than some would like to imagine, I am skeptical when an interviewed person says everything was perfect. I have never seen a monogamous family that was completely flawless! I also am concerned if a minority Latter-day Saint tells only positive experiences or only negative interactions with whites. We all have both. The best interviews result from a probing of the complexities of real life, not from either a too rosy or too cloudy picture.

Most of the interviews I have conducted have been on a specific topic. Sometimes the narrators simply answer the questions in dry, unimaginative ways. Those interviews provide good research material for papers or articles or books. But they are not fun interviews to conduct or to read. The best interviews are with people who tell stories. For example, I have interviewed women who "fought" the war from the home front during World War II. I know that Americans were encouraged to buy war bonds, but what makes the interviews valuable are stories like Gloria Robison's, who was a child living in Wyoming during the war. She recalled rationing, school clothes "made over from my aunt's old clothing," and losing all the men teachers in high school to the war. She also recalled selling her horse to help her class win a schoolwide bond drive competition. "I had a horse named Sally. I had raised her from a colt, and she was my pride and joy. I wanted my class to win the war bond drive so badly that I sold her to a neighbor who lived next door for enough to buy one war bond. That would be about $18.75. Then the rest of my stay at home I had to see the neighbor kids riding around on her. They wouldn't let me near her. That was really a sad thing." Years later she wondered if that sacrifice was really necessary.[8]

In telling stories, don't be afraid to let your emotions show. Although it may be embarrassing sometimes to cry and very difficult to express such emotions in writing, those are the very stories that add life to the interview. In an article about the stories told by his mother, folklorist William A. Wilson explained, "Reduced to cold print, the stories may not seem particularly artful. But if you could have been there during the tellings, if you could have seen my mother's gestures and facial

expressions, if you could have heard her voice rise into excited exclamation, drop now to a hushed whisper, move to a dry chuckle, break
into tears . . . you would have understood their power to excite my fancy,
engage my sympathies, and move me with joy or terror."⁹ For many of
the reasons that Wilson describes, we always preserve both the tape
and the transcript. Those who want the "facts" can quickly read the typescript; those who want the "emotion" must slowly absorb the experience through the tape.

Wilson relates one story that his mother sobbed in telling. She was
remembering when her grandfather's favorite horses, Cap and Seal,
were accidentally given poison oats meant for the squirrels. When her
uncle Jim brought word to her grandfather that the horses were dead,
she remembered, "All of us started to cry." Someone soon noticed that
Grandpa had gone. They worried. But then "Mama kind of had an idea.
She went out to the old outside toilet, and he was sitting in there crying."¹⁰ Wilson's mother loved her grandfather so much that she still
ached for him years later, remembering his sorrow that day.

As you tell specific stories and let your emotions show through, your
unique personality will radiate throughout the interview. To illustrate,
let me share some short excerpts from Shirley Moore's interview. Shirley
is a Native American who lives in Orem. Her daughter Angela was in
my oral history class and interviewed her mother. I love listening to
Shirley's oral history because it reveals her character. It's *her* interview.
She was not afraid to say what she thought!

When Angela asked her mother about living in Orem, Shirley
explained, "I really liked it a lot for a while. But I'm not liking it so much
any more. Am I allowed to be really honest? I found out that I have a
prejudice, and it's against Utah Mormons. I mean that in the true sense
of the word. It's not that I dislike all Utah Mormons. I certainly don't.
I think I prejudge because most of them I see taking things for granted.
I get the impression that they feel like if you're not a Mormon in Utah,
it's like you're not a real Mormon."

Shirley added, "I do like living here though because I feel like our
kids have opportunities to do all sorts of things that they couldn't do
back home." She recalled her experiences growing up on the Parker
Indian reservation. She was "torn between being a Wild Indian and a
good Mormon girl." She didn't want that for her children. "I think, 'Back
home what is there to do? Well, it's let's get drunk or go in the bushes.'
There are other things for them to do in Parker, but it's just there's not

that much variety. I think that if we were in Parker, our kids would be like me. I think they would lean towards being wild little Indians."[11]

I especially enjoyed Shirley's definition of heaven. When Angela asked her mother if she wanted to add anything to the interview, Shirley declared: "This is my idea of the celestial kingdom. We're going to wear long white T-shirts because they are so comfortable. We're going to eat pepperoni pizza from Pizza Hut, seafood won tons from Bamboo Hut, almond honey yogurt from the Cougareat, and maybe some of the fruit bars from the hospital cafeteria snack bar. That's going to be celestial food. We will listen to harp music because it really is beautiful, but no organ music. We'll also listen to Four Tops and Smoky Robinson. We probably won't listen to the Supremes but maybe a little Marvin Gaye. We're not going to play Monopoly or Scrabble or any competitive games. We might play a little volleyball, but it'll be just for fun." She continued: "I hope you realize I haven't been entirely serious. But I haven't really taken this assignment lightly either. If you care to, I want you to know the real me, not someone trying to make an impression by being profound. Heavens, I couldn't be profound if I tried."

Shirley concluded with a touching testimony and expressed her love for her family. And then she added: "And yes, I would like to get to the celestial kingdom, even if it may not be as I described."[12]

If family members talk to you about your life stories, I hope you will remember these keys: Be yourself, share your emotions, tell stories, and be honest. Then your posterity will not put you on a pedestal and have to reach for the impossible heights they thought you had set. And historians like me will bless you.

NOTES

1. Laurel Thatcher Ulrich, *A Midwife's Tale: The Life of Martha Ballard, Based on Her Diary, 1785–1812* (New York: Knopf, Vantage Books, 1991).

2. Maria S. Ellsworth, *Mormon Odyssey: The Story of Ida Hunt Udall, Plural Wife* (Urbana and Chicago: University of Illinois Press, 1992).

3. Caroline Eyring Miner and Edward L. Kimball, *Camilla: A Biography of Camilla Eyring Kimball* (Salt Lake City: Deseret Book Co., 1980), p. 13.

4. Natalie Palmer-Taylor Oral History, interviewed by Alan Cherry, 1985, LDS Afro-American Oral History Project, Charles Redd Center for Western Studies, Manuscript Division, Harold B. Lee Library, Brigham Young University, Provo, Utah, pp. 29–30.

5. Helen Mae Thompson Kennedy Oral History, interviewed by Alan Cherry, 1986, LDS Afro-American Project, p. 14.

6. Donna Fifita Oral History, interviewed by Odessa Neaman, 1990, LDS Native American Oral History Project, Charles Redd Center for Western Studies, Manuscript Division, Harold B. Lee Library, Brigham Young University, Provo, Utah, p. 11.

7. Imelda Lom Oral History, interviewed by Andrea Van Wagenen, 1992, LDS Hispanic Oral History Project, Charles Redd Center for Western Studies, Manuscript Division, Harold B. Lee Library, Brigham Young University, Provo, Utah, p. 3.

8. Gloria Dawn Adams Robison Oral History, interviewed by Michael Van Wagenen, 1991, World War II Home Front Oral History Project, Charles Redd Center for Western Studies, Manuscript Division, Harold B. Lee Library, Brigham Young University, Provo, Utah, pp. 2–3.

9. William Wilson, "Personal Narratives: The Family Novel," *Western Folklore* 50 (April 1991): 135.

10. Ibid., p. 147.

11. Shirley Esquerra Moore Oral History, interviewed by Angela Moore Fields, 1990, LDS Native American Project, pp. 9–10, 6.

12. Ibid., pp. 30–31.

"A Rose Is a Rose Is a . . . ?"
or
"Remember Me?"

I know that I know you . . . your name can't be lost.
Both your name and your likeness have got to be tossed
In a crevice or corner inside my computer
Where lately response to my best roto-rooter
Says a rose is a . . . Blast! If I only could name it!
Some swifter cognomer has somehow to claim it,
'Cause since I passed fifty, the best I can do
With a name of a something, a someplace, a who,
Is just to keep hoping that something subliminal
Fills in the blanks that are max in their minimal.

When meeting, I plead, right off, without jesting,
No wry accusations, suggesting, inquesting.
Just say who you are—even nephew or daughter—
Be more than a blotch on my over-blotched blotter.
And then should your matter start greying some too,
I promise, I'll do just the same, friend, for you.

Emma Lou Thayne, a native of Salt Lake City, Utah, has twelve published books of fiction, nonfiction, and poetry and is a member of the board of directors of the Deseret News. *She contributes regularly to a variety of publications. She and her husband, Melvin E. Thayne, have five daughters and eighteen grandchildren.*

Elizabeth Dennistoun Kane:
"Publicans, Sinners, and Mormons"

MARY KAREN BOWEN SOLOMON
DONNA JENKINS BOWEN

Introduction by Maureen Ursenbach Beecher, professor of English and senior research historian in the Joseph Fielding Smith Institute for Church History at Brigham Young University

For years historians have mined the diaries and journals of pioneers for their treasures of historical evidence: who was with the Prophet Joseph when; how the Saints crossed the plains; what led up to the Mormon war; how Brigham Young responded to the coming of the railroad. Raw data from the personal accounts of the participants in the Mormon movement have always been the mother lode of its history.

Especially richly veined have been the diaries and autobiographies of women. Their female voices, for all the strictures imposed on them in a male-oriented tradition, have touched the chords of human experience as men's more businesslike accounts never have. Writing themselves as subject, women present an immediate, intimate, lifesize version of the world they inhabit. No mere cataloging of historical tidbits, they are the many-dimensional reconstructions of life from the inside, and they deserve to be read as such.

Any moderately well-read student of Mormon history knows the name Thomas L. Kane, "friend of the Mormons." He facilitated the negotiations that allowed for the Mormon Battalion to send five hundred men across the continent at government expense; his published

Mary Karen Bowen Solomon teaches humanities, literature, and Russian at Colorado Northwestern Community College in Craig, Colorado, where she is associate dean of student services. She mothers her three children, plays the organ for her ward, and is a stake singles representative.

Donna Jenkins Bowen holds a degree in marketing from Brigham Young University. She is the mother of five children. She writes family histories and enjoys research. Sister Bowen served two missions with her husband, Norman R. Bowen, and she teaches the Spiritual Living course in Relief Society.

defense of the Saints created goodwill for them in government places; he mediated talks between the incoming Utah Expedition and the fleeing Saints so that the Utah War never really happened.

Little known, however, is the visit he made to Utah with his wife, Elizabeth, and their youngest children in 1872–73. Guests of Brigham Young, the Kanes rested in his St. George residence while Thomas recovered his health and gathered information on a biography of Young he hoped to write. He never wrote the book. Elizabeth, however, with less ambition but greater persistence, wrote letters to her father of such richness and interest that he collected the first batch of them and worked them into a manuscript with the ponderous nineteenth-century title *Twelve Mormon Homes Visited in Succession on a Journey through Utah to Arizona.* Elizabeth's book was published in 1874.

A second collection of Elizabeth's honest and compassionate descriptions of Mormon family life recently came into the possession of Brigham Young University Libraries though the good offices of Norman R. Bowen, who served as mission president in the area where the Church recently purchased Kane's chapel and burial site. That manuscript, now being prepared by Margery Ward and Everett Cooley, will soon be published by the University of Utah Press. President Bowen's widow, Donna, and daughter Mary Karen Solomon here present aspects of the journal accounts of Elizabeth Kane, which let us see not just what she observed of nineteenth-century Mormon life but what her observations reveal of the diarist herself. "Through her journals," concludes Mary Karen, "one comes to know this reflective yet active woman, this passionate and painstaking wife." And in knowing her, we come closer to understanding ourselves.

* * * * *

Mary Karen: Elizabeth Dennistoun Kane was a bright, ambitious woman, a perfectionist wife, and an unusual journal writer—perceptive, witty, occasionally acerbic, and spiritually centered. Those qualities may have jostled each other in contradiction—her strong sense of domestic duty seemed sometimes to struggle against her other interests and hobbies—but all bore witness to her independence of mind. A cultured and well-educated Philadelphia lady of the later nineteenth century, she wrote perceptively about herself, her religion, and her goals, as well as about new places and unusual people. Devoted to her husband, not blindly but alertly, she wrote about the nature and contradictions of her adventurous husband, Major General Thomas L. Kane, friend of the Mormons. His friendship with Brigham Young drew them southwest across the continent to St. George, Utah, to spend the winter of 1872–73 in that pioneering Mormon settlement. Elizabeth's St. George journal is a clear picture of Mormon history, sharp in human focus, a study of the people and problems, including polygamy, of newly settled St. George.

Elizabeth was a multitalented woman and a lifelong student. In her lifetime she developed considerable abilities as an early-day photographer, a physician, a northwestern Pennsylvania pioneer, and a revered "mother" of General Kane's battalion as well as of their own four children. This excerpt describing her worries about her teen-age daughter Harriet, nicknamed Harry, matches my own experience mothering my fifteen-year-old daughter: "A worse trouble is to know how to manage Harry whose temper is getting very bad. She is so contrary that I am really entirely at a loss to know what to do. She storms about nothing, insists that you say what you have not said, and frightens me lest she become like Aunt Alida in character as well as in looks. Poor pet, may God help me to bring her up rightly. She is at the same time anxious to be good, and ready to go into hysterics of penitence. But it is very seldom the 'godly sorrow that worketh repentance.'" (8 June 1861.)[1] Teenagers haven't changed! Nor have mother's hearts.

A faithful and fervent Christian, Elizabeth was always clear about her values and sure of them. She was deeply committed in her relationships: first, with her God; second, with her husband; and third, with her social responsibilities. She was deeply concerned with women's issues. Thomas believed she had a calling to improve conditions for women, and despite her self-doubts, Elizabeth grew into agreement. "Tom speaks of my being the instrument of some great work— of lecturing to women, etc. I am sure he overrates my mental powers, as well as my physical, and therefore it is not only laziness which prompts my extreme disinclination to contemplate such a mission." (16 January 1858.) Neither an apologist for traditional views of women nor an activist, Elizabeth wanted first to learn and then to teach what an ideal Christian woman should be. She believed women were equal in natural and intellectual potential with their husbands, and she wanted to elevate them to an equal level in political, social, and educational reality—the misguided and downtrodden polygamous Mormon women as well.

Elizabeth Dennistoun Wood was born in Bootle, a suburb of Liverpool, England, on 12 May 1826. At the age of six, she began a life-long enchantment with her American cousin, Thomas Leiper Kane, when he visited her family home as a young man of twenty. He brought her a French doll, which she forever treasured. Two years later, her family moved to New York, drawing closer the ties with her intriguing cousin. When Elizabeth was ten, her mother died; at twelve, she remarked to her sister that she intended to marry cousin Thomas Kane; and in 1853, when she was almost seventeen, she did. Tom was Elizabeth's only love; in 1861 when she found out that Tom had had an earlier love, she described "poor dear S—" with a mixture of generosity and jealousy. First the generosity: "A young lady who was very lovely, so amiable and charming that I have never heard her mentioned save in terms of praise, and who possessed such a genius for music that she made her piano express all the feelings of her heart, loved him very dearly. Her father was opposed to Tom, I suppose, and Judge Kane wished Tom not to marry her because there was insanity in her family. They gave each other up, and both married, and now she is dead." (13 November 1861.)

A little later in the same passage she mentioned, with perhaps a touch of jealousy over the cultivated flowers and music, that Thomas, who was then away on a military campaign, was pleased that Elizabeth's "taper" was still burning for him. She vowed, "If it please my dear love then my taper shall still shine for him (if God gives him again to my arms!) I will still try to give him pleasant associations of me with wild flowers (poor dear S— shall keep the cultivated ones, and the music) and I will earn his whole heart. And when I go home to my Father, I will not be ashamed to be friends with her who also loved him, for I will do him good and not evil all the days of my life!"

After their marriage, Elizabeth and Thomas lived in Philadelphia, where Thomas's father, Judge John K. Kane, was a prominent U. S. federal court judge, influential in national politics. Thomas soon had two promising careers, first, as a federal court clerk to his father and second, as an up-and-coming attorney. The Kanes's future, both financial and emotional, looked bright indeed.

A passage from 20 September 1857 shows Elizabeth's concerns and challenges over her "home duties." Among the duties was training the maids to be a source of help rather than one of frustration. She meditated over these concerns with typical spirituality: "I read our usual service for [family devotionals], it was however so dull and rainy a day that we could take no walk and as none of us felt well, we passed a very quiet uninteresting morning. I read Tom my diary of the week. He spoke of Elisha having clean frocks oftener. I promised to watch up Tom's tendency to 'put things through,' and we are mutually to oversee the other's dressing.

"Also we are thankful for the lessons of the last fortnight and pray that we may profit by keeping them ever in mind, day by day.

"First, and chiefly, to teach us to live as we should. Next to show me what is false kindness to Tom. Then to teach us charity. Then to show us what a mistake I might have made in falling entirely into outdoor work and overlooking home duties. I must be careful not to become absorbed in photography to the detriment of nearer things. I must keep Tom's clothes mended and in neat order, our rooms neat and clean, and my own clothes. The children's clothes must be neatly folded, and kept in their own bureau, and Jane Nelly must keep their nursery neat." Elizabeth wanted to keep her home and her family's clothes in perfect order, but her writing, reading, and photography sometimes enticed her away.

Her young country maids, Jane Nelly and Jane Pickett, needed thorough organization and instruction from her. She finally concluded that she needed to give up one maid, even though the one she let go was the tidier of the two: "I must give up Jane Pickett. I hope mother can take her. I would prefer keeping her to Jane Nelly for she is pretty dirty and slovenly." (30 December 1857.)

Though Thomas's career was flourishing, his convictions and conscience soon outweighed his material ambitions. Within the first three years of their marriage, he had given up both career paths. He first sacrificed his career as an attorney because of indignation over the fugitive slave ruling; then in 1856 he resigned his court clerkship to go to the aid of his oppressed western pioneer friends, the Mormons. A clash between Mormon and government forces seemed imminent. Both the federal government and the press misunderstood Mormon intentions and conditions in Utah Territory; the Mormons, on their part, had less than no confidence in the United States government. A history of recent unredressed persecutions in Ohio, Missouri, and Illinois intensified the Utahns' distrust of the federal government. With their backs against the walls of their new Great Basin homes, the Mormons seemed committed to defending themselves despite the odds. Thomas believed that he alone could mediate to avert open warfare and casualties; he alone had the trust of both adversaries.

Thomas's position was ambiguous. Although the Kane family records indicate that President Buchanan had strongly, though unofficially, encouraged Thomas to go to Salt Lake City, government commission and payment were only vaguely promised. Concerned for his Mormon friends, Thomas did not wait for an official commission but left quickly with only a presidential letter of introduction. His twenty-year-old wife, their toddler daughter, Harriet, and new baby son, Elisha Kent Kane, remained behind, dependent upon his parents.

Elizabeth was troubled by Thomas's mission for several reasons. Her journal entry for 18 November 1870 reveals that "13 years ago today [when Thomas decided to go to Utah] I thought my heart was broken." Her journal entries clarify her concerns. She was a new wife; she missed Thomas; and she worried especially about his delicate health and predisposition towards pneumonia. The journey was dangerous even for a strong and healthy man. Receiving few letters or messages from him intensified her anxiety, and Elizabeth conscientiously recorded her thoughts and actions in her journal; she and Thomas had both decided to keep journals—for each other's eyes only—during their separation.

She relied on God to protect Thomas. Elizabeth's strong faith, ironically enough, caused its own problems. A devout Presbyterian, Elizabeth wanted Thomas to join her faith. Religious unity was important to her, and she thought they were achieving it, writing on 26 December 1857 that "God has mercifully brought out of [recent trials] one great blessing already, in uniting Tom and me in the bonds of a common faith. Tom thinks he may be of service to Him by bringing about a peace between Utah and the United States, and went to Washington to see the president about it. May God give him wisdom to do right!"

But the prolonged separation necessarily tested such unity. Elizabeth was suspicious of Mormon influence upon her husband's religious attitudes. She felt Thomas showed entirely disproportionate interest in the Mormon religion when he was still irresolute about what she recognized as Christianity. She wrote to him on Easter Sunday 1858, "My darling, people call you a Mormon, as in the old time they called our Master a publican and sinner." Her anxiety was justified. She wrote upon Thomas's return, 20 June 1858, "I was so happy and so unhappy. . . . Tom told me the first moment we were alone, like my dear honest darling, that the hope that had dawned upon him of being a Christian was gone." Elizabeth considered Mormons heretical polygamists, not Christians; Thomas's increased sympathy for them may well have caused Elizabeth to think he had lost his "Christianity."

After learning about Thomas's "loss of faith," she wrote of her great distress that he had been traveling "without his staff," without the Christian faith she recognized as his support and protection. Soon afterwards, however, on 11 July 1858 she wrote movingly of the power of faith, as evidenced in Tom's stories of the Mormons' seemingly miraculous powers. Thomas had seen instances, scores of them, of invalids restored to health and strength through Mormon priesthood blessings. Fifteen years later in her own St. George journal, Elizabeth carefully recorded several such incidents.

A third concern, painful and immediate during the months Thomas was gone, was Elizabeth's financial position. She and her children were dependent upon her husband's family, and despite their kindness, she chafed for independence and her own home. She disliked the household tasks she felt obligated to perform dutifully. On 28 January 1858, soon after Thomas's departure (5 January 1858), she asked Judge Kane, Tom's father, for advice on an "occupation" to increase her independence. She was disheartened when he suggested studying mathematics. Wryly she noted that her feelings about mathematics resembled her attitude toward the Mormons—the more she studied them, the less she liked them.

Despite the duties burdening her spirit and the concerns that oppressed her, Elizabeth was determined to use the time apart from Thomas to overcome her "imperfections." The plan she developed to use that lonely time constructively illustrates her character and idealism. She recorded the following goals:

"1. My first duty is to watch over his children; therefore the more time intelligently given to them, the better.

"2. try to be cheerful and to grow strong, to be a help and a comfort . . .

"3. In trying to cultivate my mind, let me keep from overdoing anything and thereby injuring either my bodily or spiritual health.

"4. perform unhesitatingly all duties due to Tom's parents and family;

"5. As a help to cheerfulness, attend to my duties of society.

"6. Remember to be as much as possible with [Tom's sister,] Bess." (10 January 1858.)

By anyone's standards, those are worthy goals, marked by an absence of self-pity and indulgence. It is interesting that Elizabeth commented on the importance of time spent intelligently with the children, in contrast to time spent watching over them dutifully.

Her third goal, cultivating her mind, was an important one, though she resolved to keep her inquiring mind in check and not overdo her study. Her journal lists thirty-one books read in Thomas's absence; among them are Kingley's *Saints' Tragedy* and *Andromeda*, William H. Prescott's first and second volumes of *The History of the Reign of Philip II*, Stanley's *Sinai* and *Palestine*, Bridge's *Algebra* (evidently taking her father-in-law's advice), Thomas Macaulay's *History of England*, Merg's *Diseases of Children*, and Orson Hyde's *Mormonism*.

Elizabeth also devoted as much time as she could spare from the children and her duties to photography, a favorite hobby. But though she occupied herself with interests as well as duties, she found it difficult to distract herself from her fears for Thomas.

Elizabeth's devotion to Thomas is obvious from her writings. She resented his family and friends' beliefs, picked up by her in conversation, especially with Tom's mother and aunts, that he was "eccentric, unpractical and so forth, though a genius." (20 March 1870.) These misperceptions of her husband, she believed, were based upon some unfinished youthful projects and "passions" of his. "Though I cannot endure daws to pick at him, and it galls me so to hear it implied that 'poor Tom' doesn't attend regularly to his official duties, or hasn't kept a proper orthodox account of [his brother] Elisha's estate, or hasn't the Sunbury & Erie papers in a comprehensible form, or flirted—though that's not to the purpose—or didn't do some one of the things that people of no more intellect than Evan Thomas could and would do perfectly well."[2] (26 January 1857.)

Too often Thomas's family, perhaps unconsciously, compared him unfavorably with Elisha Kent Kane, his older brother and a noted Arctic explorer, who died a national hero soon after their marriage. It is hard to compete with a dead national hero. Elizabeth considered some of the family's concerns to be "hum-drum," as did Thomas. And yet she also wanted them to be proud of Thomas. Even little criticisms nettled.

She noted to herself: "Dear Tom, I'll ask him when he comes back to get his hum-drum affairs in order to gratify his hum-drum wife. . . .

I am trying to correct my fault. . . . I say to myself that I am not ambitious for Tom, and in one sense, I am not. I am far prouder of being Tom's chosen one than if I had been Elisha's—of whom all the world talked—because I know how much he is superior." (26 January 1857.)

Elizabeth felt that Thomas's ambition to prove himself Elisha's equal consumed his talents and energy and weakened his health. Another aspect of the problem was that Thomas himself adored Elisha. Elizabeth noted on 20 February 1868 that she was jealous of Tom's "poring over books on the Arctic Regions, fearing that he desires to go there, to prove the truth of all Elisha had discovered . . . and by a great sacrifice of his own life, to atone to Elisha's memory for having been forced to sorrow over him [Thomas and his youthful irresponsibilities] instead of being only proud of him." Elizabeth refers to vague family disapproval of something in Thomas's youth, perhaps his protective passion for the Mormons, which cost him both professionally and monetarily while Elisha's fame peaked.

The need of Thomas to prove himself in some heroic fashion continues as a source of worry and occasional discord. Ten years later, after Thomas attempted to be appointed as governor of Utah in April 1868, she commented, "Tom is not made to be happy but to dwell on cold and naked cliffs. He would make a Xavier or Loyola or Pascal, and I am utterly commonplace. . . . I told Tom he must rely on his own judgment and not on my feelings to decide his action. I will not have to endure seeing him die of discontent because I have chained him to my side here."

Later that year Elizabeth recorded, on 16 August 1868: "Sometimes he urges me to let him go away for two years, sure he would come back well off. I cannot bear to think of that—the children would be weaned from him—we ourselves would be older and independent of the misery of having him away." She explained that misery eloquently for her husband to read on his return: "Last night I yielded to the temptation of recalling how tenderly you always cared for me when my head ached, how you would take off my shoes for me, and when I was in bed, come and lay your darling head by mine and soothe me to sleep with loving words. But I found I began to cry, so I forced my thoughts off. I dare not think of your tenderness, nor dare I think how you too may be suffering for me, nor of the hardships you are undergoing. . . . [O]h my husband, it is very hard to part from you when we are so weakened by our late trials. May God keep you in the hollow of His hand, and if it be His will restore us to each other."

Thomas returned from his 1858 Utah adventure hard-pressed financially and unemployed, yet he refused a tardy and half-hearted offer of remuneration from President Buchanan. Instead, he and Elizabeth took their two small children, Harriet, four, and Elisha Kent, two, to unsettled McKean and Elk counties in the Allegheny highlands of remote northwestern Pennsylvania. There he planned to develop and manage a land company organized by his father, Judge John Kane, and some of the judge's friends. Tom himself had purchased a large parcel of land in Pennsylvania in August 1857, four months before his Utah trip. Approximately two-thirds of their time there was spent in the woods attempting to subdue nature, and one-third in Philadelphia trying to attract railroads and industry to this rural mountain area. But that is another story, one that my mother, Donna Bowen, will take up.

As women who have the same concerns Elizabeth Kane had—our children, our husbands, living true to our religion, supporting and teaching our families, both with and without husbands' support, learning to love neighbors we don't particularly like (and even math)—there is much we can learn from Elizabeth Kane's life and writings. Through her journals, one comes to know this reflective yet active woman, this passionate and painstaking wife. Elizabeth, as painfully honest as she was intelligent, never shrank from a duty or was bested by a fear. She truly was a noble and courageous woman.

Donna: Elizabeth Dennistoun Wood Kane had received an excellent education for a young woman of her time; however, having been married at sixteen to a man almost twice her age, she spent her early married life attempting to meet the challenge of becoming a vital part of a highly motivated and achieving family.

Tom arrived in Philadelphia from his Utah trip in June 1858, grieving for the death of his beloved and revered father. Complicating the situation, his mother, to settle debts, was forced to sell Fern Rock, the family home where Elizabeth, Tom, and the children had been living. Their solution was to go for the summer to the Uplands, as they called McKean and Elk counties in northern Pennsylvania, intending to build a settlement.

They were at Uplands when the Civil War began, and Tom left to serve the Union in April 1861, shortly after the birth of their third child, Evan O'Neill Kane. He had raised a regiment of hunters and loggers known as the Bucktails, which became famous for valor and endurance with Lt. Colonel Thomas L. Kane as their leader. Meanwhile, Elizabeth and the children were offered a home in Philadelphia with Aunt Ann Gray Thomas.

"July 21, 1861. A week since I wrote. Tom telegraphed to me on the 18th 'Safe from my first round.' I am terribly anxious today. Aunt Ann undertook to procure yesterday's evening paper, but as usual the precious Thomases were coming to tea, and she hurried home without it. The man has not brought today's paper and tomorrow is Sunday when I can see none, and all this time we are expecting to hear of a great battle at Manasses Junction (Bull Run) in which Pat certainly and Tom possibly will be engaged.

"Later. Tom loves me, I do believe. I don't think I ever felt the truth of it so much as in this last visit when he let me know more of his life than I have done. Oh, Father in Heaven, who hast blessed me with his love, ugly as men see me, sinful as Thou knowest me, help me to make myself worthy of the place he has given me in his heart, and make me feel the responsibility it involves."

Tom saw a great deal of fighting and was wounded three times. On 21 December 1861 at Dranesville, his regiment led the advance, and he was shot in the jaw. From that time on, he wore a beard. At Harrisonburg, 6 June 1862, he was sent with 104 handpicked men to rescue the ambushed First New Jersey regiment. He encountered three regiments of Confederate soldiers and lost 52 men. The Confederates admitted a loss of 359. Tom was wounded again, shot in the leg, clubbed in the chest, and taken prisoner. Exchanged in August, he was made brigadier general for gallant services in the field and commanded the 2d brigade, 2d Division, Twelfth Army Corps at Chancellorsville. So ill he could not walk, he rode to Gettysburg with the news that the Confederate Army had broken the Union code, and he remained to use his troops to hold Culp's Hill. For that action at Gettysburg, he was "brevetted major-general for 'gallant and meritorious services.'"[3]

Elizabeth worried incessantly. Information was hard to come by, she seldom heard from Tom, and his pay was so small that she and the children lived in poverty, despite help from others, mostly Aunt Ann. Contending with the difficulties of her life made Elizabeth more of a problem solver than a describer and observer of the beauties of nature. She wrote some of her early reminiscences of Kane for the newspaper

Kane Leader, 4 July 1896. It is the "how" and the "where" that most interested her.

"My first knowledge of this region dates from the year 1856 when . . . my husband came up to inspect the property and wrote to me in glowing terms of the delightful exhilarating air, and the freshness of the forest. He arranged a summer visit for us, and I made my first trip to the mountains. . . . [A stagecoach] highway gave me my first acquaintance with corduroy roads and places where brooks had overflowed and the bridges had floated out and not been replaced. Mile after mile of unbroken forest was traversed." The only finished structure on their land was a stable or barn, and they lived there after the war while Tom built roads and surveyed for railroad lines and coal mines. He also spent a great deal of time in Philadelphia and Washington "politicking." Their fourth child, William Wood Kane, was born in November 1863.[4]

Elizabeth wrote in the summer of 1864: "We jest to each other. Tom says that I show myself the daughter of a line of merchants, for I am a gambler who calls the game a mercantile adventure. I retort that he who risks nothing wins nothing, but Tom sighs for he would risk and win in greater games than these. . . . He feels that his health is failing and that the wife and children who are helpless without him depend on a man who is in such daily suffering as may soon end his life. He does not long for life. Were we but placed out of the reach of poverty, all he would desire would be: 'In some great cause, not in his own / To perish, wept for, / honored, known.'"

In June the sawmill burned. Prior to the war (1860–61) the Kanes had obtained lumber for a house at Flanders, thirty miles away. It had been expensive to haul. When Thomas returned to Kane, probably in 1863, ready to build his house, he found the materials he had stored for the house gone, the lime dissolved, the stone vanished, and the lumber burned. Elizabeth wrote, "Thus Tom had to commence his house by building a mill to saw his lumber." The loss of this mill so soon after its construction was a tragedy. Almost as painful to lose as the mill were the piles of beautifully finished hardwood lumber they had been accumulating to build their house. Elizabeth and Thomas scrounged, borrowed, and sold land to rebuild the sawmill.

"1865. Early in January 1865 Tom had to go to Philadelphia on business-financeering. Not many days after his departure a great snowstorm set in, which blocked up the narrow lanes that we called roads. No teams could come out to us from the settlements, for the snow lay eight feet deep on the abandoned clearings on windy Howard Hill. Travel on the railroad was suspended for ten days and for two weeks no freight was carried. Our settlement was almost starved. I doled out scanty rations of food to the teams and as to the human beings, I know that I was supplying ten families from my solitary flour barrel the day that our siege was raised. . . .

"The day following when Tom, faint and weary with his long journey 'lifted the latch and walked in,' the first object that met his eyes was my altered countenance as I lay with my own eyes closed by erysipelatous swelling in a high fever, and unable to see. . . . There was no doctor to be had. Tom telegraphed for his Brother John, who kindly left his practice and reached us in a very few days.

"My dear husband had come home sick himself and anticipating rest and my sympathy in the business discouragements he had met with. Instead of this he became my nurse (in my delirium).

"They had made a screen of sheets and old chintz curtains round my bed, partly to keep off the draughts and partly to secure a half privacy for my sickroom, as John had to sleep in one corner. There were no spare-rooms in the barn. . . .

"I was quite myself again, and able to enjoy hearing Tom read aloud, when one morning our ox-eyed Charley, replenishing the fire, slowly pronounced the words—'General, if you please, the house is on fire!'

"Tom often says he never felt such helpless misery, such desolation of spirit as when he gazed [from the burning roof] over the snowy waste. Below him [were] the frail little children and the wife to whom being turned out in that deep snow would be certain death. The drifts were more than waist deep. A wind was blowing and the thermometer stood 15 degrees below zero."

But they survived.

By 1872 Tom was in perilous health. He had never completely recovered from his war injuries. Brigham Young wrote to invite him and his family to come to Utah and winter with him in St. George. He promised his friend a complete restoration of health. Elizabeth demurred, but when Tom was adamant, she prepared for the trip. Elizabeth feared the influence of the Mormons on Tom. Accompanied by their two youngest children, eleven-year-old Evan and nine-year-old Willie, and a black servant, they took the railroad to Salt Lake City and a carriage from there to St. George.

During that carriage trip Elizabeth wrote: "I could see little of Nephi in the gathering darkness: it was evidently smaller than Provo. The carriages halted on entering town, and separated company. Ours was driven rapidly up a cross-street to a plain adobe house, standing by itself. Lights shone from every door and window; the father of the family stood waiting to help us out of the carriage, and the wives and children greeted us warmly as we crossed the threshold.

"We were first ushered into a large bedroom on the ground floor, where a superb pitch-pine fire was blazing; and two well-cushioned rocking-chairs were drawn forward for us, while half a dozen hospitable children took off my boys' wrappings, as the mother disembarrassed me of mine.

"Then we were left to rest, and begged to feel ourselves at home.

"Our present entertainers, the Steerforths, were English people. There were *two* wives, and a number of children, girls of all sizes down to the smallest elf that ever walked, and one sturdy open-faced boy, who speedily 'fellow-shipped' with my little lads, and carried them off, after supper, to the great kitchen to see their playmate, Lehi, the Indian boy.

"After supper!—To this day, when we have any special dainty at home, Evan and Will exclaim that it reminds them of the Steerforths', and describe the cozy dining-room, with the warm fire-light playing on the table-equipage, and the various good things that composed, in Yorkshire style, the hungry travelers' 'tea dinner.'

"One of the wives sat down to table, and one waited upon us, with the aid of the two elder girls. There was a young school-master there, too, who had made his home with the Steerforths since his parents died, and whose love for their quiet domestic life was duly praised by the Mistresses S. when he left the room. But I thought that the sweet face of 'our eldest'—'Noe,' I think they call her—might perhaps share the credit of the long ten-mile ride on Friday evening from his school in Nephi, and the starlight journey back which it cost the youthful pedagogue on Monday morning.

"My intercourse with the Steerforths made a strong impression on me. We stayed longer at their house than at any other on this tour, and it was difficult not to be influenced by their simple kindliness of heart and unaffected enthusiasm.

"Our conversation the evening of our arrival turned chiefly on our hostesses' experience of pioneer life. Mrs. Mary was the chief speaker, but Mrs. Sarah, a pale little lady, dark-haired and black-eyed, put in a quiet word of acquiescence, or suggested an anecdote now and then. She was from Yorkshire. Mrs. Mary was a Herefordshire woman, tall, rosy, brown-haired, and blue-eyed.

"I wonder whether the Mormon men evidence any marked peculiarity of taste in the selection of wives. Widowers with us are wont to profess that they discern a resemblance in the lady upon whom a second choice falls, to the dear departed. I asked a Mormon woman at Salt Lake how it was, and she answered that, in her opinion, men had no taste. 'In our case,' she said, 'there are *five* of us unusually tall, and *two* very short; but the rest (she did not say how many there were) are of an ordinary height, and we are all different in looks, disposition, and age.'

"In the Steerforth ménage, the wives were exceedingly unlike each other. The husband was of a Manx family, long resident in Yorkshire. He had joined the Mormons in early youth with his mother, and they had been disowned by his family, well-to-do English people.

"The Steerforths were among the first Mormons who came out to Utah. Only a select band of one hundred and forty-three men, headed by Brigham Young in person, had preceded them. These pioneers had planted posts along their route with rough boxes nailed to them containing information regarding the distances to work, water, and grass; and these guide-posts were slowly tracked out and followed by the long train of ox-wagons, freighted with the exiles from Nauvoo, women, children, and invalids. There were a few men who drove and acted as guards, but the teamsters were principally women and young boys."[5]

Sunday morning. "After breakfast I attended a Mormon meeting for the first time. I wondered whether Mr. Steerforth would walk to church alone, or between his wives. But they both accompanied me, while their joint husband (!) formed one of a group who escorted T. So there was no test of preference."[6]

"I got rid of more than one preconceived idea that morning; of none more completely than the prevailing error respecting the looks of a congregation of Mormon women. I was so placed that I had a good opportunity to look around, and began at once to seek for the 'hopeless, dissatisfied, worn' expression travelers' books had bidden me to read on their faces.

"But I found that they wore very much the same countenances as the American women of any large rustic and village congregation. . . .

"Happy or unhappy, *I* could not read histories on the upturned faces at Nephi."[7]

The journal covering the trip to St. George, entitled *Twelve Mormon Homes,* was printed by Elizabeth's father after their return to Pennsylvania. It has since been reprinted by the University of Utah Press. The journal that covered the rest of their visit to Utah and the winter in St. George is now in the process of being printed by the University of Utah Press as a companion volume to *Twelve Mormon Homes.*

From the St. George journal: "Christmas Day in St. George."

"We are in the largest house in the place. Last night when we arrived, I supposed that it was a Hotel, but it is a private house belonging to the 'President of the Stake.' We have spacious and comfortable rooms on the first floor. On one side the windows look out [south] over a vineyard belonging to our host towards the gap in the mountains through which the Rio Virgin pierces after receiving the waters of the Santa Clara. The different houses of the town stand in the midst of vineyards, each occupying the greater part of a ten-acre block. . . .

"Our host [President Erastus Snow] called upon me just now with his wife [Artemesia, wife number one]. We exchanged the usual commonplace remarks and they departed. In about five minutes more there was a knock at the parlor door.

"'Come in,' I said, and my host re-entered with another lady [apparently Minerva, wife number two], whom he presented with grave simplicity, and in precisely the same form of words, as his wife. I am not yet used to polygamy and am always taken by surprise.

"Perhaps it is because the Mormons do not say 'one of my wives' but 'my wife.' Still I imagine there is but one. I rallied, however, and we discoursed on the weather, our late journey, and the prospect of my liking St. George, while I asked myself whether Bishop Snow was remembering that I had used the same phrases in answering the same remarks a few minutes before.

"I had now seen 'Artemesia' and 'Minerva,' and after the Bishop had escorted 'Minerva' out, I reseated myself and began talking to the children, but in two minutes more, there he was back again, this time with another lady.

"She was presented with the same gravity, and we essayed the same remarks. Fortunately there was a new subject to introduce: Mrs. 'Elizabeth' [known locally as Aunt Libbie—wife number three] was my hostess, and she had kind inquiries to make relating to our comfort.

She is a gentle-looking, pale woman with dark eyes and hair, and is the mother of many of the thirty-five young Snows. When the pair rose to depart, the Bishop apologized for the infirm health of 'his wife' which would prevent Mrs. 'Julia Josephine' [wife number four] from paying her respects to me!"[8]

Elizabeth was delighted to see the improvement in Tom's health during their St. George sojourn. Early in 1873, however, he suffered a temporary setback. Elizabeth described the incident in a letter to her father included in her journal:

"Quite apart from my own longings, I am glad that T. is going to recover. The Mormons all feel as if the wonderful change in his health since he came here was caused by their prayers. He could hardly walk an eighth of a mile with the aid of his crutches when we arrived; yet just before this [most recent] illness seized him he enjoyed a mountain climb of two miles, returning scarcely more fatigued than I was. I did not tell you, hoping to give you a delightful surprise when you should see him walking without even a cane. Think! He had never done that since Harrisonburg in June of 1862.

"During this sharp sickness, it was a consolation to me to hear Elder S. [Staines] confess to the same feelings I had myself in praying. (Elder S. is the deformed gentleman whose earnest simplicity and sincerity have struck me, as much as his kindliness has done the children. He is the only Mormon man with whom I have more than a passing acquaintance.)

"I had felt that T's restoration to health was in answer to my prayers and that should he die now, this agony of pain seemed as if it would shake my faith. Poor Elder S. was even worse off than myself, because he believed that he had received the assurance of the Spirit that T. was to return home cured.

"His room is over ours, and I have always heard the tones of his voice praying for a long time at night, but when [Tom] was passing through the crisis, I could distinguish the murmuring sound nearly all night. His distress was so great that he had to be banished from the sickroom, and I pitied his wretched looks without knowing the cause, whenever I met him creeping about the house, waiting for tidings. Now he is at peace again, and more joyously hopeful and confident than I can be, yet."

"March 1873. Well, old journal; glad am I to reopen you again before leaving St. George without any further sorrow to relate!

"[Tom] was strong enough to be driven two squares to the Tabernacle to attend a farewell dinner given by the female Relief Society. The feast was spread in the basement, with 270 men and women sitting down and as many children flitting about, waiting on the company and picking up crumbs. . . .

"Erring as they may be from what I think the truth, still I cannot forget what rest and peace of soul I have enjoyed among them, and when I go back to the theoretically orthodox society of the East, with its practical infidelity that asks 'Where is now thy God,' I shall look back with tender feelings to St. George; 'for I had gone with the multitude, I went with them to the House of God, with the voice of joy and praise; with the multitude that kept holy day.'

"The fact may not have the meaning for others that I attach to it, but I mean to remember that I felt that it was right and not wrong to worship with the Mormons as with Christians. It is such a comfort to be with people who are in earnest!"[9]

Tom left his crutches in St. George, his cane in Salt Lake City, and returned to Kane, Pennsylvania, as their settlement had come to be known. There, after the panic of 1873, their financial affairs started to improve. Swedish settlers were brought in, the railroad completed, and coal lands became marketable.

In 1881 their daughter Harriet Amelia decided to attend the Women's Medical College in Philadelphia, where Elizabeth had studied shortly after her marriage. Elizabeth accompanied her, and they graduated together with M.D.'s in 1883, living in a home (1307 Walnut Street) inherited from the family. It was here that Tom died of pneumonia on 26 December 1883, at age sixty-one, and Elizabeth took him home to Kane to be buried in a plot between the two front entrances to the Presbyterian church he had built for his Aunt Ann Thomas.

Elizabeth sold the Walnut Street home and made her permanent home in Kane, where she prospered. She doctored the community and continued her charitable works. Their coal lands produced, the railroad became financially stable, and oil was discovered on her property.

Her father, to whom she had sent her journals, died in 1894, followed by her dear daughter and companion, Harriet Amelia, in 1896. That fall she finished her beautiful home, Anoatok, a superb mansion, still maintained and known as Kane Manor, and died there 25 May 1909, always gallant, gracious, and God-fearing.

NOTES

1. Journals of Elizabeth Dennistoun Kane, Special Collections Archives, 5th floor, Harold B. Lee Library, Brigham Young University. Subsequent references will be cited in the text by entry date.

2. Evan Thomas has not been identified, though obviously Elizabeth doesn't think highly of him.

3. Elizabeth was quoting from *Autobiography of the Honorable John K. Kane* (Philadelphia: College Offset Press, 1949), p. 80.

4. Willie (William Wood Kane) was born 17 November 1863. After his father's death, he changed his name to Thomas Leiper Kane.

5. Elizabeth Wood Kane, *Twelve Mormon Homes* (Salt Lake City: Tanner Trust Fund, University of Utah Library, 1974), pp. 25–28.

6. Ibid, p. 41.

7. Ibid., pp. 41–42.

8. Elizabeth Dennistoun Kane, St. George Journal; typescript in possession of Donna Jenkins Bowen.

9. Ibid.

Navigating the Rapids: Course Corrections

LEANNA SPJUT BALLARD

One of my very first memories is of being carried on my father's back through tall stands of evergreens, watching the late snow patches still hiding under a dark canopy of trees. My father is a geologist. His deep, abiding love of the land, shared with me from my earliest years, began my lasting passion for all that the outdoor world holds.

He took me along on field trips and excursions when I was very young. Because I was so close to the ground, it was easy to closely examine all the plants, the patterns in the rocks and soil, animal tracks, and the wide variety of insects crossing my small steps.

I vividly recall the shiny scales on the trout my grinning Grandmother Spjut pulled out of Yellowstone Lake on our family's yearly trek up to Fishing Bridge. On the long drive up from Salt Lake City, my grandmother entertained me with stories of her girlhood in northern Sweden. She talked of skiing across a frozen lake in winter to reach her school. The lodgepole pine forests of Yellowstone reminded her of the tall, pine-filled woods of her youth.

Both she and my Grandfather Spjut grew up in Swedish families who went fishing so they would have something for dinner. Thus, they ardently pursued the rainbow trout in Yellowstone Lake for the whole week we stayed. They understood that "it pleaseth God that he hath given all these things unto man; for unto this end were they made to be used, with judgment, not to excess." (D&C 59:20.)

Later, I took my first summer job at Yellowstone Lake, leaving even before the commencement exercises of my East High School graduation in Salt Lake City. I was delighted to arrive at the lake I loved so

Leanna Spjut Ballard is a homemaker and a research associate at Brigham Young University, where she participates on a science research team with her husband, Clark Russell Ballard. They are the parents of six children. Sister Ballard serves in her ward Primary presidency.

well and to see ice still sending chilly fingers out into the lake waters and the snow still upon the ground. Working in Yellowstone allowed me to revisit the places I had come to love as a child and explore farther into backcountry new to me.

The outside, natural world—its intricate beauties, patterns, and endless variety—has always held a fascination and riveting, boundless interest for me. This sense of awe, wonder, and gratitude to my Heavenly Father and the Savior for creating this world is a gift in my life, something lasting and significant. Contemplating and enjoying the beauty of the earth fills me with strength that helps me through difficult times.

Alone at the shore of an isolated lake in the high Uintas, I've felt deep upwellings of joy and gratitude as I contemplate the glory of creation. "The earth rolls upon her wings, and the sun giveth his light by day, and the moon giveth her light by night, and the stars also give their light, as they roll upon their wings in their glory, in the midst of the power of God. Unto what shall I liken these kingdoms, that ye may understand? Behold, all these are kingdoms, and any man [or woman] who hath seen any or the least of these hath seen God moving in his majesty and power." (D&C 88:45–47.)

In 1973, I enrolled at Utah State University in its College of Natural Resources. I entered as a wildlife biology major, hoping to conduct research in pristine, unspoiled settings, study the wild animals, and work to protect them and their wild habitats.

I was soon disillusioned. In the early 1970s, the department had a utilitarian approach to wildlife, particularly game animals. My instructors seemed to think that wildlife was a crop to raise for hunters to harvest each fall. At that time, the Department of Wildlife Resources had only two nongame biologist positions in the entire state of Utah. I did not relish the idea of counting the teeth of dead deer at checking stations or approaching poachers, with a gun strapped to my hip, to enforce regulations or give out tickets as a conservation officer.

My first plant taxonomy class changed my direction. I delighted in the sublimity of the delicate patterns and colors of wildflowers. With Art Holmgren—a kindly and wildly enthusiastic Swedish botanist—as my mentor and adviser, I switched over to the College of Science and pursued a degree in biology and botany.

Many of my high school friends married within the first two years after high school. I too wanted to marry and have children eventually, but I felt strongly that I needed to prepare myself in case that didn't happen. I wanted to be prepared for a career that I would love and enjoy.

I gravitated to the few Latter-day Saint women in the natural science fields at USU. In 1976, I shared an old white house near the campus with three roommates and dear friends who had my same passion for the natural world. Holly graduated in forestry and went on to work with the Forest Service and National Park Service. Debby graduated first in outdoor recreation and then studied nursing, which led her to Kotzebue, Alaska, above the Arctic Circle, to manage a native clinic. Ann graduated in wildlife science and is now a wildlife biologist working for the Forest Service in Loman, Idaho. We spent time together on weekends exploring wild places in northern Utah, Idaho, and Wyoming.

The summer between my junior and senior years, I began my first natural science professional position at Hardware Ranch, an elk refuge in Blacksmith Fork Canyon. Working as a biology aide, I ran the visitors center and answered questions about the elk and other wildlife. When I returned to USU for fall quarter, a long-time friend from high school, Clark Ballard, drove up from Salt Lake City for a visit. Clark had recently returned from a mission to Argentina, and we spent our first day getting reacquainted by taking a bike ride out to Newton, a picturesque little Cache Valley community.

We dated through the Christmas holidays that year while I was home visiting my family in Salt Lake City. Clark drove me back to Logan for winter quarter. He was studying English literature at the University of Utah and wrote eloquent, poetic letters that became increasingly romantic and hinted at a long-term relationship. His letters and continued visits proved convincing, and we were engaged by the end of January, just after my twenty-second birthday.

Clark shares my interests in the outdoors. He enjoys backpacking, hiking, and camping. I knew that he would be a supportive husband and would applaud and encourage whatever projects I wished to pursue. During our six-month engagement, we went cross-country skiing, backpacking with friends, hiking, and bike riding.

Clark and I were married 15 July 1977 in the Salt Lake Temple, sealed for time and eternity by Clark's father, Elder M. Russell Ballard. After an outdoor reception with lots of flowers, Clark and I spent our honeymoon backpacking in Wyoming's vast Wind River Range.

We made our first home in Millville, Utah—a small, lovely town south of Logan. Clark transferred to USU to finish his undergraduate degree in English. The first project I was interested in pursuing after our marriage was having a baby. From a biological standpoint, the whole reproductive process of combining my genes with Clark's to produce a new individual, the idea of feeling a new life growing within my own body, and going through all the stages of pregnancy fascinated me.

Nature complied quickly—our first child, Matthew, arrived ten months after our wedding. I thrilled with the surge of maternal instincts and unconditional love I instantly felt for this new son. Almost immediately I began taking my baby out on walks and hikes. I particularly enjoyed watching our new baby grow and thrive on the breast milk that my own body produced. I also found breast-feeding to be so handy—we took Matthew on a week-long camping trip in the Sawtooth Mountains of Idaho when he was two months old, and it was convenient having all his nutritional needs so close at hand.

A second pregnancy took us by surprise when Matt was only seven months old. This child was a daughter, Sara. Unfortunately, she was born with a congenital anomaly called Trisomy 18. I had studied this genetic disorder in a college genetics course; it seemed ironic that with all the knowledge science has acquired about the reproductive process, cellular structure, and cell division, nothing could be done to change the fact that our sweet little daughter had an extra chromosome in every cell of her body.

We were told that 90 percent of all babies born with this condition lived less than a year. Sara was born in September, and I remember that with all the heartache and the tragedy to come, the fall was exceptionally beautiful. The autumn leaves were vivid, and they seemed to shine with light glowing from within. On one of the few walks Clark and I were able to take during that fall, I watched the brilliantly colored leaves falling to the ground, after entering into their senescent stage to die, and I knew that so too would our precious baby daughter soon slip away.

Sara died in January, when nature is quiet and still. That winter was a time of terrible grief and longing for my missing daughter.

There is something infinitely healing in the repeated refrains of nature—the assurance that dawn comes after night, and spring after the winter.

And so I found it to be with me. With spring came a renewal of life and hope, and after the terrible sorrows of that winter, I found myself again expecting, and our third child, a healthy baby boy, Nathan, was born the next fall. I clearly recall a moment of quiet but happy recognition that fall. I had just laid Nathan back down to sleep after nursing him and then gone out to our large garden. As I dug into the brown earth, I marveled at the large potatoes and the bounteous crop that had been produced from just the small bits of seed potatoes I had planted in the spring. I thought of my new, healthy baby sleeping inside and of the satisfaction of reaping nature's harvest from the garden I had planted months before. I realized then that joy had returned to my life.

Two years later, when I was in my fifth month of pregnancy with our fourth child, we went backpacking. That summer, I also began graduate classes in botany. Once Melissa was born, I found myself once again very involved with the care of a newborn, in addition to her brothers, Church callings, and our big garden. I kept busy with crafts, sewed dozens of T-shirts for my kids, quilted, and oil- and water-painted.

We continued to travel to wild, outdoor places on vacations, and I took every possible opportunity to share my love of nature with my children. I delight in watching them make their own discoveries about the natural world and in seeing the sense of wonder within them grow.

When I was pregnant with our fifth child, Trevor, I took another challenging graduate class, "Ecologic Anatomy and Morphology of Plants," which I really enjoyed. I felt a great desire to continue with studies in that area and yet, knowing the responsibilities that would come with my new baby, I wondered how I possibly could.

One night, as I sat up late reading articles on plant ecology, I found myself pondering my old dilemma once again—if I had the aptitude and enjoyed learning about these challenging concepts, shouldn't I continue with my studies? We are here in mortality to expand and enlarge our talents, and obviously insatiable curiosity and love for all of creation is one of mine. In fact, I've come to feel that my intense love for creation was probably well developed before I entered the mortal world. As a child, I had often pondered about how wonderful it would have been to have watched the creation of the world. If these interests and talents were formed in my premortal existence, shouldn't I continue to improve them in this life?

In great turmoil over this question, I slipped out of our bed where Clark lay snoozing peacefully, knelt, and prayed for guidance. I received one of the clearest answers to prayer I have ever received: "Look to Clark and to your children first, for that is where you will find your greatest joy and satisfaction. And if you so desire, opportunities will later be given to you to continue on with this learning." I felt peaceful again and accepted that answer.

Opportunities came more quickly than I had imagined. When our sixth and last child, Tommy, was just two years old, I was invited to co-direct a new outdoor environmental education program for middle-school-aged students. This program evolved into the Outdoor Adventures in Discovering Nature program. As I researched and contacted possible instructors within the College of Natural Resources, I was offered the opportunity to make this program into a master's degree project, with a full scholarship. I accepted this offer enthusiastically, but as I began graduate coursework and continued working toward implementing the new program, I knew that I was stretching myself. Laundry, cooking, and Church callings were beginning to fall between the cracks. Clark began cooking often as I spent hours on the phone every night, lining up volunteer instructors and coordinating activities.

The Outdoor Adventures program was highly successful. Driving home after the second session, I felt I was floating. I had reached that stage of self-actualization that psychologist Abraham Maslow calls a "peak experience." Everything that I had learned over the years, including delegating in Relief Society presidencies and stake boards, as well as my course work in ecology, biology, and botany, had all come together to help create a new program that turned out to be more successful than any of us who worked on it had dreamed. I felt supremely blissful, that I had really found my niche. I loved working with children and sharing my love of nature with them. My fellow instructors became my dear friends, and I continued to take interesting classes.

A central theme of the Outdoor Adventures program was to develop a sense of stewardship for our natural resources. Unfortunately, as I became the director and chief organizer of this program, I spent less and less time on my own stewardship over the care of my children and spouse.

My energetic commitment to the project took a real toll on my family, even though I included at least one of my children in every session of the program. Clark was trying to work on his own doctoral degree through BYU, work as an elementary school principal, and serve on the stake high council. He was feeling very left out and alone.

I should have realized how serious a problem we had when Clark told me, "These past three years have been the worst ones of my life," and I thought, "But they have been the best three years of mine!" The success I had felt as an environmental educator felt so good that when I was offered another job, co-authoring and illustrating a natural history guide to Logan Canyon, I said "Yes!" Later, I accepted another project, illustrating the anatomical and morphological life stages of Dyer's Woad, a noxious weed in the mustard family that causes a lot of grief to the farmers and ranchers in Cache Valley. I justified those decisions by spending my earnings on fun vacations for our whole family and on a housekeeper, who did the housework that I had never enjoyed anyway.

Without my support of all his efforts, Clark felt increased stress and the need for a change. When he told me he would like to leave his demanding principalship and accept a position at the State Office of Education in Salt Lake City, I was incredulous. How could I leave my fledgling program when it was just catching fire? I still had a year of graduate course work to finish, and the Logan Canyon book wasn't anywhere near completion.

In what we now can see to be a foolish decision, Clark took the Salt Lake job and stayed with his parents during the work week while I stayed in Cache Valley with the children to continue with my master's degree, my book, and the botanical illustration project. With a great deal of regret, I let go of the Outdoor Adventures program, realizing that I couldn't sustain it plus act as a single parent while finishing my other projects. I felt I was abandoning one of my children: I had created it, and watched it grow and develop into something successful and greatly satisfying to me. The relationships I had formed with my fellow instructors were precious to me.

We spent a year mostly apart, with Clark commuting back to Cache Valley on the weekends while I frantically tried to get all my projects finished. During that transitional year, we made several house-hunting trips and chose to move to the town of Alpine because it reminded us of our dear Cache Valley.

The closer the time came to moving, the more precious my projects, friends, and colleagues became to me; I couldn't envision my life without them. Our children had been attending the wonderful Edith Bowen lab school on the USU campus and were enrolled in excellent on-campus art and music programs. I felt I could never replace what I was leaving behind.

The week after we moved, the children went to their new school,

Clark went to work, and I was left in a strange house looking at hundreds of boxes, so many piled everywhere that I didn't know where to begin. The days that followed, unpacking box after box after box, were some of the loneliest and saddest of my life. I would stand, entombed in the box-filled kitchen, waves of sadness rolling over me as I considered all the friends, colleagues, and interesting projects I had lost. The children, too, struggled to carve out new niches for themselves in a new school and neighborhood.

One thing that kept me going was anticipating a long-awaited two-week trip to see Alaska with my college roommates. The trip had been in the planning stages for a year and a half. Ann and I flew to Seattle and took the ferry up to Ketchikan, where Holly lives. We flew into the Misty Fiords National Monument, a magical marine wilderness of lush greenery carpeted with dogwood and other northern wildflowers. The calls of loons and mountain goats filled the air. From there, we traveled on to Juneau and then across the Prince William Sound to the Kenai Peninsula, where Debbie lives.

On an all-day hike, the four of us passed by seven lakes, gorgeous wildflowers, grouse, loons, and a lot of fresh beaver sign. How good it was to talk with my former roommates about all the changes the years had brought—marriage, children, moves, changing careers.

On our way to the Salt Lake airport, Clark had asked me to think seriously about our relationship and where we were headed as a family. I did spend time thinking about my marriage and family while I was away. I realized that the pats on the back and accolades I had received in Cache Valley had become far too important to me. Though I claimed my family was my first priority, when I honestly compared how little time I was spending nurturing my marriage and relationships with my children to how much time I was spending meeting with other environmental educators and cohorts who shared my interests, I knew that approval from colleagues had become overly important for me.

I returned from Alaska determined to work harder at building a home for us in Alpine and to attend more to my husband's and children's needs. I also determined to let go of disappointment over what I had had to leave behind. I would remind myself that the wonderful experiences and friendships of Cache Valley remain with me as part of my life's journey but are not its destination.

During that transitional summer, Clark and I attended BYU Education Week evening classes together and learned some important truths in a class on seeking personal revelation. I began to feel that while I was deeply engaged with all my projects in Cache Valley, I had lost my ability to hear the Spirit whisper to me concerning the direction my life was taking. As our lives settled down and the children enjoyed coming home for lunch, every one of them asked, "You aren't going to start your Outdoor Adventure class here, are you? Will you get back to being the kind of mom that bakes things?" As a new mother I had enjoyed learning to make specialty breads. But homemade bread, cookies, and clean floors were not the real issue, of course. I realized anew the importance of a mother's willingness to simply be there for her children.

Ecologists use the term *ecotone* for zones such as lakeshores, ocean beaches, and forest meadows where two ecosystems overlap. Much of the "action" that ecologists enjoy observing takes place in these zones of overlap. Many ecologists call this action the "edge effect." In ecotones, diversity of plant and wildlife flourishes because organisms from two different ecosystems are brought together. The area of overlapping ecosystems tends to be more complex than any single ecosystem by itself. Humans are attracted to edges. Beaches and meadows are wonderful places to be.

When I look at myself, I see that I tend to gravitate to an ecotone lifestyle. I want to combine the botanist-ecologist-teacher-artist-writer parts of who I am with my most important roles of wife and mother. But complete overlap does not work for me. I have learned that I must be very selective in what additional projects I pursue while acting in my eternally significant roles.

No one single pattern or solution, however, fits all our situations. My friend Karen Fisher, for instance, has worked very hard as a single mom to raise her four children. For seven years she has supported her family by teaching full-time as an elementary teacher. As her children grow towards being successful, happy adults, Karen feels strongly that the Lord has blessed her to balance her full-time work as a teacher with her full-time role as a parent. She feels that when parents—mothers *or fathers*—pursue professional interests for self-fulfillment or escape from stressful parenting or less glamorous family duties, they must be very careful to regularly inquire and re-evaluate if their choices are in keeping with what the Lord wishes them to do at that point in their lives.

I have learned that this process of "course corrections"— weighing trade-offs and postponing personal desires for the needs of others—

may need to be repeated often, so that the things most important are not sacrificed for short-term rewards.

In my case, I looked forward to being again a full-time wife and mother and guiding our family life back to a more stable and tranquil state, yet I still felt a terrible void from saying good-bye to all my projects. I phoned the Monte Bean Museum to find out what types of naturalist programs they offered. A team of three professors were putting together a new environmental education program for secondary school students. After they reviewed the materials I had developed for the Outdoor Adventures program, I was welcomed to the science research team, working (very part-time) to develop and write curriculum for the program.

But the happy turn of circumstances doesn't end there. Clark is also involved as part of that team. Working together, we are developing a program that we both believe in and feel enthusiastic about. We even travel together to different parts of the state, photographing and judging which sites will best serve this project.

I have learned another important lesson, one I hope I never forget. In preparing a lesson for my MIA Maids recently, I was struck by this scripture: "Search diligently, pray always, and be believing, and all things shall work together for your good." (D&C 90:24.) Shortly after this lesson, I was called into the Primary presidency. When I was set apart, the bishop blessed me with the ability to channel my gifts and knowledge to bless the lives of the children in our ward.

Every season of a woman's life holds differing limitations, compensations, and opportunities. Here at the edge of another season of life with all my children now in school, each year seems to pass more quickly, each season turns more swiftly. How important it is for me to learn how to choose the best use of each day remaining to me here, best befitting each season of life I pass through. It has been said that life is God's greatest gift to humankind, and what we do with our life is our gift to God. I'm striving to learn grace by grace as I navigate life's rapids how best to use my gifts in the stewardships I have been given.

Grace and Glory:
Strength from Our Savior

CHIEKO N. OKAZAKI

In Psalm 84:11–12, we read: "For the Lord God is a sun and shield: the Lord will give grace and glory: no good thing will he withhold from them that walk uprightly. O Lord of hosts, blessed is the [man or woman] that trusteth in thee." I testify to the grace and goodness of the Savior. I have felt his Spirit and have pondered his grace and glory.

We all know what it means to be blessed of God when we trust in him and how the Lord is a sun and a shield—but the concepts of grace and glory may seem abstract, far away, perhaps even reserved for the next life. Nevertheless, I believe that we can experience grace and glory here and now. Let me illustrate my very simple definitions of each with a story.

When I became principal of my first elementary school, the outgoing principal, among other orientation information, said, "And watch out for Kevin. He's always disruptive—in class or on the playground. He constantly slips out of class. And he's responsible for most of the vandalism that goes on around here."

I said, "Oh, thank you very much." But I thought, "Whether this is true or not, here's a fifth grader who needs another chance."

I always got to school about six-thirty or seven, so that I had half an hour or an hour to work in my office. When the teachers started arriving about seven, I'd walk through the halls and classrooms, saying "Good morning" and taking time for a quick word if any of them had problems or questions. By the time the children started arriving, I was out on the playground to meet the buses and say hello to the children

Chieko N. Okazaki, born into a Japanese Buddhist family in Hawaii, joined the Church at age fifteen. A schoolteacher and principal for thirty-three years, she serves as first counselor in the general presidency of the Relief Society of The Church of Jesus Christ of Latter-day Saints. She and her husband, the late Edward Yukio Okazaki, are the parents of two sons.

walking from their homes. Within a few days, I knew most of the children, but I made a point of meeting Kevin the first day, before anything had gone wrong, before he'd been in trouble with me even once. I saw in Kevin what he was capable of. I felt that, given respect, he would freely choose to use his boundless energy and influence over his peers to help. After two or three days, when he and I had had three or four brief conversations, I said, "Kevin, everybody says that you know this school like the back of your hand. You know where *everything* is. Is that right?"

"Yeah," he said, a little defiantly. "That's right."

"Well," I continued, "I'm new here, and I don't know the school as well as you do. Will you help me when I need it?"

His whole face shone. He wriggled with pride. I saw him grow three inches taller. "Sure, Mrs. O.," he said. "You can ask me anything."

So I did. A couple of weeks later while I was out greeting the children on Monday morning, I noticed that the playground fence had been damaged over the weekend. "Hi, Kevin," I said. "Look at our fence. Looks like something happened to it over the weekend. Did you see or hear anything?"

He planted his hands on his hips and shook his head disgustedly. "These kids!" he exclaimed. "They should know better than that. Don't worry, Mrs. O. I'll check this out." It was the last time we had damage to the fence.

Another time, the playground garbage cans had been carted to a far corner of the schoolyard. Again, I called on Kevin's expertise. "Kevin," I said, "what do you think became of our garbage cans?"

Again his response was proprietary disgust. "Some people!" he exclaimed. "Don't worry, Mrs. O. I'll take care of it." Within a few minutes, he'd organized a group of friends, and they were hauling the garbage cans back. And this time they stayed.

I knew what had happened to the fence and who had moved the garbage cans in the first place. I'd been a teacher for twenty years, so there wasn't much about kids that surprised me. But the point I want to make here is one about grace and glory.

I gave Kevin grace by believing in him, by giving him a second chance, a clean start, an unprejudiced beginning. It was something he hadn't earned, and the former principal probably would have argued that he never *would* earn it. My perception was that there was no way he *could* earn his way out of the prejudice he was laboring under. He didn't have any way of knowing, ahead of time, whether I was going to be merciful or prejudiced. His recognition of the grace produced glory—that look on his face as he drew himself up straighter, beaming with pride and delight.

This is the definition I'd like to explore. Grace is the state in which we live, surrounded by the love of God. But love is not warm, marshmallowy, indiscriminate affection. God's love is fully particular, embracing our individual beauties, strengths, and gifts. Receiving that grace leads us to give people a second chance, which means believing in them, seeing their strengths and potential for good, not simply wiping the slate clean. My conviction is that we are all different and that God loves and enjoys those differences. He *knows* us and loves what he knows. God's love is ennobling, sustaining, and personal. Glory comes when we recognize and acknowledge his love with gratitude and increased love of our own. We glorify God with our instinctive praise for his goodness when we recognize that what we have received is grace.

Let me explain in a little more detail how I think grace and glory work. God's love fills our lives every day with every breath we take. We all know that intellectually, but we don't always realize it with our hearts. Grace is a gift of love from our Father and our Savior, so tender, so loving, and so lovely that it pierces us with sweetness. At such moments, the masks that cover our everyday lives suddenly drop, and we see divine reality. If we have been shattered by sorrow and adversity, we suddenly realize that the Savior is there with us, buoying us up. If we are oppressed and wearied by many things, suddenly we realize that we are also surrounded and sustained and uplifted by the loving hands of Jesus Christ, who walks beside us and lends us his own strength. If we are overwhelmed by the feeling that we aren't very strong, very beautiful, very valuable, suddenly we realize that in God's eyes we are infinitely precious, that we are yearned over, cherished, and loved.

We realize, in fact, that we are part of a great pattern of love, that Jesus Christ willingly died for us—for you, for me. We realize that our Heavenly Father, whose love for us is boundless and eternal at the same moment that it is particular and individual, was willing to allow his Beloved Son, his Firstborn, to accept the mantle of redeemer and to accomplish the Atonement on our behalf. Think how you are moved and stirred by an act of generous love on the part of one of your children. Then think with what increased love, mingled with pride and grief, our heavenly parents accepted the willing offer of Jesus Christ. Think how that love must have drawn them even closer together. Yet in that love was the desire, even the will, to reach out and include us as well. We are brought into that family circle as an act of love and generosity and mercy. We are brought into that circle, in fact, as an act of grace. We will realize that grace fully, perhaps, in the next life, because we will be alive every moment in its radiance. But we will recognize it from the moments of piercing sweetness that we experience in this life.

If this is grace—the moment of recognizing and feeling God's love that already surrounds us—then what is glory? Again, my definition is simple. It is impossible to respond to a moment of grace with anything but an outpouring of gratitude and a welling up of love. When our rising love and joyful gratitude meet the shower of mercy and love from the Savior and from our heavenly parents, in that contact is the pure radiance and the brilliant light of glory.

The Doctrine and Covenants tells us: "The light which shineth, which giveth you light, is through him who enlighteneth your eyes, which is the same light that quickeneth your understandings; which light proceedeth forth from the presence of God to fill the immensity of space— The light which is in all things, which giveth life to all things, which is the law by which all things are governed, even the power of God." (D&C 88:11–13.)

I see that light issuing forth from our Father to fill every corner of the universe just as the light of the sun travels through the immensity of space to reach our earth. The light itself is invisible, unseen in the immensity of space, until it encounters something that it can shine upon. In the envelope around Earth, the interaction between our atmosphere and sunlight produces blue sky and golden light, warmth, and the energy that keeps the whole process of life in motion. Is the spiritual light that issues forth to fill the immensity of space any less real, any less tangible in its effects than sunlight? It falls as grace upon each of us, like a planet orbiting in the blackness of solitary space. Some of us, sadly, cannot perceive that light and recognize it for what it is. Many others receive it unthinkingly, uncomprehendingly. But when it is received with intelligent and thankful recognition, with a heart open to the direct and personal expression of love that such grace represents, then, at that moment, glory springs into being like a fountain of fireworks and rejoicing.

When Joseph Smith saw the Father and the Son, they were "two Personages, whose brightness and glory defy all description," standing in the radiance of "a pillar of light . . . above the brightness of the sun." (JS–H 1:17, 16.) There are more than eight million of us in the world today who have been stirred by the recounting of that story, who have thrilled to the love and mercy of the Father and the Son. But think of it from the divine perspective as well. How long had they waited for a beloved child to call upon them in faith? How long had they waited for a son with a heart prepared to receive them? No wonder they came in glory! Of course they are constantly surrounded by glory and dwell in glory. It is an attribute of their godhood. But we mortals perceive the glory when our hearts are prepared to see it.

I know that I have much to learn about both grace and glory and what both of those terms mean from God's perspective; but from my human perspective, grace comes in those moments when we see the divine love and acceptance that surrounds us, and glory comes when we respond to that vision with gratitude and love. At such moments, we know *who* we are because we know *whose* we are.

Do you remember Joseph Smith's vision of the celestial kingdom? In that vision, both grace and glory play a prominent role. He wrote: "And thus we saw the glory of the celestial, which excels in all things— where God, even the Father, reigns upon his throne forever and ever; before whose throne all things bow in humble reverence, and give him glory forever and ever. They who dwell in his presence are the church of the Firstborn; and they see as they are seen, and know as they are known, having received of his fulness and of his grace; and he makes them equal in power, and in might, and in dominion." (D&C 76:92–95.)

I want to explore two ideas related to grace and glory. First, faith helps us perceive grace. Second, grace is a free act of love.

THE ROLE OF FAITH

First, consider how faith helps us perceive grace. Isn't faith the purpose of mortality? Didn't we come here to the earth to walk by faith so that we might learn to see through the masks and myths of this world to the eternal reality that underlies it? That reality is that we live in a personal world created by love and agency. We are free to choose, every day and every hour, either to increase or decrease the amount of love and the amount of agency in our world. The reality is that the most solid and reliable fact in the universe is not the laws of physics or the might of armies but the personal relationship we have in our hearts with our Savior, Jesus Christ. And we can see that reality, which is the love of Christ, only through the eyes of faith.

Let me share with you a story to illustrate the strength that comes from faith and the reality of spiritual things. Malcolm Muggeridge, a prize-winning British journalist, writes of Mother Teresa's charity work among the poorest of the poor in the Calcutta slums: "Statistically speaking, what she achieves is little, or even negligible. But then Christianity is not a statistical view of life. That there should be more joy in heaven over one sinner who repents than over all the hosts of the just, is an anti-statistical proposition. Likewise with the work of the Missionaries of Charity. Mother Teresa is fond of saying that welfare is for a purpose— an admirable and a necessary one—[but that] Christian love is for a person. The one is about numbers, the other about [Christ]."[1] In other words, one is about works, and the other is about grace.

More than twenty years ago, Muggeridge filmed a documentary for the BBC about Mother Teresa's work. After much fervent persuasion, Mother Teresa finally agreed to the project and wrote: "Now let us do something beautiful for God."[2] Muggeridge arrived just the day before a general strike to find the courtyard of Mother Teresa's large, nondescript headquarters "just a bare stone space between walls with the sun beating down and, outside, the screech of the trams, the shouts, the interminable passing of bare or sandalled feet, of a Calcutta street." Even the chapel windows looked out on the street, and the noises from the street washed in steadily, a constant reminder to the sisters, even at prayer, of the poor outside. Yet the spiritual reality was quite different. Mother Teresa's courtyard, Muggeridge wrote, had "something delectable about it."[3]

A fifty-minute documentary usually takes two or three months to film, but they had only five days. There was no chance to reshoot any footage with problems. The Calcutta sun was broiling, and the cameraman worried that the film would be damaged. The physical reality was grim. But the spiritual reality was quite different. Muggeridge wrote: "It is not just my opinion but that of all concerned, that [the filming] proceeded with quite exceptional smoothness and speed. Our next move always seemed to be obvious; there were none of the usual breakdowns and crises. Above all, there were no bickering or quarrelling, which, in the circumstances of film-making, is almost unavoidable."[4]

Mother Teresa decided where they would go, when they would go, and what they would shoot, changing her mind at the last minute at one point. This remarkable ease in filming was "a kind of miracle" for these professionals and technicians, but Muggeridge also records an actual miracle. Part of the film was to be shot in the House of the Dying. This old temple, formerly dedicated to the goddess Kali, holds people from the streets of Calcutta who are too ill to be cured; the Sisters of Charity take them where they can receive simple care and, as Mother Teresa puts it, "die within sight of a loving face."[5]

Filming here posed immense technical challenges for Muggeridge and his crew; the only windows were small and high up on the walls. The lighting was so dim that Ken, the cameraman, was "adamant that filming was quite impossible. . . . We had only one small light with us, and to get the place adequately lighted in the time at our disposal was quite impossible. It was decided that, nonetheless, Ken should have a go, but by way of insurance he took, as well, some film in an outside courtyard where some of the inmates were sitting in the sun. In the processed film, the part taken inside was bathed in a particularly beautiful soft light, whereas the part taken outside was rather dim and confused. . . . [E]veryone who has seen the film [agrees] . . . that the light in the Home for the Dying is quite exceptionally lovely. . . . How to account for this? Ken has all along insisted that, technically speaking, the result is impossible. To prove the point, on his next filming expedition—to the Middle East—he used some of the same stock in a similarly poor light, with completely negative results. He offers no explanation, but just shrugs and agrees that it happened."[6]

Muggeridge's explanation is much simpler: "I am personally persuaded that Ken recorded the first authentic photographic miracle. . . . [It was,] in fact, the Kindly Light [Cardinal John Henry] Newman refers to in his well-known exquisite hymn ["Lead Kindly Light"]. . . . Mother Teresa's Home for the Dying is overflowing with love. . . . This love is luminous . . . an outward and visible luminosity manifesting God's inward and invisible omnipresent love."[7]

Mother Teresa is a pure and powerful witness to the Savior's grace, which she perceives as the love of God and which she manifests in her life as a blessing to others. These good people could see what the Doctrine and Covenants teaches us—that the light of Christ can fill the immensity of space and enlighten everyone who comes into the world. (D&C 88:12; 84:46.) I think Mother Teresa embodies the Spirit of Christ, and I think that we, too, can embody it. Every act of kindness, every generous gesture, every merciful word increases the amount of love in our world. Each of those acts recognizes the grace that surrounds our lives like a halo; and every spark of recognition ignites that halo into a blaze of glory. Faith allows us to pierce through the physical masks that tell us the world is harsh and even horrible to find the spiritual reality of love, grace, and glory underneath.

GRACE IS FREE

I was an elementary school teacher and principal for most of my adult life. One of the high points of every fall was Halloween. I've always enjoyed Halloween—and believe me, it's a big holiday in an elementary school—because the children are just aglow with joy over it. Why do children enjoy it so much? I think they love dressing up in costumes and being someone else for a little while, of course. They're trying on a different identity and exploring a dream. But I also think there's another reason: children are on the receiving end of the treats without having to work for them or explain why they want them. There aren't many occasions when a child's desires are met, literally on demand. As responsible and conscientious parents, we ask them to explain why they want to go somewhere, do something, invite someone over, buy a new item, or especially get candy. How frustrating it must be for them when we say, in effect, "Sorry, your reasons aren't good enough!"

So the whole year is a time of works for children, so to speak, but Halloween is a day of grace. Of course works are important. We know how essential it is to recognize our duties, to serve conscientiously, to work hard at righteousness, to be disciplined disciples, to endure to the end. Judging only by physical reality, we must conclude life is hard. It is filled with adversities, challenges, temptations, and sorrow. The voice of physical reality says, "We pass through sorrow." The voice of faith says, "For it must needs be, that there is an opposition in all things," and "Adam [and Eve] fell that [we] might be; and [we] are, that [we] might have joy." (2 Nephi 2:11, 25.) And the voice of grace says, "Yea, though you walk through the valley of the shadow of death, you need fear no evil: for I am with you. My rod and my staff, they comfort you." (See Psalm 23:4.)

The point I'm trying to make is that grace is a free gift to us—not something we earn or pay for or that dangles in front of us like a carrot that we can reach if we are very obedient. Nephi, in describing his labor to preserve the plates and record his own revelations, says, "For we labor diligently to write, to persuade our children, and also our brethren, to believe in Christ, and to be reconciled to God; for we know that it is by grace that we are saved, after all we can do." (2 Nephi 25:23.) Sometimes I've heard people quote that scripture in a way that gives me the impression that I am floundering in a river, being swept toward a great waterfall. As I struggle desperately toward the shore, I see a man waiting with a life preserver on a rope, but he doesn't throw me the ring. I struggle harder, more desperately, and he shouts, "Come on! I'll save you, but only after all that you can do." I wonder if there's a possibility that he'll just watch me disappear over the falls while he shakes his head sadly and says, "Isn't that too bad? She didn't do all she could do."

My feeling about Nephi's statement is very different. Christ is in the river with us, not standing on the shore. He is the master of wind and wave, the creator of the river and the falls. He can walk on the water and command the storms to obey him. Yet he is in the water with us, feeling the batterings of the same current. He lends us his strength so we can try. He gives us his vision so that we can see the shore. He whispers encouragement in our ears. When we are exhausted, his arm is there for us to lean on. It may be true that we can always do more— but not because *we* have no limits. It's because *he* has none.

Grace is not a few feet of rope. Grace is a network of support and love. It is with us, around us, under us, above us every minute of every day. When we act in an awareness of grace, we ourselves become vessels of grace. Joni Eareckson Tada has written: "Whenever those around you see God's character displayed in your attitudes and responses, you are displaying His glory. . . . God's glory isn't reserved for a temple of stone or some heavenly vista. It can shine out clearly while you're changing a flat on the freeway . . . or counseling an angry co-worker . . . or lying in a hospital bed . . . or balancing two crying babies in the church nursery."[8]

In this last year, my awareness of and my gratitude for the Savior's grace that gives me strength to live with grace myself has lengthened, deepened, and grown strong and tall. When I spoke at last year's Women's Conference, my husband, Ed, had been dead for only six weeks. I have had a year to accustom myself to the new rhythm of living without him, and it has been very hard. We had been married for almost forty-three years, and there was no part of my life he did not share. He was fully supportive of my calling, seeing my needs and meeting them as quietly and as happily as he did everything. If I took clothes to the dry cleaner's, a few days later, they would reappear in the closet. Ed had picked them up for me. He did the laundry and the shopping. While I was making supper, Ed would be sweeping the floor, emptying the dishwasher, and asking me how things had gone that day, telling me about an interesting meeting he'd attended, friends he had heard from, or remembering that a daughter in our home-teaching family had a birthday coming up and that he'd arranged for us to take her out for ice cream.

If I told him that I'd been asked to address a singles' fireside and was wondering what approach I, a long-time married woman, could take that would not sound patronizing, Ed would talk over ideas with me; a few days later, he'd hand me two or three articles and stories he thought I might be able to use. If we had guests, they walked into an orderly house, because Ed had cleaned and arranged it with an eye to their comfort. Before every meal, it was with Ed I shared a moment of gratitude to our Heavenly Father for his blessings. No day closed without uniting our hearts and our voices in prayers of gratefulness for our home and our sons, for the gospel's joyous message, and for each other. Together we petitioned the Lord for our needs, to help our children, to bless the leaders of the Church, and to keep us in his Spirit.

Now Ed is gone. If the clothes reappear in the closet, it's because I put them there. If the water heater needs either to be repaired or replaced, that decision is mine alone. I still talk over my day with Ed, and I often feel him with me, but I can no longer hear his voice in reply, in support, in questions and discussion.

Ed is gone, but I am not alone. I face my days and my nights, despite the difficult moments they contain, knowing that the Savior, whose Spirit permeated our home and whose love underlay the thousands of kindnesses that Ed performed, is still with me. I still feel that love and kindness. I have claimed in a new way the scriptural promises: "I will never leave thee, nor forsake thee." (Hebrews 13:5.) "Lo, I am with you alway, even unto the end of the world." (Matthew 28:20.) "I am the Lord, I change not." (Malachi 3:6.) I feel the Savior's grace in my life. Even in the desolation and sorrow of this last year have come unforgettable experiences of grace that have filled me with amazement at their sweetness and that have dazzled me with the glory of seeing the hand of the Lord in my life.

One of those moments came at Ed's funeral. At his request, expressed long before his death, I invited a Polynesian choir to sing at the funeral services. Sharing my sorrow, they expressed their own love for Ed in their music at the chapel. But I will never forget standing in the cemetery later with Ed's casket before me, after our son dedicated the grave, after military honors had been rendered to Ed, and feeling the whole weight of that loss towering above me, ready to fall like a wave. Quietly, lovingly, without a request or a plan, those dear Saints began singing the Hawaiian songs that Ed and I loved so much—songs of farewell and sorrow, songs of love and acceptance, songs of faith and affirmation. They strengthened me with their gift of aloha. They reached out across that terrible abyss of loneliness to tell me that I was not alone. I thanked them then, and I thank them now, for their act of grace.

CONCLUSION

We live in a world of grace; we are surrounded, encircled, enwrapped, and continually showered by grace. When we see that and let our hearts respond with the increased gratitude and love that are surely an instinctive response, we can make it a world of grace and glory. When we exercise faith, we can pierce the mask of physical reality and perceive the spiritual reality that lies beneath it. Grace is a free gift to us from a loving Father and Savior; and to honor our agency, it remains for us to accept and receive the gift.

What would it be like for us to inhabit such a world? Right now, we can see that reality only in brief moments and enter that world only as a visitor. But this will not always be so. All of the promises of the scriptures tell us that we are the children of that world, fitted to receive and to perceive the grace of God and created to dwell in eternal glory if we choose. Doctrine and Covenants 101 contains a beautiful description of the millennial world that may, I think, give us a taste of that experience. Joseph Smith wrote:

"And in that day the enmity of man, and the enmity of beasts, yea, the enmity of all flesh, shall cease from before my face.

"And in that day whatsoever any [one] shall ask, it shall be given. . . .

"And in that day Satan shall not have power to tempt any [one].

"And there shall be no sorrow because there is no death. . . .

"Yea, verily I say unto you, in that day when the Lord shall come, he shall reveal all things . . .

"Things most precious, things that are above, and things that are beneath, things that are in the earth, and upon the earth, and in heaven.

"And all they who suffer persecution for my name, and endure in faith, though they are called to lay down their lives for my sake yet shall they partake of *all this glory.*

"Wherefore, fear not even unto death; for in this world your joy is not full, but in me your joy is full." (D&C 101:26–36; emphasis added.)

May our faith in the Lord Jesus Christ grow line upon line and precept upon precept, increasing in grace until, like Enos of old, we may see His face with pleasure and dwell in His presence as partakers of His glory and in Him find a fullness of joy.

NOTES

1. Malcolm Muggeridge, *Something Beautiful for God: Mother Teresa of Calcutta* (New York: Doubleday and Co., Image Books, 1977), p. 22.
2. Ibid., p. 97.
3. Ibid., p. 28.
4. Ibid., pp. 30–31.
5. Ibid., p. 31.
6. Ibid., pp. 31–32.
7. Ibid., p. 33.
8. Joni Eareckson Tada, "Insights," *Time with God* (Dallas: Word Bibles, 1991), p. 435.

Easter Morning

MARYJAN MUNGER

1. Corpus Christi

Last night, by chance, I read old myths
of Attis and Osiris, those murdered gods,
of the Fisher Kings killed to get
one more green summer; read how New Guinea tribesmen
tear the flesh of their human offering, sharing it
like bread. What ghastly sacrament
for those first twelve—this
is my body, my blood.
Remember me.

2. Hosanna

For He rose from death
like sweet grass springing.
In the morning He rose
like the small sparrow
taking the air with a sudden
whisper, just one twig
behind him swinging.

*MaryJan Gay Munger received her master's degree in English literature from Brigham
Young University. She serves on the board of the Association for Mormon Letters and
referees poems for* BYU Studies *and* Wasatch Review International. *Sister Munger
teaches in her ward Relief Society. She and her husband, Casey H. Munger, have two
children.*

3. As We Partake

I start with spring: the tight pink bud,
the pale leaf. Something these eight-year-olds
have seen. They know it is a miracle.
They've held the small hard seeds
and buried them. This, I tell them,
is resurrection. Their eyes gaze past me,
amazed, believing; hands and feet wonderfully still.
Their eyes are seeing new life
sprouting out of graves, beautiful
bodies swaying like young cherry trees.

Living by Grace: A New Frontier

SUSAN EASTON BLACK

My struggle to understand grace began when I first memorized the Primary song "I Am a Child of God." The ending of the first verse became my childish key to celestial realms. "Teach me all that I must *know* / To live with him someday," was how I sang the stanza. I thought by quoting scripture, knowing multifaceted details of the gospel, identifying slides of the Garden Tomb and Golgotha, I could successfully pass my "final judgment." A score of 72 percent on a gospel multiple-choice test, I hoped, would satisfy my Father in Heaven, and he would say of me, "Well done, thou good and faithful servant: thou hast been faithful over a few things, I will make thee ruler over many things: enter thou into the joy of thy lord." (Matthew 25:21.)

Simply knowing about the gospel seemed sufficient for my eternal salvation. Therefore, descriptive knowledge became absorbing as the song sank deep into my heart. My bishop's admonition to leave the scriptures home and give the Sunday School teacher an opportunity to teach without rebuttal fell on deaf ears, for I knew that correct knowledge was the key to celestial glory. I viewed myself as a self-ordained scriptorian, leading my classmates to greater knowledge and ultimately greater glory.

This distorted, childish view crumbled a few years later. It was a sad day in my life when I heard that Elder Spencer W. Kimball had asked Naomi Randall to change a key word in her song: *know* was changed to *do*. He quipped, "Of course, Sister Randall wrote most of the words, but I wrote one!" Now the lyrics stated, "Teach me all that I must *do* / To live with him someday." Elder Kimball explained, "Just knowing

Susan Easton Black is a professor of Church history and doctrine at Brigham Young University. Sister Black is the BYU Eighteenth Stake Relief Society president and an ordinance worker in the Provo Temple. She and her husband, Harvey B. Black, are the parents of eight children.

the gospel is not enough. It is *doing* the will of our Heavenly Father that prepares us to return and live with him someday."[1] I have known sorrowful days but none quite so discouraging. I soon discovered that the energy required to verbally define faith paled when compared to doing acts of faith. Discussions of true charity lacked eternal import unless I visited the sick. To know the particulars of Christ's ministry without doing Christlike acts now seemed hypocritical, empty, and pretentious.

Somewhat painfully I began to emphasize doing good. Through the ensuing years, my "do-its" mounted one on top of another: wearing dresses of modest length, choosing a bathing suit my mother would not be embarrassed to be seen in, writing journal entries, and reading scripture. As I surveyed my "do-its," I also recognized my "I-didn't-do-its," my failings. It became evident that at some level I felt more worthy, but I was far from perfect. I created my own Tower of Babel, not a Jacob's Ladder, as my outward charity was increasingly laced with inward frustration. The seminary scriptures not yet memorized, journal entries missed, and endless genealogy all underscored my continuing dilemma. Nevertheless, I congratulated myself that my "do-its" did surpass the "I-didn't-do-its," and I continued to hope that the balance of justice would tip in my favor.

Little by little, I began to reach beyond the notion of *knowing* good and even *doing* good. I realized that the real challenge is in *being* good, which was not something I could achieve alone. That encompasses the love and mercy of God. This realization changes the song to, "Teach me all that I must *be* / To live with him someday." I first glimpsed the infinite implication and power of the concept "to be," which is a form of "I AM," as I reread the account of the Lord's appearance to Moses. Moses inquired: "Behold, when I come unto the children of Israel, and shall say unto them, The God of your fathers hath sent me unto you; and they shall say to me, What is his name? what shall I say unto them?

"And God said unto Moses, I AM THAT I AM: and he said, Thus shalt thou say unto the children of Israel, I AM hath sent me unto you." (Exodus 3:13–14.)

If I am to become Christlike, I must be lifted to fully accept Christ's name, "I AM." My bishop and stake president help me reach "I AM" by asking sincere questions that begin with, "Are you . . . ?" I respond, "I AM." It would be easier if they asked, "Do you *know?*" or "Do you do?" For example, "Do you *know* the definition of honesty?" My response: "I can define honesty and even give an example of George Washington and cherry trees." And if he were to say, "Do you *do* honest acts?" I could declare, "Bishop, my actions are honest." Instead he asks, "Are you honest in all your dealings?" To be temple worthy I must answer with my Savior, "I AM." A second example: "What do you *know* about tithing?" My simple response would be, "Bishop, it's 10 percent of my increase." And if the bishop asked, "Do you *do* acts of tithing?" I could respond, "I contribute by helping at home, babysitting, and listening to distressed friends." Instead he asks, "Are you a full tithe-payer?" I answer with my Savior, "I AM." He asks, "Are you morally clean?" Notice the expected response again: you and I answer with our Savior, "I AM."

This form of questioning shifts the focus from gospel knowledge and good works to being. By responding, "I AM," you and I agree to be one with Christ—to become Christlike in our consistency, in our integrity, and in our acknowledgment that we are full tithe-payers, honest, morally clean, and upright in our dealings because of Christ. How can I, so imperfect, so incomplete, answer such questions confidently with, "I AM," knowing my weaknesses and failings? The answer is in the love and mercy of Jesus Christ. We sing, "I stand all amazed at the love Jesus offers me, / Confused at the grace that so fully he proffers me."[2] For committed, striving people, his grace, his mercy, can make up the difference between what we are and what we will ultimately become. Thus, it is by and through his love that you and I can answer with assurance that we are worthy to be called children of God.

His love extends the privilege of accepting the name of Jesus Christ in the waters of baptism, making sacred covenants in his holy house, and eventually returning unspotted to our Father in Heaven. With gratitude I express my love for Jesus Christ and for his atoning sacrifice. I internalize the scripture, applying it to my own failings, "Woman, where are those thine accusers? hath no man condemned thee? She said, No man, Lord. And Jesus said unto her, Neither do I condemn thee: go, and sin no more." (John 8:10–11.)

The grace he "so fully proffers" was bought with heaviness, rejection, and deep physical and spiritual anguish at Gethsemane. The resurrected Christ reflected on 7 March 1830: "[This] suffering caused myself, even God, the greatest of all, to tremble because of pain, and to bleed at every pore, and to suffer both body and spirit—and would that I might not drink the bitter cup." (D&C 19:18.) Although he battled alone, he did not despair. His suffering brought him at one with his Father—to a completeness, a fullness of love and mercy, a fullness intended for you, for me. His grace is sufficient; the assurance of immortality and eternal life is sure.

I believe in him, and I believe his words, his teachings, and his sacrifice. With that belief comes the assurance that he invites all to come unto him. We accept his invitation by entering the waters of baptism. A new being emerges who covenants to take his name and willingly promises to "bear one another's burdens . . . mourn with those that mourn . . . comfort those that stand in need of comfort, and . . . stand as witnesses of God at all times and in all things, and in all places that ye may be in, even until death." (Mosiah 18:8–9.)

This covenantal acceptance unites with great meaning the phrases "to know," "to do," and "to be." The meaning is perhaps even more true when the phrases are reversed: "to be," "to do," and "to know." "Teach me all that I must *be* / To live with him some day." Teach me to willingly take upon myself the name of Christ and to enter and keep sacred covenants. "Teach me all that I must *do* / To live with him someday." For "when ye are in the service of your fellow beings ye are only in the service of your God." (Mosiah 2:17.) "Teach me all that I must *know* / To live with him someday." A peaceful, reassuring knowledge will fill your soul, and your hope will grow brighter as your life becomes more pleasing to our Father in Heaven.

This order of events is neither something I created nor a new insight: it is of ancient origin. When reciting the sacramental prayer upon the bread, we hear the divine order. "That they are willing to take upon them the name of thy Son," which means they take upon them the name of Christ or "I AM"—to *be*. The "to *do*" is found in the next two phrases: "And always remember him, and keep his commandments which he hath given them." The "to *know*" is found in the final phrase, "that they may always have his Spirit to be with them," which is the peaceful comfort of the Spirit of the Lord. (Moroni 4:3.) I testify that this order will make your life more meaningful because you are, you do, and you know.

I would like to share a personal experience, a brief moment with one who knew the ancient order of being, doing, and knowing. Several years ago I attended a luncheon in which Elder LeGrand Richards was the honored guest. I happened to be sitting close to him and overheard his granddaughter ask, "Granddad, how are you feeling?" He exclaimed, "How dare you ask me that?" It was an awkward moment for the granddaughter and for all who had overheard the exchange. He repeated even louder, "How dare you ask me that?" and added, "Look at me." He then invited those in attendance to look at him. He pulled a few strands from the top of his head while declaring, "This was once a full head of hair." He next removed his glasses and announced their importance to his sight. He took out his hearing aids and pronounced, "I can't hear a sound without the aid of these." He then removed his teeth, exclaiming, "None of these are mine."

After several awkward moments of silence, he turned to his granddaughter and instructed, "Ask me, How are you, LeGrand!" Her initial response was, "I don't want to." But with coaxing, she complied. "How are you, LeGrand?" she asked. Suddenly he stood so all could see him. His countenance had changed as he smiled at the guests and exclaimed, "I have never been better! I have made it! I have run the race, and I have almost finished the course. Soon I will be with my wife and with my Savior."

He taught me the joy that comes to the disciple, the follower of Christ, who knows that through the grace of God he can answer "I AM" to questions of worthiness, who knows he is on the path to return safely to Heavenly Father. He *knew* the Master because he had been His servant. He knew the Father because he had known the Son. He had *done* his works and knew by the grace of God that he could rightfully anticipate a glorious resurrection. His lifetime of knowing and doing had led to his *being* a worthy son, walking the strait and narrow path leading to eternal life. (See 1 Nephi 8:20.)

Grace on a new frontier is to venture into areas where only the righteous have traveled before. It is to accept the invitation to become constant in gospel principles and practices, having an eye single to the glory of God. It is to love him with all our heart, might, mind, and strength. It is to recognize, as Robert L. Millet so aptly stated, that "we in time gain control through being willing to relinquish control. . . . As we submit we come to know his will."[3] As you and I come to know his will, may we remember that that knowledge comes to us through the grace of God.

NOTES

1. Virginia B. Cannon, *Our Children's Songs* (Salt Lake City: Deseret Book Co., 1992), p. 83.

2. *Hymns of The Church of Jesus Christ of Latter-day Saints* (Salt Lake City: The Church of Jesus Christ of Latter-day Saints, 1985), no. 193.

3. Robert L. Millet, "The Irony of Grace," address delivered at the BYU-Relief Society Women's Conference, 29 Apr. 1993, pp. 3–4. Copy in possession of the author.

In the House of Grace

MARYJAN MUNGER

we all wash dishes. And in hot,
soapy water, until our nails soften
and come clean. Heaven's kitchen has no need
for idle overseers. With a flick of a towel
we chase them out and turn in peace
to our work. Washing our hands, reaching
for cloths, for brooms, for dirty dishes,
working like two women would
whose talk drifts up with the steam from rinse water,
whose silence settles like stoneware bowls
nesting. Two women who know
what needs to be done and how. Two,
or three, and whoever's handy
does it. Moving around the kitchen
stooping and stretching, our separate errands
wind together: a single work, a glory
of shining floors and clean plates,
the windows open to the evening air.

MaryJan Gay Munger received her master's degree in English literature from Brigham Young University. She serves on the board of the Association for Mormon Letters and referees poems for BYU Studies *and* Wasatch Review International. *Sister Munger teaches in her ward Relief Society. She and her husband, Casey H. Munger, have two children.*

Evening Balm
and Morning Manna:
Daily Gifts of Healing Grace

ELAINE SHAW SORENSEN

Grace is a powerful, personal doctrine—the essence of the inner-most personal connection between the human and the divine. We speak of it with cautious respect, even awe, taking care that a public discussion of the precious, silent gift does not distort it into common dogma rather than an issue of deep personal faith. In our intellectualizing, taxonomizing, and indexing of doctrines, we can lose personal, spiritual meaning. Our own inner "lived experience" as followers of Christ will give us our best understanding of grace.

One Easter I listened to a young man express his gratitude for the atonement of Christ. He was thankful that Jesus did not sin because, he said, "Now all I have to do is repent when I do something wrong; then I can have exaltation." This formula seems to be an immature understanding of the divine nature of Christ's atonement and of the process of exaltation. He spoke as though any one of us might have achieved the Atonement if, by some accidental miracle, we could simply have avoided sin. Similarly, we could, he assumed, achieve salvation by our good works and repentance—essentially by ourselves "with Jesus Christ as merely an advisor."[1] According to this view, we do not need the direct divine intervention of a Savior.

As a listener that day, my problems were less of major sin and repentance and more of hurt, loss, and despair. It struck me that while surely it is true that Jesus was the only one who could intervene to offer mercy for justice, because he was without sin, just as important as his *sinless* nature was his *godly* nature, "full of grace and truth." (John 1:14.) Only he could offer divine healing relief to life's trauma.

Elaine Shaw Sorensen is the mother of four children and the associate dean of the College of Nursing at Brigham Young University. Sister Sorensen filled a mission in Colombia and serves as the education counselor in her stake Relief Society.

Most of us have experienced faith-wrenching experiences that do not fit into the simple "sin-repent-be-saved" equation. Such trials require a deep personal consideration of God's healing gift of grace.

THE MEANING OF GRACE

The word *grace* itself is beautiful to ponder. Its Greek translation refers to good-will, loving-kindness, or favor. Grace has also been called the "ability to overcome the trials of the world through the love of God."[2]

Our LDS Bible Dictionary further clarifies the doctrinal principle: "The main idea of the word is divine means of help or strength. . . . It is through the grace of the Lord Jesus, made possible by his atoning sacrifice, that [humanity] will be raised in immortality. . . . It is likewise through the grace of the Lord that individuals, through faith in the atonement of Jesus Christ and repentance of their sins, receive strength and assistance to do good works that they otherwise would not be able to maintain if left to their own means. This grace is an enabling power that allows men and women to lay hold on eternal life and exaltation after they have expended their own best efforts. Divine grace is needed by every soul. . . . However, grace cannot suffice without total effort on the part of the recipient."

The New Testament and the Book of Mormon are filled with doctrines of grace. As Church members, we sometimes hesitate to discuss the principle, however, perhaps because we view grace as some complicated theological philosophy that is either among the mysteries not to be considered or a concern of the resurrection that has nothing to do with our day-to-day lives. Nothing could be further from the truth. We *need* to recognize the personal nature of grace and its power to heal in our daily living.

GRACE AND WORKS

Throughout history people have struggled to recognize the compatibility of the doctrines of works and grace. By the time Jesus came to the earth, the Law of Moses stressed almost exclusively behavioral laws and the singular value of works, especially as the Law had been distorted by the Pharisees and Sadducees. Jesus acknowledged the need for works, but moreover he "fulfilled the law," heralding the divine gift of grace. (Matthew 5:17, 19; John 14:15–21; 15:10.)

When Jesus left the earth and the Apostasy followed, the value of work for salvation again became disproportionate. By the sale of indulgences, for example, sixteenth-century churches, in effect, traded credit toward salvation for works and money.[3] The buying and selling of indulgences in itself reflected a value on the ability of a person to do (or buy) something to achieve salvation, for himself or another. The leaders of the Protestant Reformation fought this dissonance between works and grace, and indeed they overcompensated by introducing new doctrines of salvation by grace alone.

The harmony of grace and works was an important element of the latter-day restoration of the true doctrine; however, Church members of the new dispensation are naturally inclined to overemphasize works, in contrast to prevalent sectarian doctrines of salvation by grace alone. Our propensity to rely so heavily on works also reflects our present technological, behavioristic society, which places so much emphasis on achievement. We almost worship "all we can do." In business, we measure success by the bottom line. In education, the behaviorist tradition promotes a technical training model that demands specific, measurable outcomes. Such behaviorism works well for goals that are concrete, visible, and rule driven.[4]

Sometimes, in our spiritual lives, we also desire a simple set of rules to follow with a documented trail of our good actions to help us evaluate our place on the path to heaven or sometimes our more immediate and visible path of acceptance among our mortal peers. Such emphasis upon our own works gives a sense of control. We can find reasons for blessings and see our trials as consequences of failure. The world makes sense to us.

Because we believe so strongly in a theology based on works and repentance, true keystones of our religion, we sometimes risk overemphasizing the behavioristic power of our own works to achieve salvation and exaltation. Then, when adversities beyond our control prevent the perfect good works we desire, we feel we have failed somehow or that God has failed us.

As we strive toward immortality, our mortal nature hungers for a sense of power over all aspects of our lives. Trials or circumstances that leave us powerless make us feel guilty or that we have failed. We seem to prefer feelings of guilt to feelings of helplessness. Yet in many cases, to feel guilty is inappropriate, maybe even prideful. We are not omnipotent; we do not have power over all circumstances and people in our lives. To acknowledge some degree of helplessness is to invite humility and faith, to accept our dependence upon God. "God resisteth the proud, but giveth grace unto the humble." (James 4:6.) We learn more of that principle from Ether 12:27: "If men [and women] come unto me I will show unto them their weakness. I give unto [them] weakness that they may be humble; and my grace is sufficient for all men [and women] that humble themselves before me; for if they humble themselves before me, and have faith in me, then will I make weak things become strong unto them." Grace intercedes to change our focus from what we can or cannot *do* to who we *are.*[5]

Behaviorism alone does not work for things that are spiritual in nature, that cannot be measured: discernment, insight, caring, longing after goodness, creativity, ethical awareness, moral courage, love of learning, concern for excellence, love, charity—or healing. We cannot heal from life's pain, much less aspire to become godly, only by knowing and obeying commandments on a checklist. We must move one step further to submission to the Savior and acceptance of his gift of grace.

Grace is the principle that makes sense of the ironies of the Spirit: power only after submission, victory through surrender, strength by acknowledging weakness, our sin offered to his perfection, the telestial logic of justice transcended by the celestial gift of mercy.

THE NEED FOR HEALING

Grace, the divine gift of the Atonement, is a healing balm readily available to relieve our pain, a nourishing manna to assuage the hungers of our daily lives. In the arithmetic of the universe, how may grief, regret, or disappointment be accounted for when repentance does not apply or restitution is not possible? Only God's grace can balance the account. Elder Gene R. Cook taught that "Christ was sent not only to help us heal the wounds of transgression and iniquity, but also to bear our grief and sorrow and guilt."[6]

I have been haunted by countless evidences of my own negligence and inadequacies, which only Christ's atonement will redeem. I see them in the faces of my children when I disappoint them. Poor decisions may cause our families to suffer. Some of us marry the wrong person, and our children suffer; we are negligent or unconscious of acts and words that harm or destroy. The greater part of hurt, guilt, loss, and regret is borne privately, in a quiet heart, away from the warmth and casseroles of supportive friends or family. St. Exupéry wrote in

The Little Prince, "It is such a secret place, the land of tears."[7] Grace brings to that place the gift of healing that allows peace and growth.

Several years ago, I sat alone in my living room with the scriptures. For years, I had repeated apparently unanswered prayers for repair of a traumatically broken marriage. I was alone, exhausted—almost extinguished. On that night, I cried to the Lord that the only obvious answer—divorce—seemed the wrong answer, that I needed some confirmation for what I must do. That night, as no other in my life, my eyes and heart were guided to passages that gave strength and hope combined with a sweet peace and assurance of purpose for our family: the Lord was with us; we would survive.

It was a good thing that spiritual confirmation was as strong as it was, because subsequent struggles have been nearly overwhelming. Two trying years later, my children and I moved into a new home. The next few months were filled with hope, new friends, more school for me, a new job, and a wonderful welcome into our new ward. I soon settled into the hopeful myth that I had passed with faith the greatest adversity of my life, that what had been sown "in tears" could now be reaped "in joy." (Psalm 126:5.)

Before the next year was through, however, on the eve of general conference, my eight-year-old son, Todd, was killed in a shocking accident. A cog from the very gears that move the planets was gone, and for me there appeared a great dark hole in the universe.

During the months that followed, I learned that it is not enough simply to survive tragedy; trials are in vain if we gain no meaning from them, no healing, and no increase in sensitivity to the daily gifts of God's grace.

Such healing is a lifelong process. Just this last week, I was ambushed by an unexpected return of profound grief over the death of my Todd. For several days I relived the raw moments of his loss. Compounding that, I was feeling overwhelmed and deeply weary with depleting resources, loneliness, and heavy burdens of responsibility that extend into the future as far as I can see.

Through a long-distance telephone call, my mother sensed my renewed despair. She pleaded, in words I could not accept, "You must find a way to let Todd go. Allow him to be where he is, doing what he is doing. You cannot continue to try to cling to him through the veil." She ended in a wise, tearful plea, "You cannot live your whole life in Gethsemane!"

Elder Neal A. Maxwell wrote: "There is, in the suffering of the highest order, a point that is reached—a point of aloneness—when the individual (as did the Savior on a much grander scale) must bear it, as it were, alone. Even the faithful may wonder if they can take any more or if they are in some way forsaken.

"Those who, as it were, stand at the foot of the cross, often can do so little to help absorb the pain and the anguish. It is something we must bear ourselves."[8]

Anyone who would be a disciple of Christ kneels sometime at Gethsemane. But, as my mother noted, we need not stay. When we can find the courage to surrender, to accept the gift of the Savior—who already suffered there—we can stand and move on to another garden. Grace offers the quiet promise of that safe passage.

SHARING THE MANNA AND THE MEDICINE

When we serve one another, we become divine instruments for gifts of grace, vehicles by which the Savior offers love to others. By being there when another needs us, we are offering God's gifts of daily grace to the lives of others. I am just now becoming aware of the thousands of daily gifts of grace that have allowed me to survive. Foremost among them have been some unplanned precious moments with my children. I have been nourished by some of the simple things they have said.

When my son Chad was thirteen, he began to call me "Mamba La Bamba." Offended, my then-eight-year-old daughter Johanna said, "Mom, you shouldn't let Chad call you Mamba La Bamba. It sounds disrespectful." I thought about it, but aside from "I need money" and "Isn't there anything to eat?" this new nickname was the most syllables I had heard from Chad in two difficult years, so I accepted it as a sign of affection.

A while ago, my son Brian began a campaign to convince me that I should buy him a computerized synthesizer keyboard (you know, the one that costs as much as an entire Hammond organ—but fits in the backseat of the car!). As I prepared dinner, I wasn't really listening to the familiar litany of "It's a good investment," "The neighbors have one," or "It will help me into the celestial kingdom." Again, Johanna the sage patiently explained the parent-child relationship in our family: "Brian, Mom will do things like *die for you*, but she is *not* going to buy you a synthesizer!"

Other simple gifts of humor and kindness grace my life. This past month, for instance, my visiting teacher announced, "You are too busy for a lesson. We are not coming this month." As I was deciding whether to show relief or disappointment, she added, "So we are bringing dinner to you on Wednesday!" Wednesday. My longest teaching day at work, the day my children are most ignored—this week, my own personal manna on Wednesday—a gift of grace.

Or take the morning in March several years ago, when I left my house at 4:30 A.M. to commute to the hospital to teach nursing students. As I pulled out at that dark hour, my car lights lit up the secretly relettered realtor's sign at the foot of my driveway. It now read, "Happy Birthday, Elaine."

So few of the most profound events of daily life are really within our control: the bloom of the tulips, the tires on the car that last an extra winter, the needed word from a friend. All are healing gifts of grace.

THE POWER OF GRACE IN OUR DAILY LIVES

Grace transcends mortal rules of justice. Life is not a mechanical scale of effort or suffering on one side balanced by the appropriate reward on the other. Life is a process of growth, where growth itself becomes the reward. I tired long ago of hearing promises of some future mortal reward equal to my suffering, as when well-meaning friends foresee financial security or loving companionship in a future whose happiness will outweigh the sadness of my past. The deceiving logic of such an idea implies that when life goes on, droning with problems, with no glory in sight, I am not yet worthy or perhaps have not yet suffered enough. That is unsettling, when all around, those apparently less righteous or less tried seem to be reaping the glorious gifts of this earth.

The fact is that trials are neither distributed equally nor sorted according to a subsequent and matching earthly or heavenly treasure. Problems are neither price nor penance for credit toward some misconceived idea of payment. Instead, life itself, even eternal life, with growth, hope, and peace promised by the Savior's atonement, becomes its own reward, offering divine gifts of the Spirit. The proving question is not What will I gain or achieve? but Who will I become?

In the noisiness and confusion of this life, we can lose hope and cling to the obvious, the garish, the brassy, as did the tempters in the time of Elijah: "And a great and strong wind rent the mountains, and brake in pieces the rocks before the Lord; but the Lord was not in the wind: and after the wind an earthquake; but the Lord was not in the earthquake: And after the earthquake a fire; but the Lord was not in the fire: and after the fire a still small voice. . . . Elijah . . . went out, and . . . there came a voice unto him, and said, What doest thou here, Elijah?" (1 Kings 19:11–13.)

Regularly in my own life, I have "wrestled with" and tried to impress God with the storms of my life, have blindly thrashed about seeking his hand in the wind and the earthquake and the fire. (See Alma 8:10.) How many times would he have whispered, "What doest thou here, Elaine?" In the silent still reality that follows, Christ reaches out, offering the quiet peace of his grace, the gift that was *always* there. Only then comes the healing.

I have sometimes wondered why adversity has seemed to repeat itself so many times, in so many unbecoming forms, in my life of the last several years. A dear friend directed me to the following passage: "Behold, I have created the smith that bloweth the coals in the fire, and that bringeth forth an instrument for his work." (3 Nephi 22:16; cf. Isaiah 54:16–17.) Part of the problem in all our lives is that when we say, "I didn't come here for this. I didn't raise my children for this . . . Why me?" and all the other futile thrashings and flailings, we forget *who* is forging the instrument and for what purposes.

I want not to speak to you as simply a survivor of trial and tragedy. I want to speak as an instrument, as one who has been fired and may be fired again by "the smith that bloweth the coals in the fire," whom God created for his purposes. I want to know God's will for me as an instrument, not as one who simply survived.

Grace is not evident as we wrestle, though there is something important about the struggle. We must stand still, quietly endure uncertainty and troubling contradictions; then come the unexpected, surprising gifts of the Spirit.

Healing by grace is a process of daily sensing, acknowledging, and transcending pain. In my early days as a nurse, I assumed cure and healing to be synonymous. Healing is not cure. Cure is clean, quick, and *done*, often even under anesthesia. The antibiotic kills the pathogenic organism, the scalpel cuts out the malignancy, the medicine resolves the distorted chemistry. But healing is a lifelong process of recovery and growth, in spite of, perhaps because of, enduring physical, emotional, or spiritual assault.

Those life-teaching injuries of love and loss cannot occur in surgical suites, where the pain becomes only obscure memory. Cure is passive, as one submits the body to the practitioner. Healing is active. It is the active partaking of the nourishing manna, the active application of the spiritual medicinal balm. It requires all the energy of your entire being. You have to *be* there, fully aware, awake, and participating when it happens.

THE GIFT OF THE ATONEMENT

We receive the enabling grace through the Atonement, "being justified freely by his grace through the redemption that is in Christ Jesus." (Romans 3:24.) Although we cannot comprehend how it was accomplished, we can accept the marvelous gift of the Atonement. Christ set the pattern even in that. Even he knew the experience of receiving the gift of grace as a process to become more godly: "And I, John, bear record that I beheld his glory, as the glory of the Only Begotten of the Father, full of grace and truth, even the Spirit of truth, which came and dwelt in the flesh, and dwelt among us. And I, John, saw that he received not of the fulness at the first, but received grace for grace; And he received not of the fulness at first, but continued from grace to grace, until he received a fulness." (D&C 93:11–13.)

Even in perfection, Jesus was not free from anguish, suffering the bitterness and adversity of mortality. He lived without sin, the "lamb without blemish" (1 Peter 1:19), yet he knew something of the pain of mortality, and he grew "from grace to grace" (D&C 93:13). That process—grace to grace, the gift of the Atonement, the healing gift of God—is given daily and freely to each of us: "And of his fulness have all we received, and grace for grace. For the law was given by Moses, but grace and truth came by Jesus Christ." (John 1:16–17.)

Over and over the Savior affirms, "Ask, and it shall be given you; seek, and ye shall find; knock, and it shall be opened unto you," not because his treasures are hidden but simply because we must awaken and seek what is already there, waiting at the door. (Matthew 7:7; Luke 11:9; 3 Nephi 14:7.) The Savior offers his love and affirmation of our unconditional worth, *as we are now* and as we may become by acceptance of his grace. The gift of grace is freely given, awaiting our partaking every day, as morning manna, with gifts of enrichment and comfort, and as a healing balm, needed medicine in our desperate struggles to simply survive. Once we awaken to the abundance of the daily gift, we see it everywhere—like manna—in scripture, in literature, in art, in music, in culture, in our service to each other but mostly in the sweet, surprising gifts of life. "For by grace are ye saved through faith; and that not of yourselves: it is the gift of God." (Ephesians 2:8.)

NOTES

1. Stephen E. Robinson, *Believing Christ: The Parable of the Bicycle and Other Good News* (Salt Lake City: Deseret Book Co., 1993), p. 17.

2. Gene R. Cook, "Christmas Is a Time of Rejoicing in the Grace of the Lord," *New Era*, Dec. 1988, p. 4.

3. See Roland H. Bainton, *Here I Stand: A Life of Martin Luther* (New York: Abingdon Press, 1950).

4. Em Olivia Bevis, "On the Road to Excellence," *Journal of Nursing Education* 28 (January 1989): 4–5; Elaine Shaw Sorensen, "Seeds of Faith: A Follower's View of Alma 32" in Monte S. Nyman and Charles D. Tate, Jr., *The Book of Mormon: Alma, the Testimony of the World* (Salt Lake City: Bookcraft, 1992), pp. 129–39.

5. See Robert L. Millet, *By Grace Are We Saved* (Salt Lake City: Bookcraft, 1989).

6. Cook, "Christmas Is a Time of Rejoicing," p. 4; see also Edwin W. Aldous, "A Reflection on the Atonement's Healing and Power," *Ensign*, Apr. 1987, p. 13.

7. Antoine de St. Exupéry, *The Little Prince*, trans. Katherine Woods (New York: Harcourt, Brace & World, 1943), p. 31.

8. Neal A. Maxwell, *All These Things Shall Give Thee Experience* (Salt Lake City: Deseret Book Co., 1979), p. 43.

Index